Praise for *Cost-Effective Data Pipelines*

Sev's best practices and strategies could have saved my employer millions of dollars. That's a pretty good return on investment for the price of a book and the time to read it.

—*Bar Shirtcliff, software engineer*

The cloud data revolution of the mid-2010s gave data engineers easy access to compute and storage at extraordinary scale, but this sea change also made engineers responsible for the daily dollars and cents of their workloads. This is the book we've been waiting for to provide clear, opinionated guidance on monitoring, controlling, and optimizing the costs of high-performance cloud data systems.

—*Matthew Housley, CTO and coauthor of*
Fundamentals of Data Engineering

Real world data pipelines are notoriously fickle. Things change, and things break. This book is a great resource for getting ahead of costly data pipeline problems before they get ahead of you.

—*Joe Reis, coauthor of* Fundamentals of Data Engineering

This is the most readable guide I've seen in decades for designing and building robust real-world data pipelines. With plenty of context and detailed, nontrivial examples using real-world code, this book will be your 24-7 expert when working through messy problems that have no easy solution. You'll learn to balance complex trade-offs among cost, performance, implementation time, long-term support, future growth, and myriad other elements that make up today's complex data pipeline landscape.

—*Arnie Wernick, senior technical, IP, and strategy advisor*

Cost-Effective Data Pipelines
Balancing Trade-Offs When Developing
Pipelines in the Cloud

Sev Leonard

Beijing · Boston · Farnham · Sebastopol · Tokyo

Cost-Effective Data Pipelines

by Sev Leonard

Copyright © 2023 MXLeonard LLC. All rights reserved.

Published by O'Reilly Media, Inc., 1005 Gravenstein Highway North, Sebastopol, CA 95472.

O'Reilly books may be purchased for educational, business, or sales promotional use. Online editions are also available for most titles (*http://oreilly.com*). For more information, contact our corporate/institutional sales department: 800-998-9938 or *corporate@oreilly.com*.

Acquisitions Editor: Aaron Black
Development Editor: Virginia Wilson
Production Editor: Christopher Faucher
Copyeditor: Audrey Doyle
Proofreader: Amnet Systems LLC

Indexer: WordCo Indexing Services, Inc.
Interior Designer: David Futato
Cover Designer: Karen Montgomery
Illustrator: Kate Dullea

July 2023:   First Edition

Revision History for the First Edition

2023-07-13:   First Release

See *http://oreilly.com/catalog/errata.csp?isbn=9781492098645* for release details.

978-1-492-09864-5

[LSI]

Table of Contents

Preface

In my work on data pipelines, the costliest event I've seen was due to a bug: a pipeline was transforming data incorrectly for months, and the problem went undetected until our customers noticed the data was wrong.

As is often the case, many issues led to this outcome. The data was highly variable, making data quality monitoring difficult. We had test data, but it was woefully out of date. The only way to test code changes was with a full pipeline run, which was both long running and costly. We knew the data source could change unpredictably, but we didn't have data validation in the pipeline to detect when changes occurred.

We could have caught this bug with schema-based validation, which you'll learn about in this book. Instead, we spent a significant chunk of our annual cloud bill recomputing the bad data. As if that wasn't bad enough, it cost us the trust of our customers as well, to the point where the validity of the project was questioned. A multimillion-dollar contract supporting a dozen jobs to deliver a service that assisted nearly 100 million people was on the line. Errors of this scale are something every data engineer with significant responsibilities will be exposed to in their careers.

When trying to rein in costs for cloud data pipelines, you're often confronted with trade-offs. Hit performance requirements, but reduce wasted compute cycles. Use observability for debugging, reducing costs, and evolving designs, but don't over-spend on monitoring and logging. Improve test coverage, but unpredictable changes in data invalidate test assumptions and cloud service interfaces introduce additional cost and complexity. Use low-cost, interruptible compute instances, but don't sacrifice pipeline stability.

In this book, I've consolidated what you need to know to handle trade-offs like these quickly and successfully. With a focus on effective monitoring, data pipeline development and testing, and targeted advice on designing cloud compute and storage, this book will get you set up for success from the outset and enable you to manage the evolution of data pipelines in a cost-effective way.

I've used these approaches in batch and streaming systems, handling anywhere from a few thousand rows to petabytes of data and ranging from well-defined, structured data to semistructured sources that change frequently.

Who This Book Is For

I've geared the content toward an intermediate to advanced audience. I assume you have some familiarity with software development best practices, some basics about working with cloud compute and storage, and a general idea about how batch and streaming data pipelines operate.

This book is written from my experience in the day-to-day development of data pipelines. If this is work you either do already or aspire to do in the future, you can consider this book a virtual mentor, advising you of common pitfalls and providing guidance honed from working on a variety of data pipeline projects.

If you're coming from a data analysis background, you'll find advice on software best practices to help you build testable, extendable pipelines. This will aid you in connecting analysis with data acquisition and storage to create end-to-end systems.

Developer velocity and cost-conscious design are areas everyone from individual contributors to managers should have on their mind. In this book, you'll find advice on how to build quality into the development process, make efficient use of cloud resources, and reduce costs. Additionally, you'll see the elements that go into monitoring to not only keep tabs on system health and performance but also gain insight into where redesign should be considered.

If you manage data engineering teams, you'll find helpful tips on effective development practices, areas where costs can escalate, and an overall approach to putting the right practices in place to help your team succeed.

What You Will Learn

If you would like to learn or improve your skill in the following, this book will be a useful guide:

- Reduce cloud spend with lower-cost cloud service offerings and smart design strategies.
- Minimize waste without sacrificing performance by right-sizing compute resources.
- Drive pipeline evolution, head off performance issues, and quickly debug with cost-effective monitoring and logging.
- Set up development and test environments that minimize cloud service costs.

- Create data pipeline codebases that are testable and extensible, reducing development time and accelerating pipeline evolution.
- Limit costly data downtime[1] by improving data quality and pipeline operation through validation and testing.

What This Book Is Not

This is not an architecture book. There are aspects that tie back into architecture and system requirements, but I will not be discussing different architectural approaches or trade-offs. I do not cover topics such as data governance, data cataloging, or data lineage.

While I provide advice on how to manage the innate cost–performance trade-offs of building data pipelines in the cloud, this book is not a financial operations (FinOps) text. Where a FinOps book would, for example, direct you to look for unused compute instance hours as potential opportunities to reduce costs, this book gets into the nitty-gritty details of reducing instance hours and associated costs.

The design space of data pipelines is constantly growing and changing. The biggest value I can provide is to describe design techniques that can be applied in a variety of circumstances as the field evolves. Where relevant, I mention some specific, fully managed data ingestion services such as Amazon Web Services (AWS) Glue or Google Dataflow, but the focus of this book is on classes of services that apply across many vendors. Understanding these foundational services will help you get the most out of vendor-managed services.

The cloud service offerings I focus on include object storage such as AWS S3 and GCS, serverless functions such as AWS Lambda, and cluster compute services such as AWS Elastic Compute (EC2), AWS Elastic MapReduce (EMR), and Kubernetes. While managing system boundaries, identity management, and security are aspects of this approach, I will not be covering these topics in this book.

I do not provide advice about database services in this book, as the choice of databases and configurations is highly dependent on specific use cases.

You will learn what you need to log and monitor, but I will not cover the details on how to set up monitoring, as tools used for monitoring vary from company to company.

---

1 Coined by Barr Moses, *data downtime* (*https://oreil.ly/WHeye*) refers to periods of time when data is incorrect, partial, or missing.

Running Example

To illustrate different aspects of cost-effective data pipeline development, this book includes a running example of a fictitious social media site, Herons on Demand (HoD). HoD was created by Lou and Sylvia, childhood friends who bonded over their love of watching herons (*https://oreil.ly/Rdwwc*), majestic shorebirds that can be seen throughout the world. Now established software developers, they're striking out on their own to pursue their dream of helping others witness these elusive creatures through video and by recommending places to go to see herons in real life.

Using a credit card, Lou and Sylvia sign up with a cloud service provider (CSP). They immediately have access to storage, compute, databases, and web hosting, any one of which would have taken a significant amount of time to set up from scratch. While they are starting out small, Sylvia and Lou aspire to deliver heron content to avian aficionados across the globe. This makes the presence of worldwide availability zones offered by their CSP an additional selling point.

You may be skeptical that there is enough interest in herons to bet a company on, but apparently there was some serious untapped potential in this space. In a few months, HoD goes viral, with millions of users sharing data on herons. Because Lou and Sylvia built the HoD platform in the cloud, it can scale up quickly in response to demand. The cloud bill maxes out their credit card, but fortunately a heron-obsessed billionaire agrees to invest in their company. The heat is off on the cloud bill, for now.

The success of HoD results in a massive dataset of heron information. Lou, Sylvia, and their investor consider how this could be turned into new products and services. While pondering this question, a university ornithology lab reaches out. The lab is researching heron migration and believes the HoD dataset could help identify new and endangered migration sites. Lou and Sylvia are very excited about the prospect of saving herons, but the billionaire is less bullish. "There's no money in helping researchers!" she says.

Not to be defeated, Lou and Sylvia come up with a product that offers heron identification as a service (HIaaS). This service would process customer data and look for matching information in the HoD database, providing customers with high-confidence heron identification. Taking on the university project would be a great way to start building data pipelines and test out this offering.

The billionaire agrees, but she wants to see some return on investment. She challenges Lou and Sylvia to design HIaaS in a cost-effective way, limiting both cloud costs and personnel time. With these constraints in mind, they move forward with the university engagement.

Conventions Used in This Book

To try to keep things interesting I have conceived fictitious but inspired-by-real-events scenarios to illustrate concepts throughout the book. The names of the innocent have been protected. No herons were harmed in the making of this book.

When I talk about the cloud, cloud services, or CSPs, I am specifically talking about the public cloud, such as AWS, Azure, and Google Cloud.

I use the term *compute* to refer to compute instances, also known as virtual machines (VMs). When I refer to *storage*, I mean cloud object storage, such as AWS Simple Storage Service (S3).

The following typographical conventions are used in this book:

Italic
Indicates new terms, URLs, email addresses, filenames, and file extensions.

`Constant width`
Used for program listings, as well as within paragraphs to refer to program elements such as variable or function names, databases, data types, environment variables, statements, and keywords.

`Constant width bold`
Shows commands or other text that should be typed literally by the user.

`Constant width italic`
Shows text that should be replaced with user-supplied values or by values determined by context.

 This element signifies a tip or suggestion.

 This element signifies a general note.

 This element indicates a warning or caution.

Using Code Examples

Supplemental material (code examples, exercises, etc.) is available for download at *https://github.com/gizm00/oreilly_dataeng_book*.

If you have a technical question or a problem using the code examples, please send email to *support@oreilly.com*.

This book is here to help you get your job done. In general, if example code is offered with this book, you may use it in your programs and documentation. You do not need to contact us for permission unless you're reproducing a significant portion of the code. For example, writing a program that uses several chunks of code from this book does not require permission. Selling or distributing examples from O'Reilly books does require permission. Answering a question by citing this book and quoting example code does not require permission. Incorporating a significant amount of example code from this book into your product's documentation does require permission.

We appreciate, but generally do not require, attribution. An attribution usually includes the title, author, publisher, and ISBN. For example: "*Cost-Effective Data Pipelines* by Sev Leonard (O'Reilly). Copyright 2023 MXLeonard LLC, 978-1-492-09864-5."

If you feel your use of code examples falls outside fair use or the permission given above, feel free to contact us at *permissions@oreilly.com*.

O'Reilly Online Learning

O'REILLY® For more than 40 years, *O'Reilly Media* has provided technology and business training, knowledge, and insight to help companies succeed.

Our unique network of experts and innovators share their knowledge and expertise through books, articles, and our online learning platform. O'Reilly's online learning platform gives you on-demand access to live training courses, in-depth learning paths, interactive coding environments, and a vast collection of text and video from O'Reilly and 200+ other publishers. For more information, visit *https://oreilly.com*.

How to Contact Us

Please address comments and questions concerning this book to the publisher:

O'Reilly Media, Inc.
1005 Gravenstein Highway North
Sebastopol, CA 95472
800-889-8969 (in the United States or Canada)
707-829-7019 (international or local)
707-829-0104 (fax)
support@oreilly.com
https://www.oreilly.com/about/contact.html

We have a web page for this book, where we list errata, examples, and any additional information. You can access this page at *https://oreil.ly/cost-effective-data-pipelines*.

For news and information about our books and courses, visit *https://oreilly.com*.

Find us on LinkedIn: *https://linkedin.com/company/oreilly-media*.

Follow us on Twitter: *https://twitter.com/oreillymedia*.

Watch us on YouTube: *https://youtube.com/oreillymedia*.

Acknowledgments

Writing a book is a gigantic undertaking. I am extremely grateful to many folks for helping to make *Cost-Effective Data Pipelines* a reality.

Thanks to Jess Haberman, my first acquisitions editor, for all the opportunities you sent my way and for your guidance on the proposal for this book. Thanks to Jenny Kim for introducing me to Jess! Thank you to Aaron Black, my second acquisitions editor, especially for all the brainstorming around finding the right title and subtitle. Thank you to my development editor, Virginia Wilson, for answering my many questions, fielding my first-time author anxieties, and helping me become a better writer.

I feel very fortunate to have had a solid bench of technical reviewers. You absolutely made this book better. Thank you to my chapter-by-chapter reviewers, most of whom have been on this year-plus journey alongside me: Bar Shirtcliff, Nancy Lin, Milind Chaudhari, Rachel Shadoan, and Vinoo Ganesh. Thank you to my full book reviewers: Arnie Wernick, Isaac Potoczny-Jones, Joe Reis, Matt Housley, and Sam Kimbrel. Thanks also to Navin Kumar for your feedback.

This book was written on evenings and weekends, the relatively small amount of time I have for myself, my family, and my friends. I could not have done this without all your love and support. Thank you, Vanessa, for your wisdom and encouragement.

Thank you, Grey, for saying you're looking forward to this book being done so that we can spend time together again. And most of all, thank you to my amazing partner, Gibbs, for the care and feeding of an author with a full-time startup job, while also working a full-time job yourself. Thank you for your love, encouragement, and patience. Thank you for reminding me to eat, keeping our house from descending into chaos, and sharing your excitement about flora and fauna. An honorable mention to Party Cat, for busting into my office to let me know it's time to stop writing and feed her dinner.

Emotionally, this was a challenging endeavor to take on during a pandemic, while watching decades of progress for equal rights evaporate seemingly overnight. This book is dedicated to all who are targeted by fascism. May we be safe, happy, healthy, and free from suffering.

CHAPTER 1

Designing Compute for Data Pipelines

When you're developing applications that run on dedicated hardware, whether an on-premises data center, laptop, or phone, you have a predetermined, fixed amount of resources. In the cloud, on the other hand, you can configure virtual hardware to best meet workload needs, rather than working in a predefined resource envelope.

Compute design for data pipelines is about determining what resources you need for performant and reliable operation. Along with CPU, memory, disk space, and bandwidth, cloud compute has an additional axis of purchasing options, giving you the power to trade off cost against performance.

This can be a daunting topic, with millions of possible permutations (*https://oreil.ly/ _qfqz*) across compute instance types, sizes, and purchasing plans. In this chapter, I'll show you how to navigate this space, winnowing down options based on data pipeline performance characteristics and refining your choices with performance benchmarking.

The first thing to keep in mind is that cloud compute is a shared, distributed system. As a result, there are times when capacity is not available to fulfill your resource requests. I'll begin this chapter by highlighting different scenarios where you can experience resource shortfalls, because ultimately it doesn't matter how well you've designed your cluster if the resources you need aren't available.

Next, you'll see advice on various purchasing options for cloud compute and how to best leverage these options in data pipeline design.

Another step in homing in on the right compute configuration comes when you consider the business and architectural requirements of the design space. To illustrate this process, I'll walk through a scenario that starts with a business problem and takes you through identifying relevant compute options at a high level.

Having filtered down the millions of compute options to a relevant subset, in the last section of the chapter you'll see how to benchmark the performance of different cluster configurations. This is an exciting part of the chapter, where you'll begin to understand the multifaceted dependencies that go into optimizing compute, including how more cluster nodes does not necessarily mean better performance. At the end of the chapter, I'll bring purchasing options back into the picture to show you how to trade off performance against cost.

Even if you work in an environment where you don't own the infrastructure, this chapter will give you important insight into robust pipeline design, cost–performance trade-offs, and even a little architecture, which, frankly, I think is indispensable for good pipeline design.

Understanding Availability of Cloud Compute

While significant capacity is offered by the cloud, there's more to consider when it comes to the availability of compute resources. Something I try to keep in mind is that cloud resources are backed by physical hardware. It's easy to overlook the fact that the server farms and networking that back virtual compute are susceptible to capacity and reliability considerations like what you would have when running your own on-premises system. There are also aspects to consider with how cloud service providers (CSPs) make compute resources available to customers.

Outages

As more computing moves to the cloud, the impact of CSP outages can have a wide reach that includes government websites, meal delivery services, and even robot vacuum cleaner scheduling (*https://oreil.ly/y1EhH*).

CSPs provide service level agreements (SLAs) that guarantee a certain percentage of uptime, as you can see in the Google Cloud (*https://oreil.ly/LxjGY*) and Amazon EC2 (*https://oreil.ly/1eEV4*). If these SLAs are not met, you can be reimbursed for a portion of the compute spend that was impacted.

This might sound fine at first; if you can't deploy resources due to an outage, you don't have to pay for them. But consider the financial impact of your service being offline as a result of an outage. From a business perspective, you should be losing significantly more money from service disruptions than the cost of deploying cloud resources. To that point, a 2018 report from Lloyd's of London (*https://oreil.ly/RHB8E*) estimates that an incident taking down one of the top three CSPs for three to six days would result in up to $15 billion in revenue losses. Given the expansion of businesses in the cloud since the time of that publication, revenue losses for a similar event today would be costlier.

One way to stem the impact of outages is to diversify where you launch compute resources. When outages occur, they can impact a subset of regions and Availability Zones (AZs) on a CSP's network, as was the case with this outage Amazon Web Services (AWS) suffered (*https://oreil.ly/rygn4*) in 2021. Building in the option to run pipelines in multiple AZs can help reduce exposure to outages.

Keep in mind that this also has a cost: supporting multi-AZ deployments requires additional infrastructure. Furthermore, networking costs can be a consideration, as well as data pipeline performance impacts if workloads span multiple AZs.

Failover systems, as their name indicates, provide coverage in the event of a failure in the primary system. They can be implemented in a variety of ways based on how urgently you need to keep the system online. A *hot failover* is a live, redundant system that can be switched to quickly, at the cost of always keeping a redundant system online and ready.

From here, there are varying degrees of failover readiness, down to a *cold failover system*, where resources are brought online when a failure occurs. In this case, you trade system availability for cost, as you don't incur the cost of running a redundant system but you sacrifice system availability while the cold system comes online.

While failover systems can provide additional coverage in the event of an outage, these systems can be very costly. A failover strategy that runs your pipeline in a different region will require data to be replicated across multiple regions, significantly increasing your data storage and access costs.

Capacity Limits

Something that can be overlooked when working with cloud services is that resources are often shared. Unless you specifically purchase dedicated hardware, you will be sharing compute with other customers. This means that when you provision a cluster, you are making a *request* for those resources. It's not a guarantee of availability.

When you launch a compute instance or cluster, you are making a request for specific instance types and sizes. Whether this request can be fulfilled depends on the capacity available in the region and AZ you select.

If all resources are consumed when you need to initiate a batch job or add more capacity to a streaming pipeline, your resource request will go unfulfilled. I've seen this behavior when requesting compute capacity during popular times to run workloads, such as the hours after the close of business in the United States eastern time zone. Even if you have reserved dedicated compute resources, you can create this issue for yourself if you attempt to provision more capacity than you've purchased.

Segmentation can help you mute capacity impacts by splitting pipeline workloads into those that are time critical and those that can be run as resources are available. You'll learn more about this in "Architectural Requirements" on page 10.

Account Limits

There can be limits on the amount of capacity available based on your subscription level. For example, you could have access to only a limited amount of CPU capacity. Requests exceeding this amount will be unfulfilled and can result in an error (*https://oreil.ly/BaYTi*). If you are aware of these account limits ahead of time, you may be able to mitigate this situation by upgrading your subscription level, but keep in mind that you may not have access to additional resources immediately. Depending on the kind of increase you request, you may have to wait for approval from your CSP.

Infrastructure

Whether compute is available also depends on how you set up the environment where you are running pipelines. The availability of a particular instance type and size varies based on compute region and AZ, with some options being unavailable across different regions. If you are using a service like AWS Elastic MapReduce (EMR), there can be restrictions on the types of instances that are supported.

Capacity Limitations in the Wild

One way I've seen availability issues crop up in data pipelines is when an AZ runs out of a particular instance size, resulting in an "insufficient capacity" message (*https://oreil.ly/SwiIB*). In this situation, the pipeline design had to be modified to accommodate both cloud availability and customer requirements.

The pipeline ran batch jobs to ingest customer data. Data had to be submitted by the end of the month, so typically a large number of jobs would kick off close to that time. Over time, the size of the data submitted by each customer grew, which my team responded to by enabling our pipelines to scale. Eventually we started to get these "insufficient capacity" messages from our CSP that prevented the jobs from launching.

It turned out that our pipeline needs had exceeded the instance availability in the AZs we were using, which were constrained by our customers. Because the availability issues were intermittent, we never knew when they were going to crop up, and when they did, our rescheduling system would contribute to the problem by immediately relaunching failed jobs. To deal with this, we modified the job scheduling system to throttle the number of jobs submitted and back off on job retries in the event of insufficient capacity.

I like this example because it shows the multiple places constraints can come from when designing data pipelines. Had our customers not insisted on a specific set of AZs, we could have mitigated the capacity issue by running in other AZs. If the batch jobs had been spread out more evenly over the month or if the data size had stayed the same, we may never have encountered this issue.

I mentioned a few strategies for blunting the impacts of cloud availability issues including failover systems, multi-AZ operation, and job segmentation. Fundamentally, your pipelines need to operate in an environment where these situations can pop up. Good design techniques such as idempotency, data deduplication strategies, and retry mechanisms will help limit the impacts to pipeline uptime and data quality that can arise from unexpected resourcing shortfalls. These topics are covered in Chapter 4.

Leveraging Different Purchasing Options in Pipeline Design

At a high level, compute purchasing options come in three choices—on demand, interruptible/spot, and contractual discounts such as reserved instances and committed use. Table 1-1 shows the breakdown of the different prices for a fictitious instance INST3, based on an AWS pricing model.

Table 1-1. Hourly costs of INST3 instance

On demand	Reserved	Spot minimum	Spot maximum
$0.4	$0.2	$0.1	$0.2

In this book, I focus on instance hours–based purchasing options, where the underlying compute instances provide a fixed amount of resources and are charged by the number of hours used.

On Demand

As you can see in Table 1-1, on-demand pricing is the most expensive option because it allows you to request an instance whenever you need it and to retain it for the duration of your workload. It's important to remember that you can make requests for compute at any time, but there is no guarantee that what you request will be available, as you saw earlier in this chapter.

On demand is a nice option when you're trying to get a sense of your compute needs and can't tolerate service disruption or if your workloads are short, infrequent, or unpredictable. Of the available purchasing options, on demand is the easiest to manage because you don't need to evaluate reservations or handle the loss of spot instances.

Spot/Interruptible

Spot instances, also known as *interruptible instances*, are excess compute that a CSP has available. These instances offer a significant discount over on demand, as seen in the "Spot minimum" price in Table 1-1, but their price and availability are highly volatile. If demand increases, spot prices will increase (see "Spot maximum" in Table 1-1) and availability will decrease. At this point, a CSP will invoke a call-in of outstanding spot instances, providing a warning to spot consumers that the instance is about to terminate. Spot instances can be good choices for low-priority, non–time critical workloads and can also be used to provide additional cluster capacity.

Spot instances are often comingled with other purchasing options to improve performance and reduce cost based on system requirements. If you have a high-performance pipeline where interruption cannot be tolerated, you can use a baseline of on-demand or contractual provisioning, supplementing with spot instances as available to improve performance.

Some services can manage the interruption of spot instance termination for you. If you use spot instances as task nodes in your EMR cluster, you can configure settings to prevent job failure if the interruptible instances are terminated (*https://oreil.ly/WLuQO*). AWS also provides instance fleets (*https://oreil.ly/jfqM5*), where a mixture of on-demand and spot instances are configured to meet a target capacity. This gives you the benefit of lower-cost interruptible instances without the overhead of configuring them yourself. If you use an approach like this where a CSP is managing the provisioning choices, make sure to run some test workloads to validate that the choices being made for you are meeting your needs.

It's possible that interrupting a pipeline job is a reasonable trade-off. If cost is a higher consideration than performance and data availability, spot instances can be a good choice as your primary resourcing strategy. You'll see techniques for handling interrupted pipeline jobs in Chapter 4.

Other opportunities to use spot instances include development, testing, and short maintenance workloads.

Contractual Discounts

There are a variety of options for you to receive a discount in exchange for committing to purchase compute over a fixed period of time. AWS reserved instances, savings plans, and Google committed use discounts are some offerings that fall into this category. Outside of these options, companies can also negotiate private pricing agreements directly with CSPs.

Contractual discounts can be a good option if both of the following are true: you have predictable compute needs, and the way you use compute is consistent with the way the discount is applied. Understanding how the discounts are applied is very important; in the next section, I'll share a story of a time when misunderstanding this aspect of reserved instance purchases resulted in unexpected costs. So long as you are clear on this, you can save substantially over on demand, as shown in Table 1-1. Pipelines with 24-7 operation and a baseline fixed workload can be good candidates for this option.

Typically, the more rigid the reservation, the greater the discount. For example, if you commit to reserving a specific instance type in a single AZ (*https://oreil.ly/j9v8p*), you can get a better discount than if you need more flexibility, such as multiple instance types.

Something to consider with reserved contractual discounts is the historical decrease in instance hour cost (*https://oreil.ly/UftqK*). If prices drop below what you paid for with your reserved instance purchase, you do not get a refund of the difference. Committing to the minimum time period can help insulate you from overpaying in this scenario.

The area of contractual discounts is constantly evolving. To help you determine whether this is a good option, ask the following questions:

What exactly am I reserving?
Beyond the period of time you need to reserve to qualify for the discount, you want to be aware of what exactly you are committing to. Are you reserving a specific compute instance type and/or size, or are you reserving a number of CPU cores or an amount of memory? Does the contract allow you to change these choices or are they fixed?

Is availability guaranteed?
Are you reserving availability? Despite what you might think from the name, for some CSPs "reservation" does not mean that what you reserve will be available. For example, an AWS reserved instance purchase does not guarantee availability unless you also have a capacity reservation by specifying a single AZ for your reserved instance purchase.

What if I no longer need my reservation?
As resourcing needs change, you may find yourself with unused reservations. In some cases, you may be able to sell unused reservations to recoup the expense, such as on the Amazon EC2 marketplace (*https://oreil.ly/lSijx*). Additionally, some contracts allow you to convert to a different instance configuration.

How is the discount applied?

You might think that reserving a certain amount of capacity means the discount will be applied anytime you use resources matching what you reserved. This isn't necessarily the case.

Contractual Discounts in the Real World: A Cautionary Tale

To illustrate the importance of understanding how contractual discounts are applied, consider a pipeline with two workers, WORKER1 and WORKER2, using an instance type INST3. Over the past year, the pipeline was consistently using 10 instance hours per month. The pipeline is expected to process as much or more data in subsequent years, so reducing costs through a reserved instance purchase seems attractive. Based on historical use, you commit to purchasing 10 instance hours per month, for a total of 120 instance hours of INST3 over the period of one year.

The reserved instance purchase is set to start in January. In the first few months of the year, your instance hour usage is as depicted in Figure 1-1.

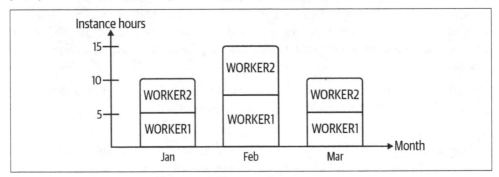

Figure 1-1. INST3 instance hours used by month

In January and March, each worker used five instance hours, adding up to the 10 you anticipated based on past use. In February, you had a bit more data to process than usual, so each node used eight instance hours, for a total of 16 instance hours. You aren't too worried; you know that if you use more than your reserved capacity, you will be charged an on-demand price for the excess. As a result, you expect the quarterly cloud bill to look something like Table 1-2.

Table 1-2. Expected bill for January through March

	Hours	Cost per hour	Total
INST3—reserved	30	0.2	$6.00
INST3—on demand	6	0.4	$2.40
	Quarterly total:		$8.40

Instead, you get the bill depicted in Table 1-3.

Table 1-3. Actual bill for January through March

	Hours	Cost per hour	Total
INST3—reserved	30	0.2	$6.00
INST3—on demand	18	0.4	$7.20
	Quarterly total:		$13.20

What happened? You were using the number of instance hours you reserved for 30 out of 36 hours, so why are you getting charged on-demand pricing for over half of the total time? And why are you charged for 48 hours?[1]

Sadly, this is not a billing mistake. The reservation is for a *single* instance, so the discount only gets applied to one INST3 instance at a time. The filled portions of Figure 1-2 show the application of the reserved instance hours. Only WORKER1 received the discount. In addition, reserving instance capacity means you pay for the instance hours reserved even if they are unused, which is why you were charged for 30 hours over three months.

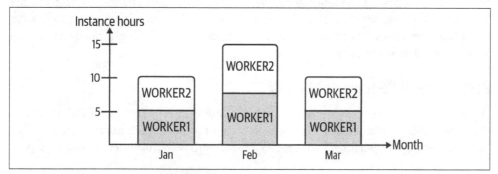

Figure 1-2. Reserved instance capacity used by WORKER1

To get the pricing you had assumed you were getting, you would have needed to purchase two reserved instances, committing to 60 hours per year for each one.

Requirements Gathering for Compute Design

As engineers, when we think about resourcing, we tend to focus on what is needed to accomplish a particular task, such as performing a set of data transformations. That is definitely part of the equation, but understanding the big, system-level picture elucidates where we can make trade-offs to harness all the options the cloud gives us.

---

1 In the scenario that inspired this story, the extra cost was well over a few dollars.

Business Requirements

Understanding the business problems that need to be solved can help you get a sense of high-level pipeline requirements. This can include identifying the data sources, setting the ingestion schedule, and specifying the desired result data. This is the time to get a sense of system uptime requirements, which will help you determine whether you need to plan for a failover system. Business requirements can also include restrictions on which regions you can use and possibly which cloud services and software you can use.

The speed at which ingestion needs to complete can also be defined at this time. Part of this is understanding how performance trades off against cloud spend; is the application something that requires real-time, zero-downtime operation, or is ingestion runtime not as critical, enabling you to trade performance and availability for reduced cost?

With the data sources and result data defined, you can get a sense of the complexity of pipeline operation. Thinking of the three Vs of big data—variety, velocity, and volume—will help you determine pipeline architecture and resourcing needs. For example, if you are working with data sources that have significant changes in data volume over time, you will want to consider how to handle that, either by provisioning the maximum amount of compute needed or by adopting a scaling strategy to reduce waste when data loads are low.

Architectural Requirements

Architectural requirements translate business requirements into technical specifications, providing a picture of what needs to be built to realize the business needs. This can include setting performance specifications, uptime requirements, and data processing engine choice.

You want to consider compute design and data processing engines together, as the configuration possibilities between the two are tightly coupled. In addition, think about the environment in which the pipeline will run. For example, in a Kubernetes environment where a single cluster is servicing several different processes, make sure you have the right namespacing in place to limit contention. This will be important to ensure that the pipeline has sufficient resources while not impairing other parts of the system.

Architectural requirements can help you identify opportunities to split pipeline operation into processes where performance is critical and processes where performance is not as much of a concern. This presents an opportunity to use some cost-saving strategies.

High-performance workloads can require a significant percentage of free memory and CPU. While this unused capacity is critical for performance, it is wasteful: you're paying for resources you don't use. One way you can recoup these unused resources without impacting performance is by using priority scheduling. Low-priority processes can run in the background to use spare cycles and can be reduced or suspended when the higher-priority processes start to ramp up. Uber used this strategy to improve utilization in its big data platform (*https://oreil.ly/azJZA*).

Workload segmentation can also help you reduce pipeline runtime by running some tasks during off-hours or in the background. For example, if the cost of deduplicating data during pipeline execution is too expensive, you can consider deduplicating post ingestion. Uber used this approach to recompress Parquet files in the background to a higher level of compression (*https://oreil.ly/rWHJP*), enabling the company to take advantage of lower storage costs without impacting pipeline runtime.

Offline processes are also an opportunity to use low-cost interruptible instances. If you have a pipeline that generates numerous small files throughout the day, you can run a compaction job offline to mitigate the impacts. I'll discuss the small-files problem and mitigation strategies in Chapter 3.

Requirements-Gathering Example: HoD Batch Ingest

Recalling the running example from the Preface, the Herons on Demand (HoD) team begins working with a university lab to help them collect and analyze migratory bird data through surveys. It is hoped that new migration sites can be identified by combining the bird sighting data from HoD users with the survey data collected by the researchers. The pipeline for processing this data is pictured in Figure 1-3.

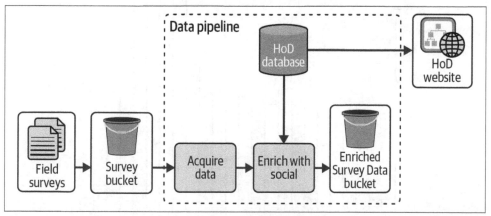

Figure 1-3. HoD batch architecture: survey pipeline

Field surveys are collected using an app that uploads survey results to cloud storage as compressed JSON. The pipeline brings in the survey data and joins it with social media collected by HoD, storing the result in Parquet format for analysis by the university researchers.

Let's first consider some of the business requirements for the survey data pipeline. The data produced by this pipeline will be used by the researchers for grant proposals and dissertations. The researchers would like to get the data as quickly as possible, particularly leading up to these important deadlines, but they also need to be judicious stewards of the grant money that will be used for cloud compute. This sounds like a potential cost–performance trade-off opportunity.

The researchers agree to receive batches of data every two weeks, or *biweekly*. Given the infrequent ingest cycle, the HoD team proposes to handle any pipeline failures through monitoring and rerunning within the same day the failure occurred, rather than spending additional money to build a more sophisticated solution that can detect and mitigate these issues in real time.

The HoD team gets access to an existing dataset of surveys from the researchers, spanning the preceding year. To get a sense of the survey data batch size, they plot the data size across biweekly bins, as shown in Figure 1-4.

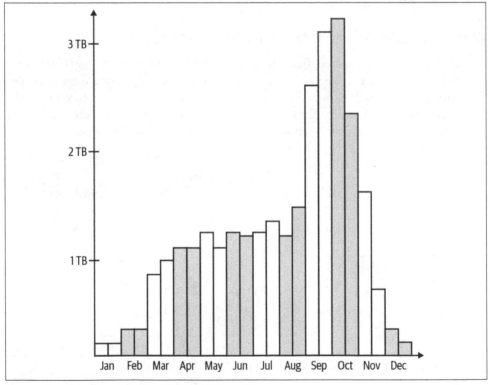

Figure 1-4. Bird survey data bucketed biweekly

From an architectural point of view, the team is already running some pipelines using Spark on EMR. They already are comfortable with that system, and the large amount of data and number of enhancements seem like a good fit for in-memory processing, so they decide to run the survey pipeline using the same tooling.

Given this scenario, let's take a look at what we know regarding the survey pipeline.

Data

The survey data is static, with a volume of a few TB of compressed JSON in cloud storage. Cloud storage provides bandwidth in the hundreds of Gbps (*https://oreil.ly/rh8aM*), which we would be well below given the expected data size per batch.

The other data source is the HoD social media database, which will be both serving content for the HoD website and providing data for the pipeline. Because there are multiple demands on this resource, contention and performance impacts are a concern for both the website and the pipeline. There may be a need to increase database resources to serve both purposes. Because the data pipeline runs biweekly, another option is to create a snapshot of the database just prior to ingestion that can be used by the pipeline.

In either case, you would want to make sure retries are built in when accessing the data, whether it comes from a cloud storage location or the HoD database.

Performance

There wasn't a specific performance spec given in the requirements, just the desire to have the data quickly but without significant cost. We will revisit this in "Benchmarking" on page 14 to get a sense of performance–cost trade-offs.

As a starting point, the Spark documentation (*https://oreil.ly/0friZ*) suggests allocating at most 75% of the available memory for Spark. Depending on pipeline resource needs and desired speed of ingest, you may need to target utilization at a lower percentage. The same applies for CPU, disk, and network utilization. This is something you will get a better sense of over time as you monitor pipeline performance.

Purchasing options

An on-demand purchasing model makes sense to start out, as this provides a fixed set of resources while getting the pipeline up and running reliably. It's too early to explore contractual discounts such as reserved instances, because you're not sure what the load looks like over the long term.

With the ability to trade cost for performance, spot instances can be added to the mix once you have a solid sense of resourcing needs. There isn't a particular time of the day or day of the week the pipeline needs to run, providing additional latitude in scheduling to run the job when spot instances are available or on-demand prices are lower.

Benchmarking

Now that you've got a sense of the subset of relevant compute options, it's time to take them for a test drive. *Benchmarking* is the process of evaluating cluster design and compute options while running a sample workload, helping you identify optimal configurations.

Something that really frustrated me early in my career was how little information I could find about benchmarking and cluster sizing, either online, in books, or by talking to more experienced data engineers. The answer was always some form of "it depends."

While I've seen some general formulas for assessing resource needs, such as the Packt approach for sizing a Hadoop cluster for data processing (*https://oreil.ly/CTPmA*), my experience has been that it really does depend (sorry!) on many things that are interrelated and that can change over time in data pipelines.

While I can't give you a magic formula, I can walk you through the process of estimating and evaluating different compute configurations, pointing out when various aspects of pipeline design impact the decisions you're making. I'll continue the example from the prior section, making some choices about different data processing engines, techniques, and cluster sizes and illustrating how they impact one another.

Because data processing engines have a significant impact on compute needs but a discussion of the topic is beyond the scope of this book, I've included pointers to resources in "Recommended Readings" on page 23.

 As you read through this section, keep in mind that not only will benchmarking workloads give you insight into cluster design, they are also a helpful tool for characterizing and debugging workloads. This can be handy if you're considering using serverless to run a process but you're unsure what kinds of resources it would need (and therefore have poor visibility into potential serverless costs). One of the trade-offs when using serverless is reduced visibility into how resources are being used, which can hide the impacts of suboptimal data processing engine configurations, low performance queries, and subpar data structures. If you find yourself in this situation, it can be worthwhile to spin up a cluster where you can monitor and introspect performance.

Even if you're using managed services, it's helpful to understand this process. You have the option to specify cluster configuration properties such as instance family, size, and number of workers in many popular managed solutions, including Google Dataproc (*https://oreil.ly/vYgFx*), AWS Glue (*https://oreil.ly/s1EbM*), Databricks (*https://oreil.ly/OJLSp*), and Snowflake (*https://oreil.ly/Dah9m*).

Instance Family Identification

Determining which instance family to use is a combination of assessing the relative needs of CPU, memory, and bandwidth and analyzing cluster performance. Once you've gone through this process a few times, you'll start to develop a sense of which families work well for different applications.

Returning to the HoD bird survey pipeline example, Spark will be used for processing the data, which primarily works with data in-memory. Another aspect of this pipeline is the join performed between the survey data and the HoD database. Joining large datasets in-memory points to a memory-optimized family or potentially a general-purpose instance with a lot of memory.

 This is a great time to consider the interdependencies among the data you are working with, how you process it, and the compute resources you need. Notice that I mentioned joining large datasets in-memory. You could choose to create this data in another way: you could minimize the size of the data being joined to reduce the amount of data in memory and disk space needed for shuffle (*https://oreil.ly/E5ht8*), or perhaps forgo the join altogether by instead performing a lookup on a sorted key-value store.

There are many knobs to optimize how data is processed. The challenge with data pipelines is that these knobs can be infrastructure design, data formatting, and data processing engine configuration, to name a few.

Because the pipeline is running in EMR, only a subset of instance types are available (*https://oreil.ly/d8yq7*). Some additional guidance from the Spark documentation (*https://oreil.ly/i8wp4*) suggests a configuration of eight to 16 cores per machine[2] and a 10 Gb or higher bandwidth, further slimming down the potential options.

The AWS instances that meet these requirements are shown in Table 1-4.[3]

---

2 This is also very dependent on how you configure Spark and your workload.

3 Data from *https://instances.vantage.sh*.

Table 1-4. AWS EMR instance type and size comparison

API name	Memory (GB)	vCPUs	Network performance	Linux on demand cost
m4.2xlarge	32	8	High	$0.40
m4.4xlarge	64	16	High	$0.80
m5.xlarge	16	4	Up to 10 Gb	$0.19
m5.2xlarge	32	8	Up to 10 Gb	$0.38
m5.4xlarge	64	16	Up to 10 Gb	$0.77
r4.xlarge	30.5	4	Up to 10 Gb	$0.27
r4.2xlarge	61	8	Up to 10 Gb	$0.53
r4.4xlarge	122	16	Up to 10 Gb	$1.06
r5.xlarge	32	4	Up to 10 Gb	$0.25
r5.2xlarge	64	8	Up to 10 Gb	$0.50
r5.4xlarge	128	16	Up to 10 Gb	$1.01
r5.12xlarge	384	48	10 Gb	$3.02

> According to Datacenters.com (*https://oreil.ly/1Pb_h*), vCPU is cal-
> culated as (Threads × Cores) × Physical CPU = Number vCPU.
> vCPU is effectively the number of threads available. More vCPUs
> can enable more parallelism by enabling more Spark executors, or
> they can provide a fixed set of executors with more resources.

In the comparison, I've selected a few general-purpose types, m4 and m5, and two memory-optimized types, r4 and r5. Notice that for the same vCPU there's twice as much memory in the memory-optimized instances and a corresponding increase in hourly cost.

Cluster Sizing

Another common question in compute design is how many nodes you should have in your cluster. At a minimum, a cluster should have two workers for reliability and performance (*https://oreil.ly/w3PRM*). To reach a desired capacity you can choose to configure a cluster with many smaller instances or use fewer larger instances. Which is better? Well, it depends. This is another case where infrastructure design, data processing engine configuration, code, and data structure come together.

The types of purchasing options you use for the cluster nodes is another consideration. In "Benchmarking Example" on page 17, you'll see some examples of mixing interruptible and on-demand instances.

Let's consider a case where you design a cluster that has a few nodes using instances with a large amount of memory per instance. When working with Spark, you can incur long garbage collection times if each worker node has a large amount of memory. If this leads to unacceptable performance and reliability impacts for your workload, you would be better off provisioning more nodes with a smaller amount of memory per node to get the desired memory capacity.

On the other hand, if your workload has significant shuffle, having more workers means there are more instances you may need to move data between. In this case, designing the cluster to have a few nodes with a larger memory footprint would be better for performance, as described in recent guidance from Databricks (*https://oreil.ly/XDvhc*).

You'll see an example of working through this trade-off in the upcoming section, "Benchmarking Example."

Monitoring

To evaluate the efficacy of a given cluster configuration, you need to monitor performance. This is covered in more detail in Chapter 11, so for now I will only highlight some of the specific monitoring areas that relate to benchmarking workloads.

Cluster resource utilization

Monitoring the usage of memory, disk, CPU, and bandwidth over the course of a workload can help you identify whether you are under- or over-provisioned. In EMR, you can inspect these metrics using Ganglia (*http://ganglia.info*). Prometheus (*https://prometheus.io*) and Grafana (*https://grafana.com*) are other monitoring tools that enable you to combine metrics from multiple deployments into a single dashboard.

Data processing engine introspection

When working with Spark, the Spark UI provides additional diagnostic information regarding executor load, how well balanced (or not) your computation is across executors, shuffles, spill, and query plans, showing you how Spark is running your query. This information can help you tune Spark settings, data partitioning, and data transformation code.

Benchmarking Example

To show you how to do benchmarking in practice, I'll walk through some example cluster configurations for the bird survey batch pipeline in Figure 1-3, describing how you would discern how the cluster is performing under load.

Looking at the data distribution in Figure 1-4, most batches have 1 to 2 TB of data. Starting the estimation using a batch in this range will provide a configuration that works in the largest number of cases. It also has the advantage of not overfitting to very large or very small jobs, which may have different performance characteristics.

Undersized

I'll start with the cluster configuration in Table 1-5. This configuration is undersized, and I want to illustrate it so that you know how to identify this scenario. GP1 denotes the general-purpose cluster configuration, and M1 is the memory-optimized configuration.

Table 1-5. Initial cluster configuration: undersized

Name	Instance type	Instance count	Total vCPU	Total memory (GB)	Bandwidth (GB)
GP1	m5.xlarge	3	12	48	Up to 10
M1	r5.xlarge	3	12	96	Up to 10

When working with large-scale data, it can take a long time to finish a single run. However, you don't have to wait until a job completes to inspect the results. In fact, it's better when benchmarking if you can check on the health of the cluster from time to time using the monitoring tools I mentioned earlier.

Distributed systems, including distributed data processing engines like Spark, will attempt to retry a variety of failure conditions such as rerunning a failed task and retrying on a communication timeout. This is a fundamental aspect of fault tolerance in distributed systems, and for your data processing jobs it means that in the presence of insufficient resources, a job could be retried several times before it is officially declared failed.

Let's consider a hypothetical scenario for running the survey data pipeline against a 2 TB batch using either of the cluster configurations in Table 1-5, as in this case they will both perform about the same.

You launch the cluster and the pipeline starts chugging away, spending quite a bit of time in the "Enrich with social" step where the join is happening. You ran a smaller batch size through the "Enrich with social" step on your laptop and it took a few minutes, whereas on the cluster it's been running for over an hour. It's time to take a look at some performance monitoring to see what's going on.

When you look at the Spark UI, you see several failed tasks and "out of memory" messages in the executor logs. You check Ganglia, and you see that 85% of the available memory has been consumed and the load on the workers is high. You also see that some cluster nodes have failed, having been replaced by EMR to keep the cluster at the requested resource level. The job continues to run as Spark tries to rerun the failed tasks, but ultimately the job fails.

Oversized

Moving on to another configuration option, GP2 and M2 in Table 1-6 add significantly more workers but retain the xlarge instance size. Fewer memory-optimized instances are used in M2 versus the general-purpose instances in GP2 given the additional memory available with this instance type.

Table 1-6. Second cluster configuration: oversized

Name	Instance type	Instance count	Total vCPU	Total memory (GB)	Bandwidth (GB)
GP2	m5.xlarge	40	160	640	Up to 10
M2	r5.xlarge	30	120	960	Up to 10

In the hypothetical 2 TB batch example, you see that these configurations perform significantly better. The metrics are well within limits throughout job execution—no out-of-memory or failed-node issues. When you look at the Spark UI, you notice there is a lot of shuffling going on. The job completes successfully, with a runtime of 8 hours for GP2 and 6.5 hours for M2.

Selecting different instance sizes is referred to as *vertical scaling*. Choosing larger sizes is referred to as *scaling up*, and choosing a smaller instance size is *scaling down*.

Right-Sized

Right-sizing refers to having the optimal number of resources to perform a task. This means there are limited excess resources (waste) and that you are not under-resourced, which can lead to reliability and performance issues.

 While this exercise goes straight into right-sizing as part of the benchmarking process, you want to be cautious about spending time too early in the design process trying to find the optimal compute configuration.

Right-sizing is something that comes over time as you gain insight into pipeline performance and resource utilization. When you are initially getting a pipeline up and running, it can be desirable to *over-provision*, that is, provide more resources than are necessary. This eliminates the issues of under-resourcing, allowing you to focus on working out bugs in other areas. Once you feel like you've got things running reliably, then you can start to consider right-sizing.

Given the shuffling you saw with configurations GP2 and M2, swapping out the small-sized instances for fewer larger instances might improve performance, giving the configuration in Table 1-7.

Table 1-7. Third cluster configuration: right-sized

Name	Instance type	Instance count	Total vCPU	Total memory (GB)	Bandwidth (GB)
GP3	m5.4xlarge	10	160	640	Up to 10
M3	r5.2xlarge	8	64	512	Up to 10

Running with this configuration, you see a reduction in shuffling versus GP2 and M2 and reduced runtimes. GP3 runs in 7 hours and M3 runs in 4.75 hours. This is an interesting outcome, as M3 has fewer resources than M2 but runs faster due to reducing shuffling overhead through fewer workers.

Now that you've identified some working configurations, let's take a look at costs in Table 1-8.

Table 1-8. Cost comparison of different configurations

Name	Instance count	Hours	On demand	40% spot	60% spot
GP2	40	8	$77	$62	$54
M2	30	6.5	$58	$49	$44
GP3	10	7	$67	$56	$51
M3	8	4.75	$24	$20	$19

Starting with GP2, it's probably not surprising that this is the costliest option given the number of instances and the runtime. Remember that GP2 and M2 both ran the pipeline successfully. If it hadn't been for inspecting cluster performance, it wouldn't have been apparent that the configuration was suboptimal.

You can see the cost advantage of the memory-optimized instances for this application in comparing M3 to GP3. Not only were fewer memory-optimized instances needed, but the job runtime was lower. As a result, the M3 on-demand cost is about 35% of the GP3 cost. With 60% of the instance hours provided by spot instances, the M3 cost could be reduced an additional 20%.

 When you're prototyping and testing out different configurations, it's very easy to forget to shut down resources when you're done with them. Look for auto-shutdown options when you launch resources; typically you can set this to shut down the resource after a certain period of idle time.

Another way to help keep track of resources is to use tags or labels, which are also set up when you launch a resource. For example, you could use the tag DEV-TEMP to identify ephemeral development resources that can be shut down if idle for more than 24 hours.

Summary

The numerous ready-to-use compute configurations available in the cloud give you tremendous power to design compute that provides an optimal balance of performance, cost, and uptime for your data pipelines. Rather than feeling overwhelmed by the millions of choices, you can confidently design compute by evaluating pricing, instance configuration, and cluster design options, and use benchmarking to refine these choices.

This understanding equips you to evaluate services and products that manage compute design for you. This includes third-party products and services that reduce cloud compute costs; CSP offerings that manage compute for you, such as AWS Fargate (*https://aws.amazon.com/fargate*); and service options that manage different pricing plans under the hood, such as AWS Instance Fleets.

As with any system design, a key part of compute design is understanding how things can go wrong. When working with cloud compute, being familiar with the sources of potential resourcing issues helps you design robust pipelines and plan for contingencies. Outages, capacity and account limits, and infrastructure design are areas to keep in mind, especially if you are working with shared tenancy compute.

Depending on the cost–availability trade-off of your application, you have a variety of ways to handle availability issues, including failover systems, job segmentation, and running pipelines in multiple AZs. Keep cost versus business need in mind when evaluating failover systems or multiregional deployments, particularly the cost of data replication.

The understanding you've gained about different pricing options will help you save costs where you can tolerate some ambiguity in compute capacity with interruptible/spot instances, and where you can comfortably commit to reservations—both strategies for saving significant costs over on-demand pricing. Interruptible instances are a great choice for development activities, opportunistically adding additional capacity, testing, or low-priority maintenance workloads. When you evaluate reservations, make sure you read the fine print! You will pay for your reserved capacity whether you use it or not, so make sure you understand how reserved capacity is applied to your workload.

To start getting a sense of what compute options are right for you, evaluate your business needs and architectural requirements. This will help you zero in on the right mixture of purchasing plans and cluster configuration possibilities for your pipelines.

Business requirements help you identify data, performance, cost, and reliability needs, while architectural requirements provide insight about data processing engines and infrastructure. During this process, acquiring sample data and gaining an understanding of where costs can be traded for system operation will give you important information to start exploring compute design options.

As you saw in this chapter, the learnings you gain from business and architectural requirements will get you ready to evaluate different cluster configurations by estimating required resources, deploying clusters to run your pipeline, and monitoring performance, resource utilization, and data processing engine behavior. Along the way, you also saw in this chapter how compute design is intertwined with many other aspects of data pipeline operation, including data processing engine configurations, approaches for transforming data, and decisions about data structure. Another element that impacts compute performance is how data is stored, which you will learn more about in Chapter 3.

As you saw in the benchmarking example, more compute power does not necessarily provide better performance. Monitoring and iterating on compute configurations is an essential practice for cost-effective design, helping you discern what configurations are most effective for a specific workload. While I focused on benchmarking to home in on cluster configurations in this chapter, this skill is indispensable for debugging and will be helpful in guiding infrastructure decisions regardless of whether you will be taking on infrastructure design yourself.

Moving on from managing cloud compute to get the best value for your money, in the next chapter you'll see how to leverage the elasticity of the cloud to increase or reduce cloud resources to accommodate different workloads and cost–performance trade-offs.

Recommended Readings

- Spark optimization resources
  - *High Performance Spark* by Holden Karau and Rachel Warren (O'Reilly)
  - Chapter 7 of *Learning Spark, 2nd Edition*, by Jules S. Damji, Brooke Wenig, Tathagata Das, and Denny Lee (O'Reilly)
  - Chapter 19 of *Spark: The Definitive Guide* by Bill Chambers and Matei Zaharia (O'Reilly)
- Dask optimization resources
  - Dask web page on optimization (*https://oreil.ly/Js5o1*)
  - *Scaling Python with Dask* by Holden Karau and Mika Kimmins (O'Reilly)
  - *Dask: The Definitive Guide* by Matthew Rocklin, Matthew Powers, and Richard Pelgrim (O'Reilly)
- AWS guide on choosing EC2 instances (*https://oreil.ly/t9Q0q*)
- AWS whitepaper on right-sizing (*https://oreil.ly/5Avbu*)
- EMR cluster-sizing tips and configurations (*https://oreil.ly/sROhE*)
- EC2 pricing data from Vantage (*https://instances.vantage.sh*) and on GitHub (*https://oreil.ly/zm0Uf*)

CHAPTER 2

Responding to Changes in Demand by Scaling Compute

When I'm not writing a book about data pipelines, I like to spend my free time exploring the woods. A big part of planning these outings involves figuring out what clothing to take. The weather forecast, how strenuous the hike is, and my pace all play a factor in this decision.

Dressing in layers is the time-honored approach to this conundrum. If I'm walking briskly up a hill, I'll remove some layers to avoid overheating. When I stop at the top of the hill to admire the view, I'll put them back on to stay warm. Being able to add and remove layers keeps me comfortable and safe in the backcountry.

Much like I can change layers to accommodate different conditions while hiking, you can customize the amount of resources for a pipeline to accommodate different workloads. Think of this as dynamically right-sizing compute, an iterative process that involves monitoring and tuning to dial things in.

In Chapter 1 you saw the definition of *vertical scaling*, which changes the capacity of a resource. This chapter focuses on *horizontal scaling*, which changes the number of resources. Adding more resources is *scaling out* and removing resources is *scaling in*, as described in "Design for Scaling in the Microsoft Azure Well-Architected Framework" (*https://oreil.ly/4xJU_*).

Scaling workloads is another realm of cost–performance trade-offs. You want to scale in resources to save cost, but not at the expense of pipeline reliability and performance. You want to scale out resources to accommodate large data loads but without allocating too many resources, which would result in wasted cycles.

This chapter focuses on how to horizontally autoscale data pipelines, illustrating when, where, and how to scale data workloads. You'll see how to pinpoint scaling opportunities, design scalable pipelines, and implement scaling plans. A scaling example at the end of the chapter brings this all together, along with an overview of different types of autoscaling services you'll see in the wild.

Identifying Scaling Opportunities

Before getting into the business of how to scale, let's start by determining where you have opportunities to scale data pipelines. Two main ingredients are required for scaling: variability and metrics.

Variability is what gives you the opportunity to scale. Without this, you have static resource use. If I'm hiking on a hot, sunny day, I'm not going to bring layers;[1] I know I'm going to be warm the entire time regardless of how strenuous the hike is or how quickly I do it. Variable conditions are what lead me to add or remove layers. In data pipelines, variation in operation and workload is where scaling opportunities abound.

Metrics are what you use to identify when to scale. Memory use increases as a large batch of data is processed, indicating that more resources are needed. The time of day when the largest jobs are processed has passed. Data volumes decrease, as does CPU utilization, providing an opportunity to scale in to reduce costs.

Variation in Data Pipelines

You can think about variation in data pipelines in terms of pipeline operation and data workload. *Pipeline operation* refers to how frequently the pipeline processes data. *Data workload* encompasses changes in data volume and complexity. Figure 2-1 illustrates a baseline case of constant operation and constant workload. In a data pipeline, this could be a streaming system that monitors temperature every few seconds. There isn't an opportunity to scale here, because nothing is changing over time.

---

1 Unless sunscreen is considered a layer.

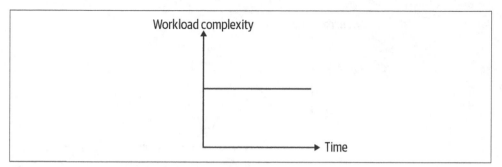

Figure 2-1. Constant workload, constant operation

As data workload and pipeline operation move from constant to variable, you have more opportunities to scale for cost and performance. You can scale in a pipeline with variable operation to save costs when there are no or few active jobs, as illustrated in Figure 2-2. This includes batch pipelines and streaming pipelines that process data intermittently.

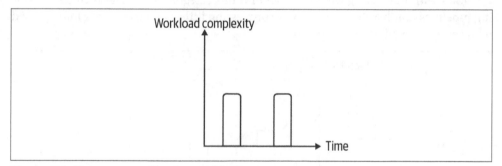

Figure 2-2. Constant workload, variable operation

A caveat in the "constant workload, variable operation" case is differentiating between scaling and triggering intermittent pipeline jobs. In the batch pipeline in Chapter 1, jobs are triggered, either on a schedule or by an external event. In another example, I worked on a pipeline that ran jobs during certain time periods. Our pipeline scaled down to a minimum set of resources outside of these time periods and scaled up when jobs were expected. Both examples have the characteristics of Figure 2-2, but one uses scaling while the other uses triggering to bring necessary resources online.

Data workload variability gives you the opportunity to service large workloads by scaling out, while also saving costs by scaling in when processing small workloads. Batch pipelines where data workloads fluctuate and stream processing with variable data loads are good candidates for scaling based on workload. Figure 2-3 shows a profile of a pipeline with variable workload and constant operation.

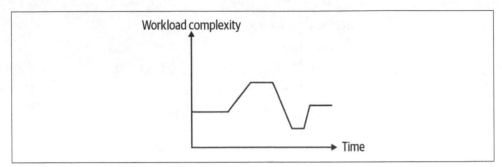

Figure 2-3. Variable workload, constant operation

You have the most scaling opportunity in pipelines that have variation in both data workload and pipeline operation, as depicted in Figure 2-4. This is where cloud billing models really shine, letting you reduce costs for smaller loads without sacrificing performance for larger loads.

Pipelines with fluctuating workloads fall into this category. Examples include streaming pipelines that have bursty behavior, processing little or constant data interspersed with spikes, and ad hoc batch pipelines.

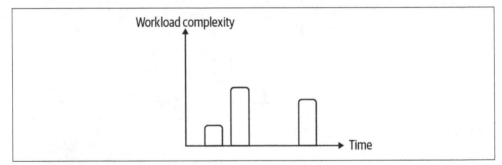

Figure 2-4. Variable workload, variable operation

These examples show variation in a system-level setting. There is also variation in how different workloads are processed within the data pipeline.

Some stages in a pipeline may be computationally intensive, requiring more compute resources, whereas other stages might not need as much firepower. You can scale in resources as data progresses past the computationally intensive stages, ensuring that you are spending for the scaled-out resources only for the duration of data processing that requires them.[2]

---

2 Spark dynamic resource allocation (*https://oreil.ly/GjNB6*) enables this kind of scaling and is supported by Google Dataproc (*https://oreil.ly/6MBko*) and AWS EMR (*https://oreil.ly/Y8LAe*).

Be sure to investigate scaling when doing *lift and shift migrations*, where you move a workload into the cloud without resizing or redesigning it. This can be a very expensive proposition if you don't take advantage of cloud elasticity to reduce costs.

Additionally, pipeline stage resource needs can vary from job to job, providing another opportunity for scaling. "Pipeline Scaling Example" on page 30 includes examples of these types of variability.

Scaling Metrics

Once you've identified where you have opportunities to scale, the next step is to determine how to know it's time to scale. In autoscaling parlance, this corresponds to thresholds and observation windows. A *threshold* refers to the value a metric is compared to when determining whether a scaling event should occur. The *observation window* is the time period for which the metric is evaluated against the threshold.

For example, a possible autoscaling rule is scale out two units if CPU utilization is above 70% for five minutes. The metric here is CPU utilization, the threshold is 70%, and the observation window is five minutes.

A scaling metric could be something as straightforward as the time of day. I worked on a data platform that was only used during the workweek, providing an opportunity to save costs by ramping down the infrastructure over the weekend. This is an example of scaling for operation variability.

As an example of scaling based on data workload variability, I worked on a streaming pipeline that consistently processed the largest workloads during a certain time period every day. The pipeline resources were scaled based on the time of day, adding more resources at the beginning of the time window and ramping down after a few hours. This cut cloud costs by two-thirds.

Don't overly rely on scaling. Thinking back to Chapter 1, aim for your baseline compute configurations to accommodate most workloads. Scaling is expensive in time and cost. It can take minutes or more depending on the capacity issues you saw in Chapter 1. This is time you may not have while running production workloads.

In "Autoscaling Example" on page 44, you'll see an example of this in which scaling out from an undersized cluster configuration did not provide relief for a struggling job.

Other metrics for scaling tend to stem from resource use and system operation. This provides a more nuanced signal based on how the pipeline processes data, providing additional opportunities to save costs. For example, if a memory-bound job falls below a certain memory utilization percentage, it could be an indication that more resources are allocated than necessary. In this case, it may be possible to save costs by scaling in.

As you'll see in "Common Autoscaling Pitfalls" on page 40, metric fluctuation can trigger undesired autoscaling events. For this reason, it can be preferable to look at metrics based on averages as opposed to a constant value. Returning to the CPU utilization example, the job may need to scale out if the average CPU utilization is above 70%, though the raw value of CPU utilization may fluctuate above and below this value during the observation window.

Depending on how the workload is run, cluster or Spark metrics can be used for scaling. You can see that several YARN-based metrics are used in AWS managed autoscaling (*https://oreil.ly/Qm3Rr*) to scale based on workload. Spark dynamic resource allocation (*https://oreil.ly/zRnwP*) looks at the number of pending tasks to determine whether a scale-out is needed, and it scales in based on executor idle time.

Benchmarking and monitoring can help you identify which metrics are good indicators for scaling. You can also get a sense of the overhead you need for reliability and performance, which will guide how much you allow a workload to scale in and determine when a workload should scale out.

To summarize, variation in pipeline operation and data workload highlights opportunities for scaling in data pipelines. Determining when to scale depends on identifying metrics that relate to these variable scenarios. With this in mind, you can evaluate a pipeline for scaling by asking the following questions:

- How does pipeline operation change over time?
- How does data workload vary?
- How does variation in data workload or operation impact resource needs?
- How do you know that resource needs are changing?

Let's take a look at applying this process to an example pipeline.

Pipeline Scaling Example

Recall the HoD batch pipeline from Chapter 1, which processes bird survey data on a biweekly basis. The data volume chart is repeated in Figure 2-5 for reference.

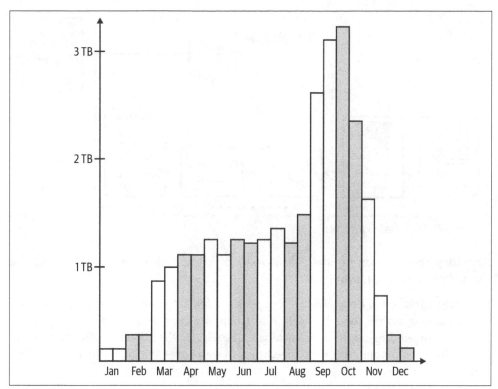

Figure 2-5. Biweekly data workload

Now let's review the scalability questions.

How does pipeline operation change over time? Pipeline operation is variable, running only every two weeks or perhaps ad hoc as needed.

How does data workload vary? The histogram shows that the data volume varies seasonally.

The survey data isn't the only data source, however. Shown in Figure 1-3 and repeated in Figure 2-6, the pipeline enriches survey data with the social media data from the HoD platform. The data volume from the social media source is unpredictable; it depends on what birds and locations are in the survey data being processed and those that are present in the HoD database.

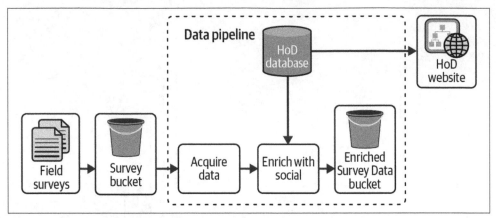

Figure 2-6. HoD batch pipeline

Revisiting the question of how data workload varies, both the survey data and the social data have varying volumes.

How does variation in data workload or operation impact resource needs? Based on the benchmarking results for this pipeline in Chapter 1, you know that memory needs are elastic depending on the data workload. There's also the biweekly schedule to consider. Most of the time, you won't need to have resources available—just when a job runs.

The overlap between the survey data and the social media data also impacts resource needs. The "Enrich with social" step could be resource intensive if there is significant overlap in the data sources, or it could require very few resources if there are no matches.

How do you know that resource needs are changing? Good question. To answer this, let's first take a look at how resource needs change as data moves through the HoD pipeline.

Thinking back to variation within the pipeline, the "Enrich with social" step in Figure 2-6 is likely to require more resources than the "Acquire data" step, owing to the merge. Resources can be scaled out at the beginning of "Enrich with social" and scaled back in when the merge is finished. Figure 2-7 illustrates this idea, where the filled background for "Enrich with social" indicates higher resource needs than the white background for "Acquire data."

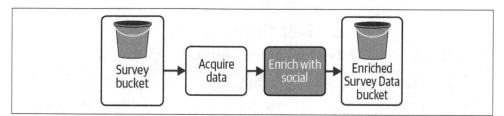

Figure 2-7. Scaling resources per stage. The filled box indicates higher resource needs.

Another source of variation is the unknown overlap between survey data and social media data, which will impact the resource needs of "Enrich with social."

Figure 2-8 shows this scenario, with the relationship between the survey data and the social data shown on the left and the corresponding resource needs of the "Enrich with social" step on the right. The darker the "Enrich with social" background is, the more resources are needed to merge the data.

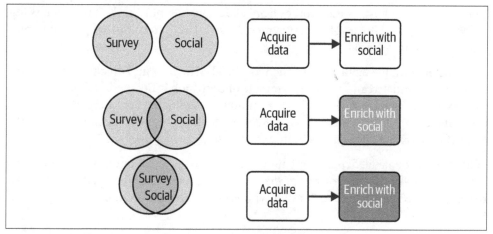

Figure 2-8. Different resource needs across pipeline jobs

To summarize, resource needs can change in the HoD pipeline based on the stage of processing and data characteristics. So *how do you know that resource needs are changing?*

Based on the benchmarking for this pipeline in Chapter 1, you know this is a memory-heavy process. As data size and survey–social overlap increase, so will memory use. With this in mind, you can look for sustained increases in memory use as an indication that more resources are needed. Conversely, a reduction in memory use can indicate that fewer resources are needed, providing an opportunity to save costs by scaling in.

Cost Reduction with Scaling

To revisit the value of scaling, consider the costs of this pipeline if you provided a fixed set of resources. If you wanted to guarantee a certain level of performance and reliability, you would need to provision resources for the case where there is a lot of overlap between the data sources in Figure 2-8. If you provide fewer resources, you run the risk of long runtimes or pipeline failures when there is a lot of data to merge.

As a result of static resource allocation, you waste a lot of compute dollars over-provisioning for the cases where there is little to no overlap in the data sources. Leveraging cloud compute elasticity with scaling lets you match the resources to the workload, saving costs on smaller workloads without sacrificing performance and reliability for larger workloads.

With all the scaling questions answered, let's work out a scaling plan.

The biggest bang for the buck comes from allocating compute at the time a job is initiated, as opposed to a 24-7 deployment. Once the job completes, the compute resources can be released.

In a cluster compute environment such as AWS EMR, you can launch a cluster at the time a job is initiated and set it to terminate once the job is finished. If you're working in Kubernetes, you may have to keep a minimum deployment running, as horizontal pod autoscaling (HPA) (*https://oreil.ly/b2bHT*) does not support scaling to zero at the time of this writing, though it is in the works (*https://oreil.ly/nU7ri*).

With the on-demand deployment model in mind, the next question is *how many compute resources are needed to run the jobs*. The variation in workload and the fluctuating resource needs of the "Enrich with social" step indicate there are opportunities to scale.

Combining the information about data volume from Figure 2-5 and the resource needs based on dataset overlap in Figure 2-8, you can see two extreme cases: low-volume survey data and no overlap, and high-volume survey data and high overlap. Benchmarking these cases will provide a starting point for minimum and maximum resource needs.

Let's say benchmarking shows you need three workers for the low-volume, no-overlap case and 10 workers for the high-volume, high-overlap case. This gives you a starting point for your minimum bound (no fewer than three workers) and maximum bound (no more than 10 workers).

Note that I said these min/max values are a starting point. Like right-sizing from Chapter 1, tuning scaling bounds is an iterative process. When starting out, pad your min and max boundaries. This will ensure that you don't sacrifice performance and reliability by under-provisioning. Monitor resource utilization and pipeline performance to see whether you can reduce these values.

Designing for Scaling

Before I got into technology, I aspired to be a jazz musician. A characteristic of jazz music is improvisation (*https://oreil.ly/vhBJW*), in which musicians spontaneously create melodies over the chord changes of a song. I remember diligently learning which scales corresponded to various chord changes as I learned to improvise.

During a lesson, I was shocked when my teacher asked me whether I knew my scales. "Of course!" I replied, and promptly busted out my repertoire of notes. He shook his head and said, "Well, why don't you use them?" It only then occurred to me that simply knowing what notes to play wasn't enough; I had to intentionally incorporate them into my playing.

Similarly, just because you are adding or removing compute capacity doesn't mean your pipeline will take advantage of this elasticity. You need to design to support scaling.

A key design consideration for supporting horizontal scaling is using distributed data processing engines such as Spark, Presto, and Dask. These engines are designed to spread computation across available resources. In contrast, single-machine data processing approaches such as Pandas (*https://pandas.pydata.org*) do not scale horizontally.[3]

In addition to using a distributed engine, the structure of data files and how you write data transformation code have an impact on scalability. Ensuring that data can be split will help distribute processing via partitioning, which you'll see in Chapter 3.

When transforming data, keep in mind the impacts of wide dependencies,[4] which can result in shuffling data. Data partitioning can help minimize shuffle, as does filtering your dataset prior to performing transformations with wide dependencies. Spark v3.2.0 and later include Adaptive Query Execution (*https://oreil.ly/Gqanp*), which can alleviate some shuffle-related performance issues by reoptimizing query plans, as discussed in the Databricks article "Adaptive Query Execution: Speeding Up Spark SQL at Runtime" (*https://oreil.ly/BjsIU*).

Another consideration with shuffle is that you can actually harm performance by scaling out too much. Recall from Chapter 1 that Spark workloads with shuffle can suffer from poor performance if spread across too many workers.

---

3 If you like working with Pandas, you can do so in a distributed way with the Pandas API for Spark (*https://oreil.ly/m60pw*), available starting with v3.2.0. You can also consider Dask (*https://oreil.ly/chKHf*).

4 Chapters 2 and 6 of *High Performance Spark* are a good reference on narrow versus wide dependencies.

Vertical Scaling

In his provocatively titled article "Big Data Is Dead" (*https://oreil.ly/-6h2E*), Google Big Query founding engineer Jordan Tigani argues that most businesses don't need huge quantities of data and, given advances in hardware, a majority of data workloads can fit on a single machine.

In addition, some data workloads perform better with vertical scaling. For example, the issues I've mentioned with Spark shuffle when scaling horizontally may be better served by vertical scaling. If a broadcast join can be used, where one side of the join is a small amount of data that can be stored on the executors, increasing the resources available by vertically scaling can perform better.

I recommend that you check out Jordan's article. It will get you thinking about the costs of gathering, processing, and retaining data versus the value it brings to your business.

Besides designing scalable data processing, you also want to think about the consumers of data processing results. If you scale out such that the throughput of data processing increases, the consumers of that data will need to scale out as well. If they don't, your pipeline can become I/O bound, stalling while it waits for consumers to catch up with increased data volumes.

Keep in mind the impacts of scaling out on services the pipeline interacts with, such as databases and APIs. If scaling out the pipeline means an increase in the frequency or size of requests, you'll want to make sure to scale out services within your control or to build in throttling and retry logic for third-party services. You'll see more about handling these types of interactions in Chapter 4.

Separating storage and compute can also help you scale more effectively, in terms of both cost and performance. For example, if the pipeline writes out to a database, scaling up the pipeline and increasing the frequency and size of database inserts can require upsizing the database. In some cases, this may require downtime to increase database capacity.

If instead you write out to cloud storage, you have the advantage of much higher bandwidth, and you don't have to pay for both storage and compute, as you would with a database. With cloud storage–backed data platforms, you only pay for compute resources when the data is accessed.

In Chapter 4, you'll see the concept of checkpointing as a fault-tolerance mechanism for data pipelines. This involves saving intermediate results during data processing to allow a job to retry due to the occurrence of a failure such as the termination of interruptible instances, as you saw in Chapter 1. If you use this technique in your pipelines, saving the intermediate data to the cloud as opposed to the cluster disk will improve scalability. With scale-in events in particular, Hadoop Distributed File System (HDFS) decommissioning overhead can take a long time to complete, as described in the Google Dataproc documentation (*https://oreil.ly/71kbw*).

HDFS decommissioning overhead is a reason why CSPs recommend scaling clusters on nodes that do not work with HDFS. In AWS EMR these are referred to as *task nodes*, while in the Google Cloud Platform (GCP) these are *secondary nodes*. Later in this chapter, I'll share a scaling strategy that involves HDFS where you'll see this issue in more detail.

Implementing Scaling Plans

To this point, you've seen how to identify scaling opportunities and advice on designing for scalability. In this section, you'll see how scaling works, which will help you design scaling configurations that avoid common pitfalls.

Scaling Mechanics

When a scaling event is initiated, the system needs time to observe the scaling metrics, acquire or release resources, and rebalance running processes over the scaled capacity. In general, autoscaling performs the following steps:

- Poll scaling metrics at a set frequency.
- Evaluate metrics over an observation window.
- Initiate a scaling event if the metric triggers the scale-in or scale-out rules.
- Terminate or provision new resources.
- Wait for the load to rebalance before resuming polling, referred to as the *cooldown period*.

This process is depicted in Figure 2-9 for a scale-out event. The circles indicate compute resources, with the resource utilization depicted as the portion of the circle that is filled. The workload is shown in the boxes below each compute resource. The difference between timepoints is just an artifact of the drawing; it is not meant to convey the relative delays between successive stages.

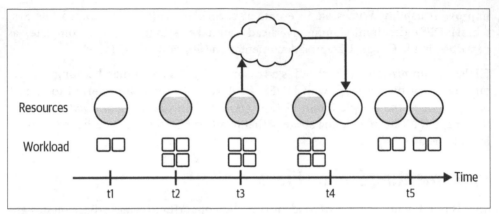

Figure 2-9. Request and rebalance timeline for a scale-out event

Starting at t1, a baseline workload uses about 50% of the compute capacity available. By point t2, the workload has doubled, increasing the load. This increase exceeds a scaling metric, and at t3 the system observes the metric and makes a request for more resources.

Recall from Chapter 1 that it can take some time for additional compute resources to be provided after a capacity request is made. The additional capacity comes online at t4, and the workload rebalances across the additional compute capacity at t5, concluding the scaling event. With the additional capacity to handle the larger workload, the resource utilization returns to the pre-scaling event levels.

You can see an example of this process in how Google Cloud Compute (GCS) uses autoscaling to service high request rates, as detailed in the request rate and access distribution guidelines (*https://oreil.ly/8b89S*). This documentation notes that it can be on the order of minutes for GCS to identify high request rates and increase resources. In the interim, responses can slow considerably or fail, because the high request rate exceeds the available capacity. To avoid this issue, users are advised to gradually increase the request rate, which will give GCS time to autoscale.

This is a really important point: *failures can occur if request volumes increase before GCS can scale out.* You will hit these same types of performance and reliability issues with data processing jobs if you don't scale out aggressively enough to meet demand for large workloads.

The order of operations is somewhat reversed when you scale in, as illustrated in Figure 2-10. This scenario starts out where things left off in Figure 2-9, with two units of compute capacity running two workload units each. The workload decreases by t2, which results in resource utilization falling for one of the compute units. This triggers a scale-in metric by t3, sending a request to terminate the underutilized compute capacity.

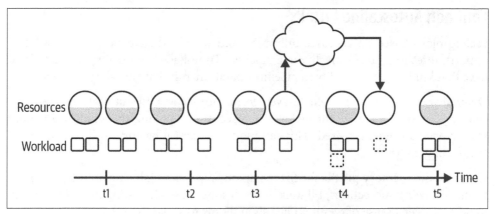

Figure 2-10. Rebalance and removal timeline for a scale-in event

Timepoint t4 in Figure 2-10 is interesting, since a few different things can happen, as depicted by the dashed lines for the workload in t4. In some cases, you can wait for active processes on a node marked for termination to complete. YARN graceful decommissioning (*https://oreil.ly/iECdq*) is an example of this, where jobs are allowed to complete before a node is decommissioned. This is a good choice for jobs that have a defined end.

The other possibility at t4 is that the compute unit is removed without waiting for processes to finish. In this case, the work being done by that process will have to be retried. This can be the case when scaling in streaming pipelines, where checkpointing can be used to retry jobs killed as a result of decommissioning. In streaming pipelines, you wouldn't want to use graceful decommissioning as part of your scale-in strategy, as this would block scale-in events.

Ultimately, one compute unit remains after the scale-in event, which picks up the workload from the removed compute unit if necessary.

 While this chapter focuses on autoscaling, there are times when you may manually scale a workload. Ideally these should be exceptional cases, such as experiments or unexpected resource shortfalls—for example, if your cluster has scaled up to the maximum number of workers but more resources are needed, necessitating manual intervention.

If these scenarios start occurring frequently, it's a sign that either you need to modify your scale-out limits or there are underlying performance issues. Don't simply throw more resources at a problem. Be sure to monitor and investigate performance degradation.

Common Autoscaling Pitfalls

Scaling plans based on resource utilization and workload state can provide a lot of opportunities to cost-effectively run a pipeline. Time-based autoscaling is great if you have that kind of predictability in pipeline operation, but that isn't always the case.

Dynamic scaling metrics, such as average memory and CPU utilization, present a challenge as they fluctuate throughout job execution, opening the window for more scaling events to get triggered. This can require a careful balance in how you set up autoscaling plans.

Consider the memory profile for the hypothetical pipeline job shown in Figure 2-11. In the following subsections, I'll walk through some possible scaling plans for this job to help you get a sense of common pitfalls and how to avoid them.

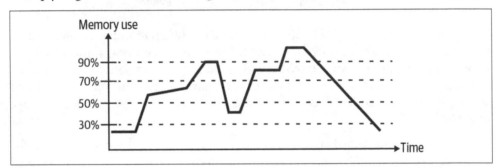

Figure 2-11. Memory profile for a data pipeline job

Scale-out threshold is too high

It's tempting to think that the scale-out threshold should be high from a cost-effective standpoint; this will prevent prematurely scaling out and wasting compute cycles. While there is some truth to this, you want to balance over-resourcing with sacrificing reliability and performance.

Recall that scaling out is not an instantaneous event; you need to wait for resource provisioning and load rebalancing. Consider the impact of setting the scale-out threshold at 90% for the job depicted in Figure 2-11. In this situation, resources wouldn't scale out until the memory exceeded this value, potentially impacting reliability.

Keep this in mind when setting scale-out thresholds, and when in doubt, set the scale-out threshold a bit lower than you think you need. You can then monitor resource utilization to see whether this results in a significant number of wasted cycles, and refine thresholds down the road.

Flapping

Not just for birds, *flapping* or *thrashing* refers to a cycle of continuously scaling in and out. This can negatively impact performance and reliability, as the load is constantly in a state of rebalancing.

Causes of flapping include:

- Scale-in and scale-out thresholds that are too close together
- An observation window that is too short

You can see flapping with the job depicted in Figure 2-11 if the scale-in threshold is set to 50% and the scale-out threshold is set to 70%. This will result in the three scaling events shown in Figure 2-12, where the lighter shaded bar shows a scale-in event and the darker shaded bars show scale-out events.

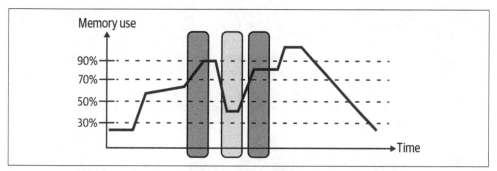

Figure 2-12. Flapping due to scale-in and scale-out thresholds that are too close

Figure 2-13 shows the resource allocation resulting from these scaling events. Looking at this view, it's clear that the scale-in event isn't necessary, as the resource needs increase immediately following it. In addition to the unnecessary workload shuffling from prematurely scaling in, you can waste compute dollars here. It takes time for resources to spin down, get provisioned, and spin up, all of which you pay for. Another consideration is the granularity of billable time. Some services charge by instance hours and some by fractional hours. Flapping can result in paying this minimum charge multiple times.

One way to resolve the flapping in this example is to increase the observation window for the scale-in event. Notice that the time period that is less than 50% during the shaded interval is much smaller than the time periods that are greater than 70%. If the observation window for the scale-in event was expanded, the 50% time period in Figure 2-12 wouldn't trigger a scale-in event, leaving resources as is.

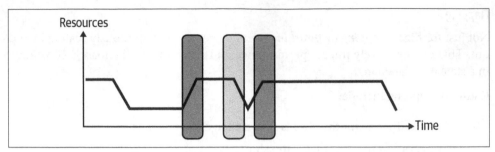

Figure 2-13. Resource fluctuation due to flapping

Another solution is to adjust scale-in and scale-out thresholds to be farther apart. If the scale-in threshold was reduced to 30%, the flapping in Figure 2-12 would not occur.

A rule of thumb for scaling is to scale in conservatively and scale out aggressively. This rule comprehends the overhead of scale-in decommissioning and rebalancing, while giving a nod to the performance and reliability needs for larger workloads.

You can achieve this by setting longer observation windows for scale-in events, and scaling in by a smaller amount than you would scale out by.

Over-scaling

When a scaling event is initiated, it's critical that you allow enough time for the load to rebalance and the scaling metrics to update. If you don't, you can end up triggering multiple scaling events that will result in over- or under-resourcing. Over-resourcing wastes money and under-resourcing impacts reliability. This is where the cooldown period comes into play.

Figure 2-14 shows a well-designed autoscaling approach with adequate cooldown. If memory use exceeds 70% for the observation window, a scale-out event is initiated that increases the number of resources by N.

Starting with Poll 1, the memory use remains above 70% for the observation window, triggering a scale-out event. The cooldown period is long enough to account for the scale-out event and resource rebalancing. As a result, the next polling event, Poll 2, occurs after the impact of the N additional resources is reflected in the memory use metric. No additional scaling events are triggered, since the memory use is not above 70%.

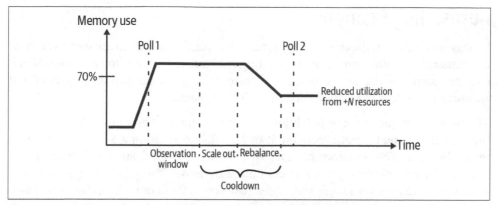

Figure 2-14. Autoscaling example with a sufficient cooldown period

Contrast this with a cooldown period that is too short, as depicted in Figure 2-15. In this case, Poll 2 happens before the impact of the initial scale-out event is reflected in the memory use metric. As a result, a second scale-out event is initiated, resulting in increasing the resources a second time.

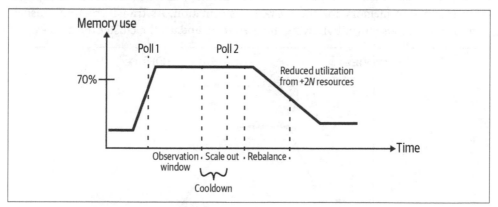

Figure 2-15. Autoscaling example with an insufficient cooldown period

There are two undesirable results here. For one thing, twice as many resources are allocated than needed, which wastes cycles. There's also the possibility of tipping over into flapping if both the scale-in and scale-out cooldown times are inadequate.

An additional concern when scaling in is under-resourcing resulting from scaling in more than warranted. This is another reason to follow the advice to scale in conservatively and scale out aggressively.

Autoscaling Example

In this section, I'll walk through an autoscaling plan I developed to show you how benchmarking, monitoring, and autoscaling rules come together to save costs. You'll also see some of the issues stemming from scaling HDFS and how suboptimal autoscaling can lead to performance and reliability issues.

The pipeline in question ran batch jobs on an on-demand basis in AWS EMR, reading data from cloud storage, copying it to HDFS, and running a Spark job to transform the data. The transformed data was written to cloud storage, where it was accessed by analytics users via a cloud data warehouse. The pipeline operation was variable, as was the workload; some jobs had very little data while others processed significantly more data. This meant scaling was possible due to variation in both pipeline operation and data workload.

Figure 2-16 shows memory and HDFS utilization over the course of the job, with HDFS use shown by the dashed line. You can see how HDFS utilization climbs during the copy step, as data is moved from the cloud onto the cluster. When the copy step finishes and data transformation begins, the memory use ramps up as data is read from HDFS into memory for the Spark transformation. As transformation finishes, memory use ramps down. Following the metastore update, the cluster terminates.

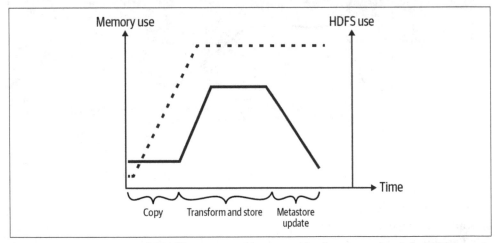

Figure 2-16. Memory and HDFS use over the course of a data ingestion job. HDFS use is depicted by the dashed line.

The pipeline experienced intermittent job failures that traced back to `BlockMissing Exception`. This issue occurs when a block of data is requested but cannot be retrieved from any of the replicas. This exception has several potential causes, but overall it indicates that HDFS is unhealthy. As data size increased, these failures became more frequent, and I took on the task of mitigating the issue.

The original cluster configuration specified an initial number of core nodes[5] and an autoscaling plan to add or subtract core nodes based on HDFS utilization. Recall from "Designing for Scaling" on page 35 that scaling HDFS capacity, especially scaling in, is an expensive operation.

You can see how it would be tempting to use HDFS utilization as a scaling parameter in this scenario. The architectural decision to copy data to HDFS and the unknown data load from batch to batch meant that it wasn't clear how much disk space would be needed until the job started running. By scaling out core nodes based on HDFS utilization, you could simply add more disk space if needed.

Known difficulties with scaling out on HDFS were only part of the issue. The source data exhibited the small-files problem, which you saw in Chapter 1. The additional overhead of having to replicate and keep track of numerous small files exacerbated the difficulties in scaling HDFS.

Another issue was that the mechanism used to copy the data didn't scale horizontally. If memory use spiked during copy, scaling out for more memory didn't provide any relief. One final confounding variable was the insufficient resource problem mentioned in Chapter 1: if a scale-out event occurred but no resources were available, the job would stall and ultimately fail.

Altogether, the data characteristics and autoscaling plan resulted in stalled jobs for large datasets. Essentially, as a large set of data was being copied, the HDFS-based autoscaling rules would attempt to scale out. The scale-out events took hours to complete, given the number of small files. The cooldown period was set to five minutes, so multiple scaling events would trigger during this time, like the issue depicted in Figure 2-15. As a result of the constant reconfiguration of HDFS space, eventually a block would not be found, causing the job to fail.

The job failures were certainly a negative, but the cloud bill costs were another issue. Hours-long autoscaling events drove up job runtime, which drove up costs and made the system unstable.

---

5 As described in the AWS documentation (*https://oreil.ly/P-VKj*), EMR clusters have three different types of nodes: primary, core, and task. Core nodes manage data storage on HDFS, whereas task nodes do not store data but can be helpful for scaling out the capacity of other resources.

Reducing failures involved improving the autoscaling rules and modifying the architecture to ensure that jobs had sufficient resources to succeed at the copy step.

On the architecture side, task nodes were added to the cluster configuration. The scaling strategy was modified to scale only the number of task nodes; the number of core nodes remained fixed. Rather than scale on HDFS utilization, the task nodes were scaled based on YARN memory and container metrics. You can see all of these metrics in the EMR autoscaling metrics documentation (*https://oreil.ly/_f4g3*).

This eliminated the issues of scaling based on HDFS, but it didn't address the fact that the amount of disk space needed varied from job to job. This is where benchmarking came in.

I plotted the various data sizes and cluster configurations for successful ingestion jobs. This gave me a starting point for identifying the number of core nodes required for a successful job. I separated jobs into high, medium, and low data size based on these metrics, and I added a step in the cluster launch process that checked the size of the incoming data. The initial cluster configuration would use the number of core nodes based on the data size falling into the high, medium, or low bucket and the min and max limits for scaling the workers. In this way, cost was optimized based on data workload, and the single-threaded copy stage would succeed because the core node count was fixed at the required capacity.

Because this process surfaced the data size, I could also set the EBS volume size to ensure that there would be enough capacity to run the job, eliminating the need to scale out disk space. I came up with a conservative approximation based on data size, replication factor, and disk space needed for data transformation.

With these changes, autoscaling events occurred only during data transformation as more resources were needed to process the data. This approach eliminated the long-running autoscaling events and significantly reduced the job failure rate. In addition, the workload-based cluster and autoscale configurations improved reliability by guaranteeing sufficient HDFS capacity from the outset.

Overview of Autoscaling Services

CSPs provide an assortment of autoscaling capabilities of varying sophistication. In some cases, much of the configuration is left to the user; in others, the CSP manages most of the configuration for the user, requiring only the minimum and maximum amount of capacity allowed. Typically the former are for more generic circumstances, and the latter operate in more customized environments where the possible scaling parameters are narrower.

Kubernetes HPA is on the bare-bones side, which you would expect from an ecosystem that can run myriad workloads, not just data processing. There is a lot of flexibility to be had here in that you can use metrics based on pod utilization or create your

---

own custom metrics. The number of replicas added or removed is calculated based on the ratio of the desired metric value to the current metric value.

The pipeline I mentioned that scaled down during certain times of the day used HPA with a simple custom metric that checked whether the current time was within the high-load window, and if so, scaled up the resources. DoorDash uses Kubernetes HPA based on CPU utilization in its real-time event processing pipeline (*https://oreil.ly/yQJtk*).[6]

For HPA strategy to be effective, pods must have resource requests defined, and they must be designed such that capacity is meaningfully changed by adding or removing pods.

Google Dataproc Autoscaling (*https://oreil.ly/YmFeE*) is more targeted to cluster data workloads. It uses YARN-based metrics to determine how many workers to add or remove, allowing you to customize the thresholds. It also has some support for various Spark autoscaling features.

EMR managed autoscaling (*https://oreil.ly/Sd4_E*) and Databricks cluster autoscaling (*https://oreil.ly/OUYjo*) take on more of the configuration burden by identifying important metrics and setting thresholds for scaling under the hood. You only need to specify the minimum and maximum bounds and the automation does the rest. Snowflake multicluster warehouses support autoscaling with predetermined scaling configurations for users to choose from (*https://oreil.ly/riN0Q*).

Finally, there is AWS predictive scaling (*https://oreil.ly/EX5O_*), which tries to forecast resource needs based on past jobs. By allocating the expected resource needs up front, you won't incur the delays of autoscaling based on dynamic cluster metrics. Essentially, this is very similar to the process I described in the autoscaling example where I used historical data to configure clusters based on data size.

Predictive scaling is best suited for pipelines with repetitive operation and a stable workload. Be cautious about applying predictive autoscaling to variable workloads, as variation in workload can make prediction less certain.

When working with more managed autoscaling services, keep in mind the observation window over which autoscaling determines whether resource use has decreased. If you have I/O-intensive processes in your pipeline, it's possible that memory utilization could temporarily drop while waiting on I/O. Managed autoscaling might attempt a scale-in during this period, when the subsequent stages may need the same or even more capacity.

---

6 This article is also a good example of the greater flexibility and scaling opportunities available by moving away from CSP-managed services to open source solutions.

Summary

Variety is the spice of life, and variation is the sign that a pipeline can take advantage of scaling, leveraging cloud elasticity to minimize costs by scaling in and to keep up with increased demand by scaling out.

Answering the following questions will help you uncover sources of variability and their predictors in data pipelines:

- How does pipeline operation change over time?
- How does data workload vary?
- How does variation in data workload or operation impact resource needs?
- How do you know that resource needs are changing?

Pipelines with variable operation provide opportunities to reduce costs when there are fewer active jobs. Variation in data workload can be leveraged to reduce costs for smaller workloads without sacrificing performance for larger workloads.

There are multiple levels at which you can scale. At the system level, pipelines with periodic operation can take advantage of scheduled autoscaling, reducing costs during known quiescent times. When operation variability is less predictable, resource use and system metrics can be used to trigger scaling events.

At the level of data processing, workload variation can provide opportunities to scale in for less complex workloads while scaling out to support higher volumes and complexity. You can also scale within data processing jobs, such as with Spark dynamic resource allocation, to take advantage of differing resource needs across data processing stages.

Determining when to scale involves identifying meaningful metrics that indicate whether more or fewer resources are needed. Benchmarking different workloads can help you identify a starting point for these metrics, as well as appropriate thresholds and observation windows for making scaling decisions.

Designing pipelines to take advantage of distributed data processing is essential for horizontal scaling. Careful code design, partitioning, and being aware of shuffle will help you get the most out of this strategy.

When scaling out data processing, account for the impacts of increased data volume and size on services the pipeline interacts with. Take care to ensure that consumers can manage increased workloads, and be cognizant of impacts to quotas and throttling limits.

Favoring cloud storage will improve pipeline scalability and can reduce costs. Scaling HDFS is not recommended due to long decommissioning times; furthermore, databases couple storage and compute, necessitating scale-up of both. Separating storage and compute gives you the faster bandwidth of cloud storage and eliminates the compute cost associated with databases.

Automatically adjusting resource allocation is a delicate balancing act. When developing scaling plans, leave adequate time for the following:

- Scaling events to conclude, such that resources have been added or removed

- Workloads to rebalance across the changed resource envelope

- Metrics to update, ensuring that the next scaling decision is made based on the impacts of the previous scaling event

Scaling out aggressively helps you keep up with rapidly increasing workloads, while scaling in conservatively minimizes decommissioning overhead, under-resourcing, and double costs for terminating compute just to request it again.

Common issues stem from setting thresholds too high or too close together and from not having adequate cooldown and observation window durations. The following recommendations will help you avoid degraded performance and reliability when scaling:

- Set scale-out thresholds low enough to allow time for new resources to come online and load rebalancing to occur before critical performance or reliability limits are hit.

- Provide enough time between scaling events (i.e., cooldown) to give resources time to rebalance.

- Set scale-in and scale-out thresholds sufficiently far apart to avoid flapping.

- Ensure that your observation window is wide enough to avoid premature scaling events. Scaling too early can cause flapping, and scaling too late can miss cost optimization opportunities.

This and the preceding chapter focused on navigating the cost–performance trade-offs of cloud compute, with strategies for resource sizing, pricing, and scaling specifically for data pipeline workloads. The themes of size, cost, and scaling continue in the next chapter on cloud storage, where you'll see how to minimize storage costs and structure files for efficient data processing.

Recommended Readings

- The "Autoscaling" article (*https://oreil.ly/1GWmE*) in the Azure Architecture documentation, which does a particularly good job of describing autoscaling best practices
- The "Design for scaling" article (*https://oreil.ly/FxOZr*) from the Microsoft Azure Well-Architected Framework
- Scaling in Kubernetes
  - "Horizontal Pod Autoscaling" (*https://oreil.ly/6ZtV4*)
  - Issue about scaling to zero (*https://oreil.ly/opiP4*)
- Spark adaptive query execution explainer from Databricks (*https://oreil.ly/G9au5*)
- DoorDash's "Building Scalable Real Time Event Processing with Kafka and Flink" (*https://oreil.ly/cfEmu*)
- *High Performance Spark* by Holden Karau and Rachel Warren (O'Reilly)

CHAPTER 3

Data Organization in the Cloud

Organizing data in the cloud has a lot in common with organizing clothes in a closet. Some folks arrange clothes based on season, shape, or color, making it easy to quickly find a pair of blue pants or an overcoat. Others may forgo organization altogether, haphazardly chucking clothes into a rumpled pile and resorting to heap search when they want to find something.

You can see these same scenarios in cloud storage. At its best, data is neatly organized and managed to reduce costs and improve performance. At its worst, it can be a bit of a black hole where disorganized piles of data accumulate, driving up costs and dragging down performance.

It's very easy to put data into cloud storage, close the (figurative) door, and forget about it. That is, until performance starts to suffer or someone starts to complain about the bill. Fortunately, there isn't a physical avalanche of data when you start combing through the forgotten corners of cloud storage, unlike an overstuffed closet.

This chapter covers cloud storage techniques to help keep data organized, performant, and cost-effective. To begin, you'll see the different ways storage costs add up in terms of both the cloud bill and engineering overhead. Before you say "Storage is so cheap! Why should I care?" and decide to skip this chapter, I encourage you to read on. You'll see several real-world situations where cloud storage costs accumulate and how to mitigate these scenarios.

After an overview of storage costs, the rest of the chapter focuses on cost-cutting strategies. You'll see how to use the services provided by CSPs to organize and maintain cloud storage and when it makes sense to trade performance for lower-cost options.

Based on this foundation of organization and automation, the last section of the chapter focuses on file structure design for performant data pipelines and data analysis. Because file structure is a case-by-case decision, you'll see general advice in this section and receive suggestions on where you can learn more about this topic in "Recommended Readings" on page 62.

Cloud Storage Costs

When it comes to cloud storage, the bulk of costs tends to come from three areas:

- The amount of data you store
- The amount of data you transfer
- The number of operations performed on cloud storage objects

In this section, you'll see how different aspects of data pipeline design and operation impact costs in these areas.

Storage at Rest

At the risk of sounding obvious, data pipelines store and process data, sometimes vast quantities of it. Cloud storage can be involved in many parts of this process, including but not limited to:

- Ingested data, which can be raw as well as processed
- Intermediate data created during ingestion or analysis
- Historical data for machine learning, compliance, or product offerings
- Data for development and testing
- Logs from pipeline operations

It's very easy to store data in the cloud, much like thoughtlessly chucking a sweater into your closet. Unlike databases, there are no schemas to set up or tables to define. As long as you've got permission to write and read, you can pile as much data as you like into cloud storage. This can lead to massive amounts of data accumulating as the near-infinite closet of cloud storage continuously expands.

In addition to using cloud storage as a primary data repository, it can also augment other data storage mechanisms. As an example, I worked on a pipeline that wrote to a database. Over time, we added more enrichments in the pipeline, increasing the size of the data to the point that it dominated the database resources. Not only did this lead to database performance issues, but this approach was also wasting money.

The data was only accessed occasionally, yet because of its size, the database had to be upsized. Using a common pattern of separating compute and storage to optimize cost–performance trade-offs, our team decided it would be better to store the pipeline data in the cloud. This reduced our costs, as adding storage is cheaper than adding more resources to the database. In addition, the bandwidth of cloud storage improved the reliability and performance of writing the data.

With the CSP client library in hand, the developers were ready to start shoveling terabytes of data into the cloud.

As our team discussed this change, I could hear our infrastructure engineer nervously clicking his pen. "We need to determine how to organize the data, and we need to think about lifecycle policies," he said. Our infrastructure engineer wisely raised these concerns knowing that managing both the data and its costs could easily get out of control.

Egress

Putting data into cloud storage is free, but getting it out is another story. While storing data at rest is inexpensive, egress costs can be significantly greater. Say you need to move 10 TB of data to another AWS region. Based on the AWS S3 pricing chart (*https://aws.amazon.com/s3/pricing*) at the time of this writing, moving this data once will cost four times the amount it costs to store it. This is why it's important to process data in the same region where it's stored; otherwise, every time the data is read, you pay for roughly one month of storage costs!

Egress costs show up in data pipelines when replicating data for backup or failover systems, especially if you move data across geographical regions. If you have failover, you can reduce costs by combining your backup and failover data, keeping in mind the impact to backups if the failover system is activated. For example, if backups are used in a failover environment and data is added, modified, or deleted, the backup no longer represents the state it initially captured.

The End of Exports?

Storing data in the cloud gives you more opportunities for sharing data, something cloud data platforms (CDPs) have taken advantage of to provide zero copy clones (*https://oreil.ly/APrXA*) and data sharing in Snowflake (*https://oreil.ly/7ojPw*) and Databricks (*https://oreil.ly/3F82r*).

Under the hood, these product features couple cloud data storage with service layers and metadata. Instead of exporting data, you can share access to it, assuming the recipients can access data from your CDP.

While CDPs provide a lot of nice features, you aren't limited to this option to reap the benefits of sharing data instead of exporting it. Some options for surfacing queryable,

---

cloud-backed data include Hive metastore, which is supported by Azure via Databricks (*https://oreil.ly/UAxxd*), AWS EMR (*https://oreil.ly/tUFFz*), and Google Dataproc (*https://oreil.ly/9YVhS*), and open table formats including Delta Lake (*https://oreil.ly/bftei*) and Apache Iceberg (*https://oreil.ly/sRXRB*).

You can also incur egress costs if you export data for customers. One way to reduce these costs is to export *deltas*, that is, just the data that has changed since the last export, rather than providing a full dataset every time. In addition, AWS S3 (*https://oreil.ly/xOPis*) and GCS (*https://oreil.ly/eh-Bx*) provide the option to have the requester (i.e., user) pay for transfer and data access costs, which you'll see in the next section.

Compression is another approach for reducing the costs of egress as well as storage at rest. If you use compression as a strategy to reduce egress costs specifically, make sure you check whether decompressive transcoding will be applied when data is accessed. For example, GCS will decompress gzip files with specific headers (*https://oreil.ly/nPuZ7*), which is handy if clients want the uncompressed data but will result in egress fees for the uncompressed version of the file.

Data Access

Every time you interact with a cloud storage object, you incur a fee for data access. In AWS S3 parlance, a PUT operation occurs when you create an object and a GET operation occurs when you read an object. There are also actions for listing objects and deleting objects, among others.

A lot of the time these data access costs are minimal compared to storage and egress, but I've seen several conditions where data pipelines run up these costs either due to design or because of data processing.

Generally, situations that result in creating many small files result in undesirable behavior for cloud data pipelines. Retrieving all the objects from a bucket that has many small files results in many data access operations, which could be reduced to a few operations if the files were compacted into a few larger files.

Not only can this increase cloud costs, but it can impact performance and reliability in data pipelines and analytics platforms. The small-files problem exists across various big data systems, including Map Reduce (*https://oreil.ly/EVMAK*), HDFS, and Spark (*https://oreil.ly/xtob1*). To summarize; in distributed systems there is more overhead when dealing with many small files.

Where do small files come from? Streaming pipelines can produce small files during periods when not much data is coming into the stream. I've also seen this happen in batch pipelines if the input data is small. In one case, the small-files problem was present in the data source. The pipeline didn't compact the data, causing the small-files problem to be perpetuated.

Overaggressive partitioning strategies can also cause small files by dicing data into small pieces. You'll see some suggestions on partitioning and file structure in "File Structure Design" on page 58.

Managed services are not immune to the small-files problem. In one example (*https:// oreil.ly/tvYXY*), an AWS Glue job at AI-powered software company Taloflow created a multitude of small files. As a result, over half of the cloud storage costs were due to object access operations. Moving off managed services gave the team the control to prevent this issue.

In another case, I was working with a Spark CDP to surface ingested data to analytics users. The users were experiencing slow queries that defied the usual course of investigation; query plans looked reasonable, there were few small files in the underlying dataset, and data skew was minimal. After several volleys with the CDP account reps, it turned out that the platform itself was creating a small-files problem because of how it managed tables in cloud storage.

This is all to say that there are a lot of reasons to avoid small files due to both data access costs and big data processing performance. I'll talk through some approaches to this in "File Structure Design" on page 58.

As you've seen in this section, a variety of elements impact cloud storage costs for data pipelines:

- Large amounts of data processed and stored
- Data replication for disaster recovery
- Customer data exports
- Data access fees due to the small-files problem

The good news is that cloud storage has a lot of features to help you tackle these issues. In the next section, you'll see how to get the most out of cloud storage organization and automate cost-savings strategies.

Cloud Storage Organization

In *The Life-Changing Magic of Tidying Up* (*https://oreil.ly/p6ilY*) (Ten Speed Press), Marie Kondo describes how to declutter and organize your home. The process of tidying up can be tough if you've accumulated a lot without an organization strategy. It's possible to declutter by following Kondo's advice; it's just more painful than starting with an organized approach.

This is similar to organizing cloud storage. It's ideal to think of organization from the outset, like the pen-clicking infrastructure engineer in the story I shared earlier. You can also use the methods in this chapter to retrofit existing cloud storage; it will just be a bit more involved.

Each CSP has their own unique ways to manage cloud storage. For specific clouds, you can refer to AWS S3 management (*https://oreil.ly/VI-j9*), Google Cloud Storage (GCS) (*https://oreil.ly/2F4Ay*), and Azure Blob Storage (*https://oreil.ly/x8a23*).

Storage Bucket Strategies

A good place to start organizing is by defining buckets in a way that best suits your application. One approach is to create buckets by function and environment. For example, let's say you have three different types of data to store—logs, raw data, and processed data—and you have two environments where the pipeline is running—test and prod. You would end up with six different buckets: `logs-test`, `logs-prod`, `raw-data-test`, `raw-data-prod`, `processed-data-test`, and `processed-data-prod`.

When creating buckets, consider adding tags and labels (*https://oreil.ly/xlVSf*) to help you track resources and cost in the same way tags and labels are used for compute, as described in Chapter 1. Be aware that some of these services may include extra costs, such as GCS bucket tags.

Keep in mind that the granularity of the tags and labels correlates to how finely you can stratify reports and permissions. If you want to look at the cost of raw data, add a label for raw data to each raw-data bucket. If you want to look at raw data cost per environment, you would want to add another label denoting the environment for each bucket. In larger organizations, looking at cost by department is desirable, which can be another label.

The next thing to consider is versioning, which can really save the day if things go haywire. With versioning enabled, each time you write to a storage location, a new object is created. A pointer keeps track of the latest version, so from the data consumer point of view, it appears that the old version of an object has been replaced. With versioning, you can go back in time to prior data.

As an example, versioning could be helpful if you're processing time-series data that is stored based on timestamp, such as by the prefix YYYY-MM-DD. In the event of a job rerun or backfill, the same prefix would be used to store the new data.

At a previous job, I used versioning to create a recovery mechanism for failed data ingestions. If the latest ingestion created bad data, our team could quickly roll back to a last known good state because versioning gave us access to prior data. The Azure Blob Storage documentation (*https://oreil.ly/GN0if*) has a nice description of the mechanics of object versioning and rollback.

Versioning is a powerful tool, but it can be costly. As an example from the FinOps foundation (*https://oreil.ly/v2knE*), one company reduced its storage costs by 60% after its developers realized stale object versions were not being deleted.

Lifecycle management (*https://oreil.ly/R3J0t*) can help with this issue. Lifecycle configurations can be applied at the bucket or prefix (*https://oreil.ly/3nMJZ*) level to control object expiration, storage class (more on storage class in a bit), and other properties.

Lifecycle Configurations

Lifecycle configurations are helpful for keeping costs in check by automatically deleting objects or moving them to a lower-cost storage class. Returning to the earlier example of the different data buckets, you can see that the breakdown by function and environment allows for different lifecycle policies to be applied. Table 3-1 shows a possible lifecycle configuration and versioning strategy for these buckets.

Table 3-1. Versioning and expiration lifecycle for example storage buckets

Bucket	Versioning	Expiration
logs-test	No	7 days
logs-prod	No	30 days
raw-data-test	No	7 days
raw-data-prod	No	30 days
processed-data-test	No	7 days
processed-data-prod	Yes	365 days

Notice that versioning is only enabled for the `processed-data-prod` bucket. For the sake of example, I'm assuming the pipeline overwrites existing objects in `processed-data-prod`.

For the test environment, I'm assuming there isn't a need for versioning; if the pipeline generates bad data in the test environment, you can rerun the test.

The lifecycle configuration in Table 3-1 expires objects after seven days across the test buckets. Expired objects get deleted, reducing the cost of storage.

The prod tiers have longer expiration times—30 days for logs and raw data and one year for processed data—to reflect the longer period you may want to keep data in production. These retention periods can be defined by how much data you want to provide to users, regulatory requirements, and the amount of data you want to retain for debug, monitoring, and analysis.

Especially with debug information such as logs, it can be a careful trade-off with the cost of retention versus the ability to look at bugs over time. Log retention in particular can be very costly; you'll see techniques for minimizing log costs without sacrificing debug capabilities in Chapter 11.

I mentioned that storage class was another object attribute that can be controlled by lifecycle policies. *Storage class* refers to the tier of service an object is stored in, which can range from high-performance "hot" tiers to reduced-performance "cold" tiers.

Hot tiers are good for objects that are being actively used, where you are willing to pay more for better performance. Cold tiers trade performance for cost, being less expensive for storing data at the cost of higher data access latency. Colder tiers are better suited for backups or historical data that isn't actively used but is needed for compliance or regulatory reasons.

You can automate the transition from hot to cold storage classes to take advantage of cost–performance trade-offs as data ages. Table 3-2 illustrates this transition as a lifecycle configuration for `processed-data-prod`, similar to this example for AWS S3 (*https://oreil.ly/OtO1-*).

Table 3-2. Lifecycle configuration moving from hot to expired

Data age at lifecycle transition (days)	Class
0	Hot
90	Warm
180	Cold
365	Expire

Objects in `processed-data-prod` start out in the high-performance, hot-storage class, transitioning to warm after 90 days, followed by a transition to cold storage at 180 days, and finally expiring after one year.

One more cost-saving lifecycle policy is cleaning up failed multipart uploads (*https://oreil.ly/TJiyy*). This is an issue that can crop up in data pipelines if you're uploading large (greater than 100 MB) files. While multipart uploads are a smart technique to overcome temporary network issues while transferring large files, failed uploads can accumulate objects in cloud storage. Automatically cleaning up failed uploads with a lifecycle policy helps keep things tidy. Otherwise, you must find and manually delete the partial uploads.

File Structure Design

Cloud storage organization and lifecycle configurations are the foundations of cost-effective storage for data pipelines. How you structure data within cloud storage builds on this. Recalling the closet analogy from the beginning of the chapter, if organization and lifecycle are closet organizers, file structure is how clothes are grouped within an organizer.

Let's say one of your closet organizers is for socks. If you store your socks as matched pairs, it's much faster to find a pair of socks in the organizer than it would be if you stored each sock individually. Since humans only have two feet, the performance of this sock-pairing algorithm isn't all that impressive, so consider instead if you were an octopus and had to scan for eight individual socks instead of one group of eight socks.

Similar to searching for socks, how you structure files generated by data pipelines can reduce or increase the time and resources it takes to find what you're looking for.

File Formats

Columnar file formats such as Parquet (*https://parquet.apache.org*) and ORC (*https://orc.apache.org*) can help you reduce costs in both storage and compute. On the storage side, these formats offer superior compression to flat files such as JSON or CSV, enabling you to store more data for less cost. On the compute side, the ability to *prune* columns, that is, read only the data in columns referenced in a query, cuts down on data processing overhead, reducing resource costs for querying data.

File formats are a place where you may see performance trade-offs between writing and reading data. For example, writing a JSON file can be faster than writing a Parquet file, but reading the JSON file may be less performant than reading the Parquet file if you're using a data processing engine that is optimized for columnar data.

While columnar formats have performance benefits, you may want to have data in another format for visual inspection or use by other services. One data pipeline I worked on created data for use by a React frontend, where JSON was converted to UI elements. In this situation, storing data as JSON was necessary for product functionality. For larger files, our team developed a pagination strategy, breaking up the JSON into multiple files to reduce load times on the frontend.

If you can't use columnar formats, you can still benefit from compression to reduce file size. Keep in mind that some compression types are not splittable, as described in *Spark: The Definitive Guide*. Splittable files can be divided into chunks to parallelize data processing. Choose a compression type that minimizes data size while still allowing the data to be processed in parallel.

Partitioning

Partitioning refers to splitting a block of space into smaller pieces, allowing you to use resources more effectively. This technique is used across mediums, from disk partitioning for operating systems to table partitioning in databases.

Partitioning can also be applied to data, where data with a common element, called a *partition key*, is grouped together. Similar to column pruning, partitions can also be pruned to filter out irrelevant data based on query parameters to improve performance. In the earlier sock analogy, the partition key would be the sock color or pattern.

A common question I received when teaching PySpark was how should data be partitioned. The choice of partitioning and file format is driven by data characteristics and how the data is used, so without knowing a lot about those things, I can't make a recommendation. In general, the following advice applies when thinking about partitioning:

- Be conservative. The more partition keys you create, the finer you will slice your data, which can negatively impact performance.
- Choose keys that are at the intersection of common query filters and low cardinality.
- Monitor queries and query performance to find optimization opportunities (which I'll cover in Chapter 11).

For example, the HoD pipeline in Chapter 1 ingests bird migration data. This could be queried in a variety of ways: searching for a particular species, location, or observation date range, to name a few. Let's say that primarily, queries look at observations over months: for example, "How many night herons were observed from May through July?" This hints at a date-based partitioning strategy in which partitions outside the months of May, June, and July could be ignored.

When you choose a partition granularity, look for a gradation that meaningfully breaks up the data into smaller chunks, while not tipping over into small-files territory. Let's say the bird survey data has very few observations on weekdays. If the data were partitioned by day, most partitions would have very little data, creating the small-files problem. Increasing the granularity to a month aggregates these values and results in larger partitions that provide the desired query granularity.

Generally, data partitioning gives you the biggest bang for your buck when it comes to file optimizations. If you have well-characterized data, it can be worth investigating finer-grained optimizations, such as choosing an encoding approach (*https://oreil.ly/r88TO*).

Compaction

Data compaction, in which multiple files are consolidated into a single larger file, is a common remedy for the small-files problem you've seen throughout this chapter.

Modern table formats include support for compaction, such as Delta Lake (*https://oreil.ly/QCdwQ*) and Apache Iceberg (*https://oreil.ly/c3UKu*). You can set up scheduled jobs to compact and repartition data to consolidate small files. This is an approach I used when working on a microbatch pipeline on Delta Lake. The compaction job ran nightly, which was sufficiently frequent for analytics users to see performance benefits. You may need to compact more frequently based on query patterns and data characteristics.

If you're not working in an environment that supports compaction out of the box, you can write a script to perform the compaction job. A simple approach would be reading the small files into a DataFrame and writing out larger files.

Summary

I think most people would agree that a tidy, organized closet is preferable to a disorganized jumble of clothes. Rather than spending a lot of time in the closet, you can quickly find what you need and get on with your life.

Similarly, data pipeline costs and performance improve when you organize cloud storage and thoughtfully structure data, enriching the experience of data users, finance teams, and fastidious infrastructure engineers.

Data pipelines can use the cloud as a primary means of data storage, or as a way to augment other data storage mechanisms such as databases. As data grows, look for opportunities to separate storage from compute to save costs.

Defining buckets by environment and function provides more granular control for both access management and cost efficiency. Within these buckets, lifecycle configurations automatically tidy up for you, saving engineering hours and cost by moving objects to different storage classes and deleting stale data, including obsolete versions, temporary development and test data, and the fragments of failed multipart uploads.

Tags and labels can help you track costs based on criteria such as function, environment, and department. At the object level, versioning gives you a time-travel option to revert to a prior state. Because versioning creates more objects, use this approach judiciously and make sure you limit version history.

Keep an eye on egress fees when creating backups, seeding failover systems, or exporting data for customers. Combining backup and failover storage can help reduce these costs, as well as exporting deltas and using requester pays settings in AWS and GCS.

Much of the time, data access costs are a drop in the bucket compared to egress and storage at rest. If you see an uptick in data access costs, this could be indicative of the small-files problem, which can also impact performance. Small batches of data, streaming pipelines, and overaggressive partitioning strategies can create small files. These issues also occur in managed services and cloud data platforms, as you saw in the examples in this chapter.

Organizing cloud storage provides the foundation for cost-effective design; the next layer is how you structure the data. Columnar formats can improve costs in both storage and compute by offering better data compression and query performance than flat files when using data processing engines that take advantage of columnar formats.

Regardless of the format, file compression is another lever to reduce storage at rest and egress costs. Be sure to choose a splittable compression type to benefit from parallel processing, and be aware of how compression (or decompression) impacts egress fees.

If you have data that has low-cardinality characteristics that often appear in analytical queries, partitioning is a file structure strategy that can reduce compute costs by improving performance. Don't go overboard creating partition keys; more is not necessarily better and may result in small files and poor performance.

Finally, compacting files into larger blocks can improve performance and reduce data access costs. Whether you write compaction code from scratch or take advantage of compaction support in modern table formats, a scheduled job can run this process in the background.

In this and the preceding two chapters, you learned about cost-effective practices when working with compute and storage in the cloud. Whether you're working on a scratch-built pipeline, using managed services such as AWS Glue or Google Cloud Dataflow, or running jobs on a fully managed CDP, the fundamentals of how cloud infrastructure impacts data pipeline cost and performance will help you root-cause these issues, make savvy decisions, and identify where you can improve.

In the next chapter, you'll see design and development techniques to help you really take advantage of the cost-effective strategies explored to this point. Understanding the trade-offs in infrastructure is a great baseline; how you design and develop data pipelines is where you truly harness the benefits of this work.

Recommended Readings

- The Data Efficiency Playbook from the FinOps Foundation (*https://oreil.ly/_i5WA*) mentions some of the topics covered in this chapter.
- The article "Data partitioning guidance" (*https://oreil.ly/bPC-b*) from the Azure Architecture Center is a nice guide to data partitions.
- The "Big Data File Format Optimizations" section of the article "Cost-Efficient Open Source Big Data Platform at Uber" (*https://oreil.ly/LRZGy*) details Uber's cost optimization strategies.

CHAPTER 4

Economical Pipeline Fundamentals

In the preceding chapters, you learned how to design cloud compute and storage solutions that make the right cost–performance trade-offs given your overall product goals. This gives you a strong foundation for cost-effective design.

The next step is to design and implement data pipelines that scale effectively, limit waste by making smart use of engineering and compute resources, and minimize data downtime. The first part of this process involves some fundamental design strategies for data pipelines: idempotency, checkpointing, automatic retries, and data validation.

In this chapter, you'll see common data pipeline issues and how to mitigate them using these four strategies. Rather than simply defining idempotency, checkpointing, retries, and data validation, I'll illustrate how to implement these strategies across batch and streaming environments as well as discuss some of the trade-offs you will encounter. You'll also get to see how these strategies (or lack thereof) contributed to real-world pipeline failures and successes.

Idempotency

The first place to start is designing your pipelines to be idempotent. *Idempotency* means you can repeatedly run a pipeline against the same source data and the results will be exactly the same. This has benefits on its own and is a prerequisite for implementing retries, as you'll see later in this chapter.

Preventing Data Duplication

The definition of idempotency can vary based on how the pipeline output is consumed. One way you can think about idempotency is an absence of duplicated data if the pipeline runs multiple times using the same source data.

For example, consider a pipeline that inserts data into a database by looping through the dataset and inserting each line into the database. If an error occurs, such as a networking blip that interrupts the connection to the database, you wouldn't be able to tell which portion of the data was written to the database and which was not. If you retry from this state, the pipeline could end up creating duplicate data.

To make this process idempotent, you can wrap the database inserts in a transaction, ensuring that if any of the inserts failed, any prior inserts would be rolled back.[1] This eliminates the possibility of partial writes.

You can also build data sinks that reject duplicated data. If you can create a unique key for ingested data, you can detect duplicate entries and decide how to handle them. In this case, you want to be absolutely sure the key you come up with is truly unique, such as a natural key (*https://oreil.ly/Hl9Vm*). Keep in mind that unique constraints can slow down inserts, as the database needs to validate that the key is unique and update the index. In columnar databases and data lakes, you can enforce uniqueness by hashing, preventing updates and inserts if the hash matches existing data. Some data lakes support merge keys, such as Delta Lake merge (*https://oreil.ly/mm3gh*), where you can specify a unique key and instructions for how to handle matches.

> Reducing data duplication will reduce costs by limiting your storage footprint. Depending on how data is used, this can also save on compute expenses.

When working with cloud storage, you can use an overwrite approach, also known as delete-write. Consider a pipeline that runs once a day, writing data out to a folder named for the current date. Prior to writing out the data, the pipeline can check whether any data already exists in the current date folder. If so, the data is deleted and then the new data is written. This prevents partial data ingestion as well as duplicated data.

For streaming processes, you can achieve idempotency through unique message identification. You can accomplish this by setting up the data producer to create the same ID when the same data is encountered. On the consumer side, you can keep a record of message IDs that have already been processed to prevent a duplicate message from being ingested.

Especially for streaming or long-running processes, consider maintaining a durable record of the information you need to ensure idempotency. As an example, Kafka

---

1 This assumes that the database is ACID compliant.

persists messages on disk (*https://oreil.ly/PcgHH*), making sure messages are not lost across deployments or due to unexpected outages.

Idempotency can be hard to ensure, particularly in streaming processes where you have a lot of options for how to handle messages. Keep your message acknowledgment (ack) strategy in mind; do you acknowledge messages when they're pulled from a queue or only when the consumer is finished? Another consideration is where your consumers read from; is it always the end of the stream or are there conditions where you may reread previously consumed messages?

For example, if you ack a message when the consumer reads it from the queue, a failure in the consumer means the message will go unprocessed, dropping data. If instead the messages are ack'd only when the consumer has finished processing, you can have an opportunity to reprocess the message if a failure occurs.

This opportunity to retry can also create duplicated data. I saw this happen in a pipeline where occasionally the data source would produce a large message that significantly increased processing time. These processes would sometimes fail partway through, creating partial data similar to the database example you saw earlier. Our team remedied the issue by setting a max message to prevent the long-running processes.

Tolerating Data Duplication

Given that idempotency can be difficult to achieve in the sense of preventing data duplication, consider if you need data deduplication. Depending on your pipeline design and data consumers, you may be able to allow duplicate data.

For example, I worked on a pipeline that ingested and evaluated customer data for the presence of specific issues. In this case, it didn't matter whether the data was duplicated; the question was "Does X exist?" If instead the question was how many times X had occurred, data deduplication would have been necessary.

Another place you may be able to tolerate duplication is time-series data where only the most recent records are used. I worked on a pipeline that, ideally, generated records once a day, but if there were errors, the pipeline had to be rerun. This made it particularly tricky to detect duplicates, as the source data changed throughout the day, meaning the results of an earlier pipeline run could generate different records than a rerun later in the day. To handle this case, I added some metadata that tracked the time the job was run and filtered records to only the most recent runtime. In this case, there was data duplication, but its effects were mitigated by this filtering logic.

If you can tolerate eventual deduplication, you could create a process that periodically cleans up duplicates. Something like this could run as a background process to make use of spare compute cycles, as you learned about in Chapter 1.

Checkpointing

Checkpointing (*https://oreil.ly/ydj0U*) is when state is saved periodically over the course of pipeline operation. This gives you a way to retry data processing from a last known state if a fault occurs in the pipeline.

Checkpointing is particularly important in stream processing. If a failure occurs while processing the stream, you need to know where you were in the stream when the failure happened. This will show you where to restart processing after the pipeline recovers.

You can benefit from checkpointing in batch pipelines as well. For example, if you have to acquire data from several sources and then perform a long, compute-intensive transformation, it can be a good idea to save the source data. If the transformation is interrupted, you can read from the saved source data and reattempt the transformation rather than rerunning the data acquisition step.

Not only does this cut down on the expense of having to rerun pipeline stages prior to the failure, but you also have a cache of the source data. This can be especially helpful if the source data changes frequently. In this case, you may altogether miss ingesting some of the source data if you have to rerun the entire pipeline.

> Clean up checkpointed data as soon as you no longer need it. Not doing so can negatively impact cost and performance. As an example, I worked at a company where a large Airflow DAG checkpointed data after every task, but it didn't clean up after the job was completed. This created terabytes of extra data that resulted in high latency, made DAG execution excruciatingly slow, and increased storage costs. While I am not familiar with the details, I suspect that checkpointing after every task was overkill, which is a good reminder to be judicious about where you use checkpointing.
>
> Remove checkpointed data after a job has completed successfully, or use a lifecycle policy, as you saw in Chapter 3, if you want to let it persist for a short time for debugging.

Intermediate data can also be helpful for debugging pipeline issues. Consider building in logic to selectively checkpoint, using criteria such as data source, pipeline stage, or customer. You can then use a configuration to toggle checkpointing as needed without deploying new code. This finer granularity will help you reduce the performance impacts of checkpointing while still reaping the benefits of capturing state for debugging.

For even finer granularity, consider enabling checkpointing on a per-run basis. If a job fails, you can rerun with checkpointing enabled to capture the intermediate data for debugging.

As an example, I built checkpointing into a pipeline stage that retrieved data from an API. The checkpointing was enabled only if the pipeline was running in debug mode, allowing me to inspect the retrieved data if there were problems. The state was small, and it was automatically purged after a few days as part of the pipeline metadata cleanup cycle.

Automatic Retries

At best a rite of passage and at worst a daily occurrence, rerunning a failed pipeline job (or many) is something that I think most data engineers are familiar with. Not only are manual job reruns mind-numbing, they are also costly.

One project I worked on had a dedicated on-call engineer whose time was mostly spent rerunning failed jobs. Consider that for a moment: the cost of one full-time engineer and the cost of the resources for rerunning failed jobs. A lot of times this cost isn't accounted for; as long as SLAs continue to be met, the cost of rerunning failed jobs can remain hidden. The cost of reduced team velocity due to one less engineer is harder to quantify and can lead to burnout. In addition, this manual overhead can reduce your ability to scale.

In my experience, a significant driver of failed pipeline jobs is resource availability. This can be anything from a CSP outage taking down part of your infrastructure, a temporary blip in the availability of a credentials service, or under-provisioned resources, to data source availability, such as getting a 500 error when making a request of a REST API. It can be extremely frustrating to lose an entire job's worth of computation because of a temporary issue like this, not to mention the wasted cloud costs.

The good news is that a lot of these pipeline killers can be handled with automated processes. You just have to know where these failures occur and implement retry strategies. Recall that retrying jobs can lead to duplicate data, making idempotency a precondition to implementing retries. Checkpointing can also be needed for retries, as you'll see later in this section.

Retry Considerations

At a high level, a retry involves four steps:

- Attempt a process.
- Receive a retryable error.
- Wait to retry.
- Repeat a limited number of times.

Generally, a *retryable error* is the result of a failed process that you expect to succeed within a short time period after your initial attempt, such that it makes sense to delay pipeline execution.

 Consistent, repeated retries can be a sign of under-resourcing, which can lead to poor pipeline performance and can limit scaling and reliability. Logging retry attempts will give you insight into these issues and help you determine whether additional resources are needed to improve pipeline performance.

As an example, I worked on a pipeline that differentiated the kinds of database errors it received when making queries. An error could be due to either connectivity or an issue with the query, such as running a SELECT statement against a table that didn't exist. A connectivity error is something that could be temporary, whereas a query error is something that will persist until a code change is made. With separate errors, the pipeline could selectively retry database queries only if the error received was related to connectivity.

Retrying involves waiting a period of time before attempting the process again. Where possible, you want to make this a nonblocking event so that other processes can continue while the retried process is waiting for its next attempt. If instead you allow a waiting process to take up a worker slot or thread, you will be wasting time and resources.

You can prevent blocking at various execution levels, such as by using asynchronous methods or multithreading. Task runners and scheduling systems such as Airflow and Celery support nonblocking retries using queues. If a retryable task fails, these systems place the failed task back onto the queue, allowing other tasks to move forward while the retryable task waits out the retry delay.

Retry Levels in Data Pipelines

You can think about processes in a data pipeline as falling into three levels: low, task, and pipeline. Low-level processes are where you interact with a resource, such as making an API request or writing to a database. A retryable error in these cases could be a 429 from an API (*https://oreil.ly/Y8U5u*), indicating that too many requests have occurred in a set time period. Another potential retryable error is resource contention, such as waiting for a pool slot to write to a database and exceeding the timeout period.

When working with cloud services, retries can be a bit more involved. For example, I worked on a pipeline where data was written to cloud storage. The data size was small, and the requests were well within the bandwidth and request limitations. Uploads succeeded most of the time, but occasionally an upload would fail, not because of issues with the storage service but because there was an issue with the credentials service that granted access to the storage bucket.

> This is an important consideration when working with cloud services: while you may think you're interacting with a single service, such as cloud storage, several services can be involved in handling your request.

This issue was particularly hard to nail down because the retry mechanism was encapsulated in the CSP client library. I was using the Google Cloud Storage (GCS) client, which had its own retry strategy (*https://oreil.ly/godFl*) that applied only to the storage service. Because the credentials service was a different service, the GCS retry didn't handle cases in which the credentials service was temporarily unavailable. Ultimately, I had to wrap the GCS client retry in a custom retry using the *tenacity* library (*https://oreil.ly/JWldg*) to retry on the credentials service issues.

In the next level above low-level processes are task-level processes. You can think of these as different steps in the pipeline, including tasks such as running a data transformation or performing validation. Task-level processes often include low-level processes, such as a task that writes data to cloud storage. In these cases, you have two levels of retry: a low-level retry that may attempt for seconds to a few minutes, and the opportunity to retry at the task level over a greater time period.

As an example, a pipeline I worked on included a task that sent email to customers after data processing was complete. The request to send the email went to an internal API, which prepared a customized email based on the customer data. The pipeline had task-level retries on the "Send email" task and low-level retries on the request to the Internal Email API, as depicted in Figure 4-1.

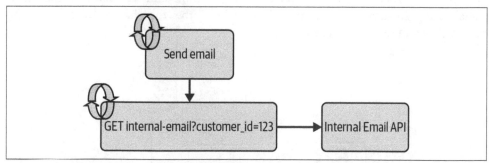

Figure 4-1. Email sending process with retries

The timing of the task and low-level retries is depicted in Figure 4-2. The "Send email" task started at the beginning of the time window, making a low-level request to the Internal Email API. If a retryable error was received, the GET request was retried using an exponential backoff (*https://oreil.ly/BFCpc*). You can see this as the increasing length of time between the first, second, and third retries on the "Low-level API retries" timeline.

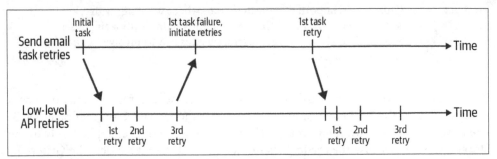

Figure 4-2. Retry timeline for "Send email" task and API request

If the GET request was still failing after three attempts, the "Send email" task would fail. This triggered the task-level retry, which retried over a longer time period. Whereas the low-level process would be retried several times over the course of a few minutes, the task-level process would retry once starting at 10 minutes and would exponentially increase the wait period with every retry. As long as the errors returned from the API were retryable, the task-level retry would continue until a specific time of day, after which the email was no longer relevant.

Task-level retries are a place where checkpointing can be especially helpful. Consider the HoD pipeline from Chapter 1, where bird survey data is joined with data from the HoD social media database. Figure 4-3 shows this process with checkpointing added, where the data is saved to the cloud in the Temp Storage bucket after extracting the species information, before the "Enrich with social" step. If "Enrich with social" fails because the HoD database is temporarily busy, the pipeline can retry "Enrich with social" using the data in the Temp Storage bucket, rather than having to reacquire the survey data and rerun "Extract species."

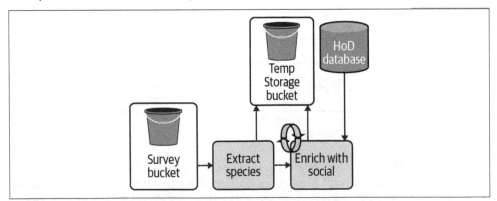

Figure 4-3. HoD batch pipeline with checkpointing and retry

Finally, you can also experience retryable failures at the pipeline level. If you think about the probability of different levels of recoverable failures, with low level being the most common, pipeline level is the least likely level, in part because you've already built in low-level and task-level retries to handle most temporary failures.

Largely, retryable errors at a pipeline level result from temporary infrastructure issues. One possible source is the termination of interruptible instances. As you learned in Chapter 1, these are among the cheapest compute options, but they can be terminated before your job completes. In a containerized environment like Kubernetes, temporary resourcing issues could occur if your containers overrun their resource requests (*https://oreil.ly/RS6c6*).

Building retry strategies for these situations can make it easier to use cheap interruptible instances by building in a self-healing mechanism. It can be tricky to determine whether a pipeline failed due to resourcing shortfalls and whether these shortfalls are due to a temporary service issue or a nonrecoverable problem such as a job that exceeds the provisioned resources and will continue to fail. In some cases, you can get information from the compute infrastructure to help you figure this out.

If you're using interruptible instances, you can subscribe to termination notifications to help you identify resulting pipeline instability. When I was working on the pipeline that experienced out-of-capacity issues described in Chapter 1, I was able to capture the failure reason when the AWS EMR cluster terminated. If the job failed due to insufficient capacity, a retry mechanism would kick in, alerting the team to a failure only if the job continued to fail after a few hours of waiting for capacity to improve.

Human Operational Costs

Something I've observed a lot is the lack of attention to the human costs of poor design. I've seen engineers get saddled with the job of manually chasing down and remediating data pipeline failures in lieu of teams investing time to implement automated approaches. Often the cost fails to be noticed if SLAs continue to be met. Meanwhile, team members burn out and quit, and fewer resources are available for maintaining and building new pipeline features. In addition to this approach being bad for people, it's also very costly for organizations that have to attract, interview, and retain talent.

There were a few key elements to this solution. First, I knew from experience that these resource issues typically cleared up in a few hours. Second, I accounted for the possibility that the job was simply too large for the capacity that was allocated. I capped retries at two to limit wasting resources in this scenario. Another way a large job could be detected is by comparing the data size to historical values, as you saw in "Autoscaling Example" on page 44.

This retry mechanism reduced manual intervention, human errors, and alert fatigue. It also reduced the cost of rerunning jobs and improved pipeline throughput. Previously, every failed job would generate an alert, and an engineer would manually restart the process. If the issue was insufficient capacity, the rerun would also fail, leading to a cascade of failures and wasted resources. Because retries were a manual process, inevitably our team would miss one of the reruns while waiting out the capacity issues, leading to missing data.

Thus far, this chapter has covered design strategies focusing on the mechanics of data pipelines that will help you avoid data corruption and recover from common intermittent failures. The last topic in this chapter, data validation, is a technique to build into pipeline execution to help you catch data issues before they occur.

Data Validation

The 1970s sitcom *Laverne and Shirley* opens with the duo heading off to their jobs at Shotz Brewery, where they inspect beer bottles coming down an assembly line. As the bottles stream by, Laverne and Shirley look on, pulling out the defective ones to ensure a high-quality product.

Data validation is a bit like the quality control Laverne and Shirley performed at their jobs: inspecting the data as it goes by and getting rid of defects before they make it into the hands of data consumers.

A lack of data validation is what led to the multimillion-dollar mistake I shared in this book's Preface. The data source our team was ingesting added new columns of data. We were relying on manually updating schemas to capture changes in the source data, a practice I'll show you how to avoid in this section. The schema had not been maintained and didn't include the new columns, causing them to be excluded from ingestion.

Before getting into specific data validation techniques, I want to get you thinking about data validation at a high level. This will help you build a data validation plan where you'll use the techniques in this chapter.

In my experience, data validation has three main goals:

- Prevent data downtime.
- Prevent wasting cycles processing bad data.
- Inform the team of bad data and pipeline bugs.

To meet these goals, think about the source data, how it is being processed, and the expectations for the result data. You can start with these questions:

- What constitutes valid source data? For example, are there attributes that must be present for you to be confident the source has provided good data?
- Should you ingest all data from a source, including new attributes, or do you only ingest a subset?
- Does data need certain formats, data types, or attributes for successful ingestion?
- Are there deterministic relationships between pipeline stages, such as data shape, that you can use to identify possible issues?

Thinking through these questions will help you identify areas where data validation would be useful. In addition, consider the overhead of adding validation in the pipeline; this is another process that acts on the data as it moves through ingestion and can impact performance depending on how you approach it.

Finally, think about what you want to do if a data validation failure occurs. Should the bad data be discarded? Should it be set aside for review? Should the job fail?

Validating Data Characteristics

Rather than trying to capture every individual data issue, which is an impossible task, think about validation as identifying patterns in the data. "Know thy data" is the first step to successfully processing and analyzing data. Validation involves codifying what you know and expect to prevent data bugs.

In this section, you'll see some basic checks that are relatively cheap to compute and easy to implement but pay big dividends in rooting out common data issues. These checks include:

- Inspecting data shape and type
- Identifying corrupt data
- Checking for nulls

Whether you're cleaning data or analyzing it, checking the shape of data as it moves through different pipeline stages is a good way to check for issues. The issue of missing columns from the book's Preface could have been prevented by a simple check comparing the number of columns in the input data to the number of columns in the DataFrame that processed the data. In fact, this was one of the first validation checks our team added to mitigate the problem.

While comparing the number of columns can identify missing attributes, additional checks on column names and data types are necessary when attributes are added. For example, the "Extract species" step from Figure 4-3 adds a new column, `species`, to the raw data. To verify that "Extract species" performed as expected, you could start by validating that there are $N + 1$ columns in the "Extract species" data. Assuming this checks out, the next step is to ensure that the data produced by "Extract species" has the same column names and types as the input data from the Survey bucket, in addition to the new `species` field. This verifies that you added the new column and that you didn't drop any input columns.

Getting the DataFrame shape gives you a second piece of information: the length of the data. This is another helpful characteristic to check as data passes through the pipeline. For example, you would expect "Extract species" to produce the same number of rows as the input data.

In some cases, you might be working with data sources that could provide malformed data. This is especially true if you work with data sources external to your organization where you have limited or no visibility into potential changes. One data pipeline I worked on ingested data from dozens of third-party APIs, which was the backbone of the company's product. If the pipeline came across malformed data, it would raise an exception, alerting the team that something was amiss.

Let's take a look at some methods for dealing with malformed data, which you can see in this book's validation notebook (*https://oreil.ly/iRL5B*) under the heading "Identifying and acting on malformed data."

Here's an example of some malformed JSON where the last record was partially written:

```
bad_data = [
    "{'user': 'pc@cats.xyz', 'location': [26.91756, 82.07842]}",
    "{'user': 'lucy@cats.xyz', 'location': [26.91756, 82.07842]}",
    "{'user': 'scout@cats.xyz', 'location': [26.91756,}"
]
```

If you try to process this with some basic Python, you'll get an exception on the entire dataset, though only one record is corrupt. Processing each row would let you ingest the good records while allowing you to isolate and respond to the corrupt ones.

PySpark DataFrames give you a few choices for how to handle corrupt data. The `mode` attribute for reading JSON data can be set to `PERMISSIVE`, `DROPMALFORMED`, or `FAIL FAST`, providing different handling options for bad data.

The following sample shows the `mode` attribute set to `PERMISSIVE`:

```
corrupt_df = spark.read.json(sc.parallelize(bad_data), mode="PERMISSIVE",
                             columnNameOfCorruptRecord="_corrupt_record")
corrupt_df.show()
```

`PERMISSIVE` mode will successfully read the data but will isolate malformed records in a separate column for debug, as you can see in Figure 4-4.

	_corrupt_record	location	user
0	None	[26.91756, -82.07842]	pc@cats.xyz
1	None	[45.2341, 121.2351]	lucy@cats.xyz
2	{'user': 'scout@cats.xyz', 'location': [45.2341,}	None	None

Figure 4-4. Reading corrupt data with PERMISSIVE mode

PERMISSIVE mode is a good option if you want to inspect the corrupt records. In a medical data management system I worked on, the pipeline isolated records like this for a data steward to inspect. The data management system was used in patient diagnosis, so it was critical that all data was ingested. Debugging the malformed data gave medical staff the opportunity to fix the source data for reingestion.

DROPMALFORMED does what it sounds like: the corrupt records would be dropped from the DataFrame entirely. The result would be records 0–1 in Figure 4-4. Finally, FAIL FAST would throw an exception if any records were malformed, rejecting the entire batch.

If certain attributes are required for you to successfully ingest the data, checking for nulls during ingestion can be another validation activity. You can do this by checking for the required attribute in the source data or doing a null check on a DataFrame column. You can also do null checks with schemas.

Schemas

Schemas can help you perform additional validation, such as checking for data type changes or changes in attribute names. You can also define required attributes with a schema, which can be used to check for null values. DoorDash uses schema validation to improve data quality, as described in "Building Scalable Real Time Event Processing with Kafka and Flink" (*https://oreil.ly/aOZ8J*).

Schemas can also limit data to just the attributes you need for ingestion. If you only need a few attributes from a large dataset, using a schema to load only those attributes will cut down on compute and storage costs by not processing and storing extraneous, unused data.

Another use of schemas is as service contracts, setting an expectation for both data producers and consumers as to the required characteristics for ingestion. Schemas can also be used for synthetic data generation, a topic you will see in Chapter 9.

In the following subsections, I cover how to create, maintain, and use schemas for validation. You can find the corresponding code in the validation notebook (*https://oreil.ly/Vt3Uk*).

In an ideal world, data sources would publish accurate, up-to-date schemas for the data they provide. In reality, you're lucky to find documentation on how to access the data, let alone a schema.

That said, when working with data sources developed by teams at your company, you may be able to get schema information. For example, a pipeline I worked on interacted with an API developed by another team. The API team used Swagger (*https://swagger.io*) annotations and had an automated process that generated JSON schemas when the API changed. The data pipeline could fetch these schemas and use them to both validate the API response and keep the pipeline test data up to date, a topic you'll learn about in Chapter 9.

Creating schemas

Most of the time you'll have to create your own schemas. Possibly more important than creating the schemas, you also have to keep the schemas up to date. An inaccurate schema is worse than no schema. Let's start by looking at ways to create schemas, and in the next section you'll see ways to keep them up to date with minimal manual intervention.

As an example, let's look at creating schemas for the survey data pipeline in Figure 4-3. Table 4-1 contains a sample of the raw survey data.

Table 4-1. Example bird survey data

User	Location	Image files	Description	Count
pc@cats.xyz	["26.91756", "82.07842"]		Several lesser goldfinches in the yard today.	5
sylvia@srlp.org	["27.9659", "82.800"]	s3://bird-2345/34541.jpeg	Breezy morning, overcast. Saw a black-crowned night heron on the intercoastal waterway.	1
birdlover124@email.com	["26.91756", "82.07842"]	s3://bird-1243/09731.jpeg, s3://bird-1243/48195.jpeg	Walked over to the heron rookery this afternoon and saw some great blue herons.	3

The survey data contains a row for each sighting recorded by a user of a bird survey app. This includes the user's email, the user's location, and a free-form description. Users can attach pictures to each sighting, which are stored by the survey app in a cloud storage bucket, the links to which are listed in the "Image files" column in the table. Users can also provide an approximate count of the number of birds sighted.

In "Validating Data Characteristics" on page 73, I mentioned that the location field is used by the "Extract species" step in Figure 4-3. Here's the code that extracts the species, which you can see in *transform.py* (*https://oreil.ly/6-DnF*):

```
def apply_species_label(species_list, df):
    species_regex = f".*({'|'.join(species_list)}).*"
    return (df
        .withColumn("description_lower", f.lower('description'))
        .withColumn("species", f.regexp_extract('description_lower',
                    species_regex, 1))
        .drop("description_lower")
    )
```

The expectation in this code is that `description` is a string that can be made lower-case and searched for a species match.

Another step in the pipeline extracts the latitude and longitude from the `location` field and is used to group users into similar geographic regions. This is an important feature of the HoD platform as it helps fellow bird lovers flock together for birding trips. The location is represented as an array of strings, where the underlying code expects a format of [`latitude, longitude`]:

```
df
  .withColumn("latitude", f.element_at(df.location, 1))
  .withColumn("longitude", f.element_at(df.location, 2))
```

So, at a minimum, a schema for the survey data should include constraints that the `location` field is an array of string values and the `description` field is a string.

What happens if either of these attributes is null? This is an interesting question. A better question is how *should* the pipeline process the data if these attributes are null. For example, if the `location` field is null, the code for extracting the latitude and longitude will throw an exception. This could be a code bug, or it could be that `location` is a required field within the survey data, meaning a null `location` value is a sign of a problem with the source data and should fail data validation.

For this example, let's say `location` is a required field, and a null `location` indicates a problem with the data. In addition, `user` is a required field, and `count`, if provided, should be coercible to an integer. In terms of which attributes should be ingested, let's say that just the current five columns in Table 4-1 should be ingested, and if new attributes are added to the survey data they should be ignored.

With these criteria in mind, let's take a look at a few different ways to generate a schema using the data sample in *initial_source_data.json* (*https://oreil.ly/d_kjJ*). You can find this code under the "Schema validation" heading in the validation notebook (*https://oreil.ly/hSy3o*).

If you're working with DataFrames, you can read the data sample and save the schema. You may need to change the nullable information to meet your expectations. Based on the data sample in *initial_source_data.json*, the inferred schema assumes the nullable value (*https://oreil.ly/f04sf*) for the description field should be `True`:

```
df = (spark
       .read
       .option("inferSchema", True)
       .json("initial_source_data.json"))
source_schema = df.schema
source_schema

> StructType(
   [StructField("count", LongType(),True),
    StructField("description", StringType(),True),
    StructField("user", StringType(),False),
    StructField("img_files", ArrayType(StringType(),True),True),
    StructField("location", ArrayType(StringType(),True),False)]
)
```

If your data transformation logic assumes the description field will always be populated, you will want to modify this value to False for validation.

Another way you could validate the bird survey data is with a JSON schema, which allows for more definition than the Spark schema. You can generate a JSON schema from sample data using some online tools (*https://oreil.ly/i8OOT*), or by hand if the data attributes are few.

Validating with schemas

These schema generation methods give you a starting point. From here you'll need to refine the schema to ensure that it will raise validation errors, such as changing the nullable values in the generated Spark schema.

For example, using a JSON schema generator tool for *initial_source_data.json* provided the schema shown in the "Working with JSON schemas" section of the validation notebook (*https://oreil.ly/sAxiG*). Notice how the schema generator defined location:

```
# "location":["26.91756","82.07842"]

"location": {
   "type": "array",
   "items": [
      {"type": "string"},
      {"type": "string"}
   ]
}
```

Recall that the code extracting the latitude and longitude expects two elements in location.

Validating this schema against some test data, you can see that this definition isn't sufficient to ensure that the location field has two elements. For example, the short_location JSON has only one string, but there is no output when executing this line, meaning the validation succeeded:

```
validate(short_location, initial_json_schema)
```

To use this JSON schema for data validation, you need to specify the minItems in the location array, as in this updated schema definition for location:

```
"location": {
        "type": "array",
        "minItems":2,
        "items": [
            {"type": "string"}
        ]
    },
```

Now comes the exciting part: check out all the bad data that gets flagged with this new definition.

The following validation errors from the Python *jsonschema* (*https://oreil.ly/bw_JM*) library tell you exactly what was wrong with the data, giving you a way to both halt execution if bad data is found and provide helpful debug information:

Not enough elements
```
validate(short_location, updated_schema)
> ValidationError: ['26.91756'] is too short
```

If the location *data type changes from an array to a string*
```
validate([{"user":"someone", "location":"26.91756,82.07842"}],
        updated_schema)

>ValidationError: '26.91756,82.07842' is not of type 'array'
```

If the survey data provider decides to change the data type of the latitude and longitude values from string to numerical
```
validate([{"user":"pc@cats.xyz", "location":[26.91756,82.07842]}],
        updated_schema)

>ValidationError: 26.91756 is not of type 'string'
```

These last two errors of the location changing from an array to a string or from an array of strings to an array of floats can also be identified when using a Spark schema. If you're working with Spark datasets in Scala or Java (*https://oreil.ly/MUImY*), you can use the schema to raise an exception if the source data doesn't match.

In other situations, you can compare the expected schema to the schema that is inferred when reading in the source data, as described in the "Comparing inferred vs explicit schemas" section in the validation notebook (*https://oreil.ly/U4xU-*).

As an example, let's say you have an expected schema for the bird survey data, source_schema, where location is an array of strings. To validate a new batch of data against `source_schema`, read the data into a DataFrame and compare the inferred schema to the expected schema. In this example, the `location` field in *string_location.json* (*https://oreil.ly/VHAti*) is a string:

```
df = (spark
        .read
        .option("inferSchema", True)
        .json('string_location.json'))
inferred_schema = df.schema
> StructType(
    [...
    StructField("location", StringType(),True)
    ...])

inferred_schema == source_schema
False
```

This check is useful for flagging a validation failure, but it's not great for reporting the specific differences between the schemas. For more insight, the following code checks for both new fields and mismatches in existing fields:

```
source_info = {f.name: f for f in source_schema.fields}
for f in inferred_schema.fields:
  if f.name not in source_info.keys():
     print(f"New field in data source {f}")

  elif f != source_info[f.name]:
     source_field = source_info[f.name]
     print(f"Field mismatch for {f.name} Source schema: {source_field},
            Inferred schema: {f}")

> Field mismatch for location
        Source schema:
            StructField(location,ArrayType(StringType,true),true),
        Inferred schema:
            StructField(location,StringType,true)
```

Another useful validation check you could add to this code is to flag fields in `source_schema` that are missing from `inferred_schema`.

This kind of schema comparison logic was another validation technique used to fix the missing-columns bug. If the pipeline had a validation check in place like this to begin with, our team would have been alerted to new columns in the source data from the very first batch where the change occurred.

Keeping schemas up to date

As I mentioned at the beginning of this section, it is absolutely essential that schemas are kept up to date. Stale schemas are worse than worthless; they could cause erroneous validation failures or miss real validation failures due to out-of-date data definitions. This section describes a few methods for automating schema upkeep.

For schemas that are generated from source code, such as with the Swagger example I mentioned earlier or by exporting a class to a JSON schema (*https://oreil.ly/bckkY*), consider automated builds and centralized schema repositories. This provides a single source of truth for everyone accessing the schemas. As part of the automated build process, you can use the schemas to generate test data for unit tests. With this approach, breaking schema changes will surface as unit-test failures. I promise this is the last time I'll say "as you will see in Chapter 9." Schemas are great, and there are more great uses for them in addition to their noble use in data validation.

Validation checks can also be used to keep schemas up to date. If a pipeline is designed to ingest all data source attributes, you could spawn a process to update the schema when nonbreaking changes occur in the source data. For example, if the pipeline in Figure 4-3 is designed to ingest any fields provided by the bird survey data, so long as the user and location fields are present and valid any new columns could be added to the source schema.

If you adopt a practice of automatically updating schemas to contain more or fewer attributes based on source data, make sure you account for nulls. Particularly with semistructured formats like JSON, it's possible to get a few batches of data where an attribute value hasn't been dropped from the source; it just happens to be null.

Another thing to keep in mind is the impact of changing the schema. If new attributes are added, do you need to fill in values for older data? If an attribute is removed, should old data retain this attribute?

Finally, a pseudo-automated approach of schema updates can be effective, in which you get alerted to schema-breaking changes in the source data. This could be from a validation failure, or you could set up a scheduled job to periodically compare the schema against a sample from the data source. You could even work this check into the pipeline, acquiring a data sample, running schema validation, and exiting without any subsequent steps.

I urge you to avoid relying on manual updates to keep schemas up to date. If none of the preceding options work for you, strive to keep your schemas to a minimum to limit what you have to maintain. Additionally, make schema upkeep part of the release process to ensure that they are regularly attended to.

Summary

The combination of cloud infrastructure, third-party services, and the idiosyncrasies of distributed software development pave the way for a cornucopia of potential pipeline failure mechanisms. Changes in source data or pipeline code, bad credentials, resource contention, and blips in cloud service availability are just a few possibilities. These issues can be temporary, as in a few seconds during the exact moment you try to write to cloud storage, or more permanent, such as the data type of an important source data field changing without notice. In the worst cases, they can result in data downtime, as with the multimillion-dollar mistake.

If this landscape sounds grim, don't despair. You are now well equipped to build pipelines that can prevent and recover from many of these issues with a minimum of engineering overhead, reducing the cost of cloud resources, engineering time, and loss of trust in data quality by data consumers.

Idempotency is an important first step for building atomic pipelines that support retries and limit data duplication.

For batch processes, delete-write and database transactions support idempotency by ensuring that the batch is processed in its entirety or not at all, giving you a clean slate to retry from without the potential of data duplication. You can also prevent duplication at the data sink by enforcing unique constraints, such as with primary keys, which will prevent duplicate data from being recorded.

For stream processing, building producers that guarantee unique IDs based on the source data and consumers that process each unique key only once provides idempotency. When building these systems, make sure you consider how messages are being consumed, acknowledged, and retried. Durable storage for idempotency data will help you ensure idempotency across outages and deployments.

Keep in mind that you may be able to tolerate some data duplication depending on how pipeline data is used. If the data is used to verify the absence or presence of particular features, duplicated data might be OK. Consider deduplicating data post-ingest if you have a time gap between when ingestion completes and when data is accessed. Attaching metadata to filter out duplicates when data is queried is another option, as you saw in the example of using data from only the most recent runtime for analysis.

With idempotency in place, the next foundational design element is checkpointing, providing a known state to retry from if a fault occurs, as well as debug information when investigating issues. You can benefit from this technique without sacrificing performance and cloud spend by automating the deletion of checkpoint data.

Checkpointing and idempotency lay the groundwork for automatic retries, which enable pipelines to recover from temporary issues. This reduces wasted resources and manual intervention and can also help you take advantage of cheap, interruptible compute.

When looking for opportunities to use retries, think about processes that could temporarily fail and recover within a reasonable window of time based on your pipeline throughput needs. Something like database connectivity could be a temporary issue and may recover, whereas an invalid database query would not succeed no matter how many times you try it.

Overcoming temporary issues involves waiting between retry attempts. Nonblocking retries will help you maintain performance and limit wasted cycles. Don't forget to log retry attempts, as this can help you introspect for performance and scalability issues.

Idempotency, checkpointing, and automatic retries are like the hardware of an assembly line—components that work together to keep things running efficiently. This is necessary but not sufficient to produce a quality product. You also need a keen pair of eyes checking product quality, ejecting bad products before they reach customers, and raising alarms if there is a problem on the assembly line.

Data validation is like Laverne and Shirley, diligently inspecting and, if needed, rejecting data as it moves through the pipeline. If you've ever had to debug bad data by hand, combing through logs and datasets to determine what when wrong and when, you can definitely appreciate the automated approaches described in this chapter, from checking data shape and format to using schemas to validate attribute name, type, and existence against expectations.

Schemas can be powerful tools for data validation and other data pipeline activities I'll describe in later chapters, but they must be kept up to date to be an asset and not a liability.

Just as the strategies covered in this chapter provide a foundation for pipeline design, an effective development environment provides the foundation for pipeline implementation and testing. In the next chapter, I'll cover techniques to reduce cost and streamline development environments for data pipelines.

CHAPTER 5

Setting Up Effective Development Environments

Just like any other software system, data pipelines require development and testing environments as part of the software development lifecycle. With the combination of cloud services, data sources, sinks, and other dependencies, environments for data pipelines have a lot of moving parts that can be costly and confusing to juggle.

In this chapter, you'll see how to create effective development environments, from techniques for local development to advice for setting up test and staging tiers that prepare pipeline changes for production.

The chapter opens with an overview of the differences between data environments and software environments and how to bring these concepts together to create environment tiers for data pipelines. You'll see how to plan out these environments while balancing cost, complexity, and functional needs with the needs of development, testing, and data consumers.

The second part of the chapter focuses on the design of local development environments and includes best practices to help you get the most out of containers and avoid common pitfalls.

While the term *local development* implies an environment that runs exclusively on a developer's machine, the reality of working with data pipelines and cloud services is that you may have to connect to external resources in local development. To help reduce these costs and complexities, you'll see strategies for limiting dependence on external services.

For those times when you need to create cloud resources for local development, it's critical to have reliable ways to clean up these resources when they are no longer needed. The chapter closes with tips on spinning down resources and limiting ongoing costs associated with development.

Environments

If you develop software, you're likely familiar with the concept of staging code across different environments and promoting the code as it passes various testing and quality requirements. The same is true when developing data pipelines, with additional consideration for the data you use across these environments. This section illustrates how to merge the needs of data environments and software development environments, enabling you to ensure reliability from both a code and data processing point of view.

The approach you take to setting up environments is extremely situation dependent. The release schedule, development process, and opinions of those involved will impact the number of environments and the activities you use them for. Think of the examples in this section as a guide rather than something that must be replicated exactly.

Software Environments

Figure 5-1 shows an example of software environment tiers. There are four tiers—DEV, TEST, STAGING, and PROD—where code is progressively deployed as it passes through additional levels of testing and verification until ultimately being released to the production environment (PROD). To get a sense of how code moves through various tiers, let's take a look at an example process for testing and promoting code.

The promotion process typically starts with a merge request. When you create a merge request, a continuous integration (CI) pipeline runs unit tests as a first check of code functionality. If these tests pass, the code can be merged.

Once the code is blessed by your merge request reviewer and is committed, it gets deployed to a DEV environment. The DEV environment can be used for running integration tests, where you validate that the code operates as expected while connecting to databases, APIs, and any other required services. Once your integration tests are passing, the code would then be promoted to a TEST environment. Code that makes it to the TEST environment is stable enough for quality assurance (QA) testing.

When you're satisfied with the QA results, it's time to create a new release candidate. The code is moved from the TEST environment to STAGING, where it can run for an additional time period before being deployed to PROD.

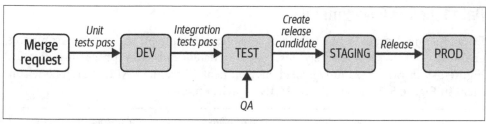

Figure 5-1. Example development environments

This practice of progressively evaluating a system before releasing code updates to end users helps build quality into the development process.

Data Environments

The same environment system is also present when developing data logic. One of the projects I worked on was an analytics platform where we ingested and surfaced data to third-party analysts. Similar to the code promotion process in Figure 5-1, the analysts wanted different tiers of data environments to test their queries. This included a development tier, which contained a small amount of sample data, a test tier with a larger sample of data, a validation tier with a copy of production data, and finally a production tier.

You can see this process in Figure 5-2. Initially when the analysts were figuring out their queries, they worked against a small dataset in DEV. This allowed them to easily verify the query results by hand. When they were satisfied with the initial designs, the analysts promoted the queries to TEST, where a larger dataset was available to test and refine the queries.

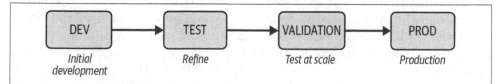

Figure 5-2. Example data environments

In the same way that code has to move through multiple levels of testing and QA before release, the analytical queries had to follow the same process on the data side. The analysts were creating reports that would be used to drive policy decisions by the US government, so it was essential to ensure that the queries surfaced the exact data that was expected. Because of this, the data in VALIDATION was the same as the data in PROD. This gave the analysts an exact comparison to validate the results they got when running queries in PROD.

Data Pipeline Environments

Data pipelines benefit from a hybrid of software development and data environments, enabling you to progressively test code updates and data processing fidelity.[1] Figure 5-3 shows an example hybrid environment where the VALIDATION environment in Figure 5-2 maps to the STAGING environment.

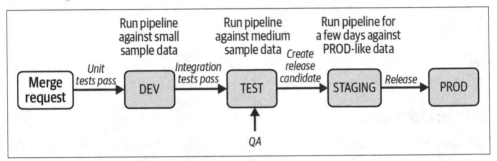

Figure 5-3. Environments for data pipeline design

As code is promoted to higher environments (i.e., closer to PROD), it runs against progressively more data. In Chapter 7 you'll learn specifics about data pipeline testing, but for now it's sufficient to think about validating pipeline operation at a high level.

Similar to the analysts, you first want to make sure the pipeline runs well against a small set of data. Typically you don't just run the pipeline in DEV and TEST; you would also validate that the results are what you expect.

In STAGING, it's best to use data that is as close as possible to your production data, although this may not be possible because of limited resources, customer agreements, or regulations. In the analytical platform I mentioned earlier, we could not run PROD data using our STAGING pipelines due to government security regulations. By testing with full-scale PROD-like data, you can have high confidence that pipeline updates will work as expected when you deploy them to PROD.

> One does not simply copy production data into lower environments. If you're working with sensitive data, such as protected health information (PHI) or personally identifiable information (PII), consult with your privacy and legal teams.

---

1 Both based on my experience and corroborated by an aptly named guide to data pipeline testing in Airflow (*https://oreil.ly/nDZf-*).

In addition to running pipelines against PROD-like data, a STAGING environment gives you a place to let the pipeline run for a longer time period before a release. For example, if you are expanding from running a single pipeline job to several in parallel, a STAGING environment can let you run these pipelines concurrently over a few days to assess performance issues that are harder to pin down (e.g., resource contention) before releasing the update to PROD.

Environment Planning

With dual requirements to support software development and data environments, it's important to think about what you will need to support both data pipeline testing and data consumers.

Without considering this up front, you can end up being painted into a corner. Figure 5-4 depicts the environment design for the analytical platform I mentioned earlier, where our team had insufficient development and data environments.

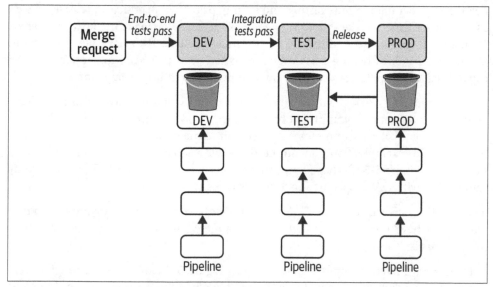

Figure 5-4. Implications of inadequate environments

This design began with three environments. The team had two uses for the DEV environment. One was to deploy merged code for further testing, as in Figure 5-1. We also used DEV to test branches, giving us an opportunity to try out changes before initiating a merge request. TEST was used as both the test and staging environment, and PROD was used for production.

Initially we ran the pipelines in each tier. The input data came from another pipeline owned by a different team, so we could use the data from their TEST environment to run our pipelines. Things became problematic when the analysts requested that TEST data be a copy of PROD, depicted in Figure 5-4 with the arrow going from the PROD bucket to TEST.

With PROD data synced to TEST, these environments became coupled. Our team could no longer run the TEST pipeline, as the data would overwrite the PROD copy. Instead of making the changes necessary to continue having a TEST environment, the decision was made to stop running the pipeline in TEST.

As a result, the only full pipeline tests we could run before a release used the small sample dataset in DEV. When bugs inevitably occurred with medium- to large-scale data in production, the analysts lost trust in the system, no longer believing it to be accurate or reliable.

Design

Experiencing the drawbacks of the environment setup shown in Figure 5-4 was a good lesson on the importance of environment design. You already learned about the need to support full pipeline testing and staging prior to a production release, as well as the role of different data tiers. While the examples so far have included four environments, there's no set number of environments you need to have. It's really more about what kinds of testing and development activities you need to support and the capabilities you have to create, maintain, and update in multiple environments.

An Ops engineer I worked with once remarked that if you don't have to communicate about environment use, you probably don't have a good environment setup. This is a nod to the fact that environments have a cost in terms of both resource use and engineer time. For example, you may not need to have a separate environment for QA, as pictured in Figure 5-3. Perhaps you could instead use a single DEV/TEST tier, communicating with QA as specific functionality is ready to validate.

The pipeline environment in Figure 5-3 presents somewhat of an ideal scenario, where you have the same number of development environments as data environments. This isn't always possible.

A three-environment setup like that shown in Figure 5-4 can provide enough coverage for testing and data needs if you design it adequately. Another project I worked on had three environments—DEV, STAGING, and PROD—where DEV was used to run full pipeline tests on merged code and STAGING was used to test infrastructure updates and stage release candidates (RCs).

While there are plenty of jokes about testing in production, that is the only place we had access to full-scale data. We leveraged the fact that our product surfaced only the most recently computed data to customers to deploy and run full-scale pipeline tests at off-hours. If we ran into a problem, we could revert the deployment knowing that a later, scheduled pipeline job would create a newer batch of data for customers.

Costs

The costs of standing up multiple data pipeline environments can be considerable. For one thing, to run the entire pipeline, all the resources the pipeline uses must be present, including cloud storage, databases, and compute resources, to name a few. You have to pay for both the cloud resource consumption and the time your infrastructure team spends managing multiple environments.

There is also the cost of data to consider. Returning to the analytical platform team I mentioned earlier, the regulations that prohibited us from running PROD data with our TEST pipelines also meant we had to create a copy of the data for the analysts to access PROD data in the TEST environment. This was petabytes of information stored in the cloud, the cost of which doubled because we had to create a copy in the TEST tier. There was also a job that synced data from PROD to TEST, which was another process to design, monitor, and maintain.

You can reduce some of these costs by applying the advice from Chapter 1 through Chapter 3. For example, you can use autoscaling settings to ramp down compute resources in lower tiers when they aren't in use. It's likely you won't need as much capacity as production, so starting out by allocating fewer resources to lower tiers will also help. Coincidentally, this can also provide a load testing opportunity, where fewer resources in lower environments can help you debug performance issues. I've seen this used to figure out scaling formulas, testing out a miniature version in DEV or TEST before rolling out to PROD.

Having appropriate lifecycle policies in place will mitigate costs as well. For example, you can consider deleting data created by testing that is older than a few days or a week. You can do this with bucket policies for cloud storage objects or with maintenance scripts to clean up database objects.

Back to the analytical platform, the security position that required us to make a replica copy from the PROD bucket to TEST was especially disheartening in terms of cost efficacy. As you learned in Chapter 3, cloud bucket access policies can be set up to allow access from other environments. Had we been able to do this, we could have provided read-only permission to PROD buckets from the TEST environment. This ability to provide read-only access is how some fully managed data platforms make "copies" of data available for testing and machine learning without the cost of replication.

Environment uptime

Something to keep in mind is that an environment doesn't have to be constantly available. For example, the infrastructure team for the analytics platform had a very strong infrastructure as code (IaC) practice. They created scripts to create and destroy sandbox environments, which developers could use to stand up a mini version of the pipeline infrastructure for running tests.

This approach can reduce costs compared to having a permanent environment, so long as you make sure these one-off environments get destroyed regularly. Another advantage of this approach is that it tests some of your disaster response readiness by regularly exercising your infrastructure code.

Keep in mind the complexity and size of the environment. For the analytics platform, our ephemeral environments could be ready in about 15 minutes, as they had a limited number of cloud resources to bring online and there was no database restoration involved. However, you could be looking at hours of time for an ephemeral environment to come online if you're restoring a large database, for example. A long startup time doesn't mean you shouldn't use an ephemeral approach, just that you should keep in mind the startup and teardown times when you evaluate your use cases.

You can also save costs by setting up environments to be available based on a schedule. For example, the analytics platform surfaced data in Hive, using cloud storage for the backing datafiles. To access the data, we had to run clusters for the analytics users, but they often only worked about 10 hours out of 24. We used this to cut costs by setting up clusters to turn on when the first query was issued and to auto-terminate after a specific time of day.

One project I worked on served data to analytics users that worked a set number of hours during the week. Rather than keep the supporting infrastructure running 24-7, we set up scripts that would start and stop the clusters near the beginning and end of the customer workday.

Local Development

When you're working on a development team, having a consistent, repeatable development practice will help you move quickly and reduce mistakes and miscommunication. This is especially true in microservices environments, where a pipeline interacts with a variety of services developed by different individuals or teams.

One way to help keep your team in sync is to document your development approach and reinforce it with automated communication mechanisms. For example, if you rely on connecting to databases, APIs, or cloud services while doing development, share mechanisms for doing so among the team. For the cloud, this can include the creation of credentials, such as using Google auth configuring AWS credentials (*https://oreil.ly/3LJaY*).

If you need to share credentials among the development team, such as for APIs, have a standard way to store and share this information, such as with a password manager or secrets management tool.

Containers

One approach for ensuring a consistent and repeatable development environment is to use containers. *Containers* (*https://oreil.ly/pNfqs*) bundle code and dependencies into a single package that can run anywhere. This means code runs in the same environment whether you are developing locally or running in production, which helps alleviate problems arising from differences between how you develop code and how it behaves when deployed.

Containers have become popular in large part due to the work of Docker (*https://www.docker.com*), both in its product offerings and in its work on the Open Container Initiative (*https://opencontainers.org*), which develops standards for containerization. I'll be using Docker examples throughout the rest of this chapter to illustrate working with containers.

To get a sense of the importance of having a consistent development environment, imagine if you were working on a data transformation job running in Spark. Without containers, you might approach local development by installing Spark and its dependencies locally. Perhaps after a few months, another developer starts working in Spark and downloads a newer version. In the meantime, your production environment is pegged to a specific Spark version because of a dependency needed by data consumers running Spark queries. You now have three different versions of a dependency across development and production environments. This can result in code behaving differently in each environment in ways that can be difficult to reproduce and investigate to determine the root cause of the differences.

I've seen a case of this where a developer was working on some code that used a new feature of a database we were running. We had a production image of the database, but because this wasn't used in the development environment, the developer did not realize the new feature was not available in our production version. In the end, we had to scrap the work.

 When using containers you'll need to perform some additional steps to access the debugging tools in your IDE. Check the documentation for your IDE about debugging with Docker for specific instructions on setting this up.

Container lifecycle

While it is true that using containers helps create a consistent, repeatable development process, the realities of the container lifecycle can spoil this claim in practice.

Docker containers and images can be like bad houseguests. Once you invite them in, they won't leave until you force them out. In my experience, this tends to be the primary culprit of mismatches between containerized environments. It makes me sad just thinking about the amount of time I've spent with colleagues trying to figure out the "it works on my machine" issue, only to realize one of us is running an out-of-date container.

To get a sense of how this can happen, let's take a look at the lifecycle of a container. Containers are created from images. An image can be specified as a link to a prebuilt image in a repository, or by specifying a Dockerfile that will be built to create an image. In both cases, the first thing Docker does when it creates a container is to see whether the desired image is present in the local repository on your machine. If it isn't, it pulls or creates the image, adding it to your local repository.

Let's consider what happens over time. Figure 5-5 shows a view over time of running a container from the Postgres image tagged `latest`.

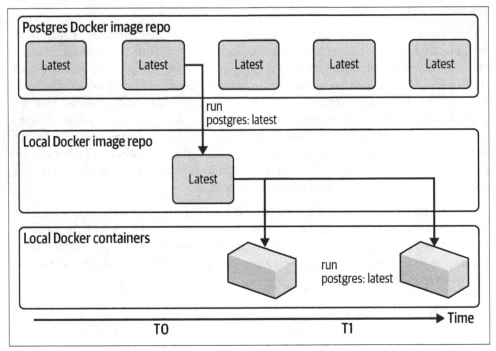

Figure 5-5. Container lifecycle showing how an image with a `latest` tag may not truly be the latest version of the image

At the top of Figure 5-5, the official Postgres Docker repository is shown, where the `latest` tag is periodically updated with the most recent stable Postgres version. At T0, a container is created by issuing a `run` command for the image `postgres:latest`. Because there is no image for `postgres:latest` in the local Docker image repo, the current latest tagged image is pulled from the Postgres Docker repo. The container runs for a while before it is destroyed when it is no longer needed.

Sometime later at T1, you need to run Postgres again, so you issue the same `run` command, but because a `postgres:latest` image is already in your local repository, Docker will create a container based on the image that was downloaded at T0. This image is no longer the latest, as there have been two updates to the `postgres:latest` image in the Postgres Docker repo since T0.

This is exactly how Docker is expected to operate, but it's very easy to forget that you could be running old containers and/or old images. For this reason, it's important to get into the practice of regularly deleting and re-creating your images and containers.

Much like you may pin a code library or module to a specific version to prevent unexpected breakages when the "latest" version changes, using specific versions of Docker images works in the same way. In both cases, you have to navigate the trade-off of using the most recent, up-to-date versions of a dependency versus an upgrade process, where pinned versions need to be monitored and evaluated for updates.

When working with containers that use images, use `docker pull` to download a new image, and then re-create the container. If you're using a Dockerfile to build an image, running `docker build —no-cache` will rebuild the image without relying on any existing layers, guaranteeing that you are rebuilding from scratch. If you're using `docker-compose`, which you'll see more about in this chapter, you can specify "pull_policy: always" (*https://oreil.ly/fnQjd*) in the service definition to always get the most up-to-date image.

When in doubt, you can always inspect the images and containers to check creation timestamps. For example, let's say you want to see what Postgres images you have locally:

```
$ docker images
REPOSITORY          TAG       IMAGE ID        CREATED        SIZE
postgres            latest    f8dd270e5152    8 days ago     376MB
postgres            11.1      5a02f920193b    3 years ago    312MB
```

To determine what images a container is running, you can first list the containers, using `-a` to show stopped containers. It's important to check for stopped containers so that you're aware of containers that could be restarted instead of re-created:

```
$ docker container ls -a
CONTAINER ID   IMAGE           CREATED          STATUS
2007866a1f6c   postgres        48 minutes ago   Up 48 minutes
7eea49adaae4   postgres:11.1   2 hours ago      Exited (0) 2 hours ago
```

You can see the name of the image in the `container ls` output. To get more detailed information on the image used for the container, you can run `docker inspect`. In this case, you can see that the latest Postgres image was created on August 12, 2022:

```
$ docker image inspect postgres
"RepoTags": [
        "postgres:latest"
    ],
    ...
    "Created": "2022-08-12T00:44:14.711354701Z",
```

In addition to keeping your containers up to date, regularly running docker prune (*https://oreil.ly/zYm45*) on volumes, containers, and images will help minimize the resources Docker is taking up on your local machine.

Container Conundrums

In addition to stale containers and images, there are a few other causes of "it works on my machine" that I've seen when working with containers:

Local volume differences
Later in this chapter you'll see an example of mounting a local volume so that you can run your code updates in a container. I once spent a good hour trying to figure out why the version of a Python library was mismatched between two containers using the same base image.

The cause? In one container, I had mounted a local directory that contained code updates, but it also included a wayward local Python module installation. The mount was part of the PYTHONPATH as it included some custom libraries, so it picked up the older version of the package in question as well.

Different hardware
I was working at a company where developers chose what kind of laptop they wanted. We ended up with a mix of Linux and Mac hardware and had different Docker issues across these different machine types. This created some chaos in our Docker Compose files, as updates from Linux users wouldn't work on the Mac and vice versa.

Things got really interesting when we started getting a mix of Intel and Mac M1 chips. If you find yourself in this situation, look to the platform attribute (*https://oreil.ly/PrRv3*) in docker-compose.

As you can see, containers don't solve all the inconsistencies of local development environments. Another approach to consider is to develop in the cloud, such as with Google Cloud Workstations (*https://oreil.ly/cMMo9*). This provides another layer of isolation that mitigates the impacts of different hardware and local settings or state among developers.

Although developing with cloud VMs adds to the cloud bill, consider the cost of engineer time spent debugging issues with local environments. One time, while helping a new engineer through the onboarding process, I spent several hours a day for the better part of a week to help them get all the dependencies set up and the Docker environment running. Altogether this cost over a week of one full-time engineer.

Container composition

With multiple services to set up for data pipeline development, bringing together multiple containers can be necessary. This functionality is provided by Docker Compose (*https://oreil.ly/zm2As*).

As an example, consider the streaming pipeline shown in Figure 5-6.

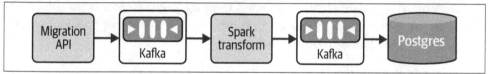

Figure 5-6. Bird migration tracking pipeline

The pipeline in Figure 5-6 is part of another offering from HoD: migration tracking. Researchers studying bird migration habitats have tagged birds with tracking devices that are picked up by towers near popular migration sites. To study the impacts of habitat destruction, the researchers want to collect and analyze information about the birds coming back to these sites on a yearly basis.

When a bird flies near a tower, the tracking information is registered and published to the Migration API. This data is captured by Kafka and streamed to a Spark transformation stage, the result of which is streamed into a Postgres database.

With this architecture in mind, let's take a look at how to build a Docker Compose environment. Rather than focusing on the syntax, in this section you'll learn how to approach the design of Compose files. If you are interested in learning more about Docker Compose, check out the Compose file specification (*https://oreil.ly/KPc4E*).

The Docker Compose files in the GitHub repo for this book are not intended to be run, but rather are provided as high-level examples. If you'd like to try applying these techniques in a live Docker Compose setting, you can check out the Compose examples provided by Docker (*https://oreil.ly/Fa82O*).

At a high level, the Docker Compose file for the pipeline in Figure 5-6 would include services for Kafka, Postgres, and the data transformation. Each service entry creates a new container, as shown in the following code sample (the full Compose file can be found in *transform-docker-compose.yml* (*https://oreil.ly/kAxS2*)):

```
services:
  kafka:
    image: confluentinc/cp-kafka:7.2.1
    . . .

  postgres:
    image: postgres:latest
    . . .

  transform:
    image: image/repo/transform_image:latest
    . . .

networks:
  migration:
```

In the preceding code, `networks` identifies which services can talk to one another in a Docker Compose environment. It's omitted from the high-level view, but every service is on the `migration` network. This ensures that `transform` can publish to `kafka` and `postgres` can read from `kafka`.

Running local code against production dependencies.   Let's start by taking a look at the transform container definition:

```
transform:
  image: container/repo/transform_image:latest
  container_name: transform
  environment:
    KAFKA_TOPIC_READ: migration_data
    KAFKA_TOPIC_WRITE: transformed_data
  volumes:
    - ./code_root/transform:/container_code/path
  networks:
    migration:
```

The image is built from the transformation code and stored in the HoD image registry. This is the same image that runs in production. The environment variables `KAFKA_TOPIC_READ` and `KAFKA_TOPIC_WRITE` are used by the Spark job to determine which Kafka topics to read from and write to.

To test local code changes there is a volume mounted to the directory where the local transformation code resides, *./code_root/transform*, mapping it to the expected location within the container for the Spark job, */container_code/path*.

Using a production image and mounting your local code gives you the ability to modify code while still using the environment in which the code runs in production. If you need to upgrade or add new libraries, you need to either build the image with those new dependencies or create a Dockerfile for development that adds the dependencies to the existing image:

```
FROM container/repo/transform_image:latest

WORKDIR /
COPY requirements.txt requirements.txt
RUN pip install -r requirements.txt
```

To use the Dockerfile with the new dependencies instead of the original image, you would update the `transform` container to build from the Dockerfile:

```
transform:
    build: Dockerfile
    container_name: transform
```

This is a bit more involved than if you were developing locally without containers, where you could just install a new library and move on. This has the advantage of making dependency modification more explicit to a developer. If you're working with Python, as in this example, it can be a helpful reminder to make sure you keep requirements files updated.

Using environment variables.   Taking a look at the `postgres` container definition, there is also a volume defined—this is for a location for Postgres to save data to. The `POST GRES_USER` and `POSTGRES_PASSWORD` values are set based on the environment the Compose file is run in, using the environment variables `PG_USER` and `PG_DATA`:

```
postgres:
    image: postgres
    container_name: postgres
    environment:
      POSTGRES_USER: ${PG_USER}
      POSTGRES_PASSWORD: ${PG_PASS}
    volumes:
      - pg_data:/var/lib/postgresql/data
    networks:
      - migration
```

Using environment variables encourages good practices, such as not hardcoding credential information into Compose files. To keep your local environment clean, you can use a *.env* file (*https://oreil.ly/movig*) to define the environment variables needed for Docker Compose.

Sharing configurations.   When you have services that are reused across different Compose files, you can consolidate them into a single shared file. This is a good practice for keeping shared resources consistently defined across teams.

To see shared configurations in action, let's look at an additional dependency for the transformation process in Figure 5-6. Part of the transformation process involves acquiring bird species information from a `species` table in the Postgres database. This is provided by an API developed by another team. Figure 5-7 shows the API layer added to the migration tracking pipeline.

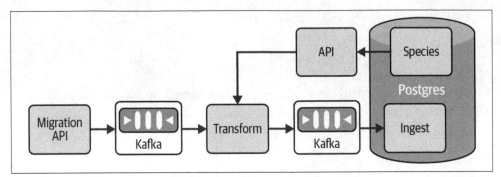

Figure 5-7. Bird migration tracking pipeline with API dependency

There are now two different teams that will use the `postgres` container and the `api` container for development. In scenarios like this, it is helpful to share Compose configurations (*https://oreil.ly/-OA6L*). Consider the Compose file for API development, which you can find at *api-docker-compose.yml* (*https://oreil.ly/4NPM3*):

```
services:
  postgres:
    image: postgres
    . . .

  api:
    image: container/repo/api_image:latest
    container_name: api
    environment:
      POSTGRES_USER: ${PG_USER}
      POSTGRES_PASSWORD: ${PG_PASS}
      POSTGRES_PORT: ${PG_PORT}
      POSTGRES_HOST: ${PG_HOST}
    volumes:
      - ./code_root/api:/container_code/path
    networks:
      migration:
    depends_on:
      - postgres
```

This uses the same Postgres service as the transform Compose file, and an API service with a local mount for development. Notice that the API service needs the Postgres credentials so that it can access the database.

For the transformer environment, you would need to add the `api` container to access the species information while developing the transformer, which you can find at *transform-docker-compose.yml* (*https://oreil.ly/xTz83*):

```
services:
 kafka:
   image: confluentinc/cp-kafka:7.2.1
   . . .

 postgres:
   image: postgres:12.12
   . . .

 transform:
   image: image/repo/transform_image:latest
   . . .

 api:
   image: container/repo/api_image:latest
   environment:
     POSTGRES_USER: ${PG_USER}
   . . .
```

In this situation, you have repeated configurations for the API and Postgres services, which can easily get out of sync. Let's take a look at how to share configurations to minimize this overlap.

First, you can create a Compose file that contains the shared resources, such as in the following *dev-docker-compose.yml* (*https://oreil.ly/eiTrG*). For the `postgres` container, you can share pretty much the entire service definition. The network is also shared, so you can include that here as well:

```
services:

 postgres:
   image: postgres
   environment:
     POSTGRES_USER: ${PG_USER}
     POSTGRES_PASSWORD: ${PG_PASS}
   volumes:
     - pg_data:/var/lib/postgresql/data
   networks:
     - migration

volumes:
 pg_data:
   name: postgres

networks:
 migration:
```

For the API service, you would want to share the environment but leave the image setting to the developers (you'll see why in the next section):

```
api:
    environment:
        POSTGRES_USER: ${PG_USER}
        POSTGRES_PASSWORD: ${PG_PASS}
        POSTGRES_PORT: ${PG_PORT}
        POSTGRES_HOST: ${PG_HOST}
    networks:
        migration:
    depends_on:
        - postgres
```

With the common setup shown in the preceding code, the next step is to create new transform and API Compose files. These will be fairly minimal now, as a lot of the setup is in the shared file.

The API Compose file, *api-docker-compose.yml* (*https://oreil.ly/RirxM*), contains only the following lines; the rest will be supplied by the shared file. Note that the image tag has changed here to convey that the API team might be working against a different image than the transform team as well as mounting local code:

```
services:
  api:
    image: container/repo/api_image:dev_tag
    container_name: api
    volumes:
      - ./code_root/api:/container_code/path
```

Because the api container in the shared file includes the depends_on clause for Postgres, you don't need to explicitly add the Postgres service in the API Compose file.

For the transform Compose file, *transform-docker-compose.yml* (*https://oreil.ly/fFZ3k*), the kafka and transformer sections are the same. The primary difference is that the Postgres service is removed and the API service definition is minimal. Note that the transformer team is using the latest image tag for the API service and there is no local code mounted:

```
services:
  kafka:
    . . .

  transform:
    . . .

  api:
    image: container/repo/api_image:latest
    container_name: api
```

Sharing Compose configurations is an important practice for teams that work on shared elements, such as the Postgres database in this example.

This example is inspired by a scenario where two teams were developing against, ostensibly, the same database container but were using slightly different settings in the Compose files. It eventually became clear that the different configurations weren't compatible and that the database creation wasn't accurate for one of the teams. Moving to a shared configuration alleviated this issue.

Now that you have a common Compose file and the reduced transform and API Compose files, you can start the containers.

For the `transform` containers:

```
docker compose -f transform-docker-compose.yml -f dev-compose-file.yml up
```

For the `api` containers:

```
docker compose -f api-docker-compose.yml -f dev-compose-file.yml up
```

The order in which you specify the Compose files is important: *the last file you apply will override values specified in earlier files.* This is why the image was not included in the API service definition in `dev-compose-file`; it would have forced the same image to be used for both API and transformer development.

Consolidating common settings. In the previous example, you learned how to share container configurations across multiple Compose files. Another way you can reduce redundancy is by using extension fields (*https://oreil.ly/hVGQK*) to share common variables within a Compose file.

Looking at the shared *dev-docker-compose.yml* (*https://oreil.ly/3SRAZ*) from the previous section, the `PG_USER` and `PG_PASS` environment variables are referenced by both the `api` and `postgres` containers. To set these in a single place, you can create an extension field, as this snippet from *dev-docker-compose.yml* (*https://oreil.ly/3OraD*) shows:

```
x-environ: &def-common
  environment:
    &common-env
    POSTGRES_USER: ${PG_USER}
    POSTGRES_PASSWORD: ${PG_PASS}

services:
 postgres:
   image: postgres
   environment
     <<: *common-env
   . . .
```

```
api:
    environment:
        <<: *common-env
        POSTGRES_PORT: ${PG_PORT}
        POSTGRES_HOST: ${PG_HOST}
    . . .
```

The extension field, x-environ, contains the shared environment variables in the common-env anchor. For the Postgres service, we only need the USER and PASS variables, but you can see how common-env can be used as a supplemental value for the api container, where you also want to define the PORT and HOST.

Resource Dependency Reduction

You've now got some good tools for creating a reproducible, consistent development environment with the Docker techniques from the previous section. There's a good chance you will have to interact with dependencies outside your local environment. You'll see a lot more on this topic in Part III.

Reducing the external dependencies you interact with will help you reduce costs and speed up development. To understand why, let's revisit the ephemeral environment setup I described earlier, pictured in Figure 5-8. I've split the environment into two sections, the portion that ran locally and the portion that ran in the cloud.

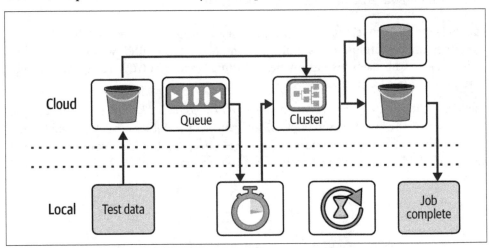

Figure 5-8. Ephemeral development environment setup

Before launching the pipeline job, a small sample dataset was copied to cloud storage. To initiate a job, a message was submitted to the cloud queue, most often using the corresponding cloud UI. The scheduler ran locally, extracting the job information from the message and launching the pipeline to run in a cluster. At the end of the job, the result was written to cloud storage, which backed a Hive metastore. The metastore definition was created in an RDS instance. Once the metastore was updated, the cluster terminated, sending a response back to the local environment.

Notice that a lot of cloud resources are being created to run a small amount of sample data. In addition to the associated cloud costs, I found debugging to be much more involved versus running locally in containers. For one thing, if the environment creation script failed to create all the resources, I had to figure out what went wrong and sometimes delete individual services by hand. For another, when you are running services in containers locally, you have access to logs that can be hard to find and access in the cloud, if they are created at all.

Remember the capacity issue I mentioned in Chapter 2? That could happen here as well. Without capacity to run the cluster, you couldn't run a pipeline test.

A lot of the reason for the heavy cloud setup in Figure 5-8 was due to how the pipeline had been developed. While our production environment used images, we weren't using containers to develop locally. Instead, we were using virtual machines, which were limited to running the workflow engine and mounting local code.

Another issue was code design, which you'll learn about in Chapter 6. The pipeline was set up to run as a series of steps on a cluster, without any way to run the pipeline locally. Had there been stubs for testing, we could have bypassed a lot of this setup. You'll learn more about mocks in Chapter 8.

The environment in Figure 5-8 is a pretty extreme example of running cloud services as part of a development environment. In a lot of cases, you can limit the cloud resource overhead, particularly if you are using containerization and good coding practices. You'll see advice on coding practices in Chapter 6 and learn how to reduce dependencies on cloud services in Part III.

In some cases, you may need to connect to external services as part of local development. For example, I worked on an analysis pipeline that sourced data from the results of an internal ingestion process. We had the internal ingestion running in a test environment, populating the source database for the analysis pipeline. I connected to this source database while working on the analysis pipeline. Running a large Spark job could be another case where you can't run locally. In this case, you might need to submit to a cluster to run a job.

A hybrid approach can be a good middle ground, where you build in the capability to run services locally or connect to them. I did this when augmenting a pipeline to add functionality to write part of the transformed data to cloud storage. At first, I simply needed to validate that the correct data was getting saved, something I could do by writing to a temp file and examining the results. For the portion of the work where I was designing the cloud storage interface, I connected to cloud storage because I needed to ensure that the interactions between the code and the cloud APIs were working as intended.

This approach both expedited development by not having to take an extra step to download the new object from the cloud to inspect the results, and minimized object interaction events and the associated costs. On top of this, the ability to write the file locally was useful for running unit tests.

You can also use a hybrid approach like this with some managed cloud services. For example, let's say the Postgres database in Figure 5-6 was hosted in Google Cloud SQL. You could use a local Postgres container for development instead of connecting to Cloud SQL by providing an alternative set of database credentials for local development.

Setup Scripts and Mock Options

I worked on a pipeline that operated in a microservices environment where internal APIs and data sources were leveraged as part of the data transformation process. One of the engineers scripted a test environment setup script, which populated local database containers with a minimum amount of information so that the APIs could be used. This improved productivity by creating a repeatable setup and allowed us to develop locally.

In another situation, our Airflow DAGs were set up based on the tier of service a customer was subscribed to. For example, customers who paid for a premium account would have their data processed at a higher priority than customers on free accounts. Customer account information was pulled from an internal API by the DAGs.

Rather than creating accounts with different tiers of service in the database container to force the API response, I added an option to mock the API response for local development. We could check the integration of the DAG and the API in the TEST environment, so this approach let me develop quickly without sacrificing test coverage. This too had the secondary benefit of enabling unit testing, as with the cloud storage mock environment I mentioned earlier.

Resource Cleanup

One task that's often cited in cost-cutting initiatives is cleaning up idle and unused resources. These resources can accumulate in the development and testing process if you don't take specific steps to clean them up after you are finished using them.

If you're creating clusters as part of your development process, setting auto-termination will ensure that these resources are cleaned up after a period of inactivity, such as with auto-termination (*https://oreil.ly/s9jEq*) for EMR clusters. Similarly, using autoscaling on development resources to reduce capacity in quiescent times will also help save costs. For example, you can set pod autoscaling (*https://oreil.ly/yKa3F*) in Kubernetes to scale down when not in use.

You can also take advantage of idle resource monitoring to find and terminate resources that are no longer in use. This is provided for free[2] for Google Compute Engine (*https://oreil.ly/Hv5pI*).

Many cloud databases also have scaling settings, such as reducing read and write capacity for DynamoDB (*https://oreil.ly/3o3So*) and scaling down RDS (*https://oreil.ly/9h8Fa*). This lets you limit resource consumption when these services aren't being used.

Even in cases where resources should get cleaned up, you may need to add some extra guardrails. The ephemeral environments I mentioned had a teardown script, but due to some entangled security permissions, they didn't always tear down entirely. Every so often, someone would audit the existing "ephemeral" environments and harangue developers to shut them down, if they could even figure out who was responsible for creating them in the first place.

You can use labels and tags on your cloud resources to identify them as development related and eligible for automatic cleanup. This is especially useful for automated cleanup scripts that look for orphaned or idle resources. On one project, we had a job that looked for EMR clusters that were older than a certain number of days and terminated them. Keep in mind that you pay for partial hours, startup time, and teardown time, so don't be overaggressive with termination.

Keep an eye out for tools that will help you run things locally versus using cloud services. I was working on a Google Cloud build config (*https://oreil.ly/NP45W*) to run unit tests as part of CI. When you submit a job, Cloud Build runs Docker commands in Google Cloud. While I was figuring out the individual Docker steps involved, I ran them locally rather than submitting the builds. This was faster since I didn't have to wait for Cloud Build to run the job, and I wasn't paying to run Cloud Build.

A former colleague likes LocalStack (*https://oreil.ly/K8cWq*) for emulating cloud services locally. If you use AWS, this could be worth checking out.

---

2 As of the time of this writing.

Summary

In this chapter, you learned how to create an ecosystem to develop, test, and deploy data pipelines in an efficient, repeatable, and cost-effective way from local development to test and staging environments.

Data pipelines need a combination of environments that merge the software development lifecycle with data size and complexity to incrementally test pipelines for functionality and performance under load. A staging environment where a pipeline can run for an extended period prior to release can help you observe issues such as resource contention or lag buildup in streaming pipelines, helping you identify infrastructure impacts before a release.

Planning out environments will help you balance data and testing needs with the costs of cloud resources and infrastructure engineering overhead. Look for opportunities to share environments across multiple purposes rather than creating many single-use environments, and consider whether you need an environment available all the time or could use an ephemeral environment to limit cloud cost and maintenance overhead.

Developing locally with the numerous external dependencies of data pipelines can be intimidating. A containerized approach will help you break down a pipeline into discrete services and help you minimize differences between development and production by using the same images. You can test local code changes against this environment by mounting your code in a Docker Compose file.

A consistent, repeatable approach to development will help keep engineers in sync across teams, including how you connect to services and how credentials are shared. You can populate a *.env* file with this information to reference from Docker Compose, allowing you to connect to the resources you need without the fear of committing sensitive information to your code repository.

Using a common Docker Compose file for shared services and configurations will help multiple teams work in tandem and minimize repeated code, reducing the likelihood of mismatch across teams. You can also share settings within Compose files using YAML anchors and extension fields, allowing you to set variables once and reuse them across multiple services.

To make sure your containerized environment really does mirror production, make sure you regularly wipe out local containers and pull or rebuild images. Cleaning up images, containers, and volumes will also help you minimize how much space Docker consumes locally.

Look for opportunities to minimize cloud resource usage by adding alternative code paths and setups, such as using a Postgres container instead of connecting to Cloud SQL or writing files locally instead of to cloud storage. When you want to test connections, you can switch to using these resources directly or use a test environment to run integration tests. This hybrid approach can have the benefit of also setting up mocks for unit testing, as you saw with the API and cloud storage examples.

At times, you may need to use or create cloud resources as part of your development process. Keep in mind that anything you create you will need to tear down, so tag and label resources so that they are easily identifiable as temporary development collateral. In general, you can reduce costs by using fewer resources in lower environments, such as less compute capacity; using more frequent lifecycle policies to clean up cloud storage; and turning on autoscaling to reduce resources when not in use.

Don't fear the reaper (*https://oreil.ly/a4Mgg*). Instead, use auto-termination and scaling where available and automate processes to look for orphaned or idle resources, cleaning them up when they are no longer actively in use.

Now that you've seen how to get set up for development, the next chapter dives into software development strategies for building nimble codebases that can keep up with the changes inherent in data pipeline development.

CHAPTER 6

Software Development Strategies

One of the foundational concepts in *The Pragmatic Programmer* (*https://oreil.ly/3ESjN*) by David Thomas and Andrew Hunt (Addison-Wesley) is that code should be Easy To Change (ETC),[1] a concept I'll expand on throughout this chapter. I find this advice to be especially relevant when working with data pipelines, where change is a way of life. When developing data pipelines you need to support changes in a multitude of areas: data size, format, and shape; data acquisition and storage; and evolving needs for data transformation and validation, not to mention changes in cloud services, providers, and data processing engines.

With all these vectors for change, even the best-intentioned codebases can turn into spaghetti, making it difficult to modify, extend, and test functionality. This in turn will negatively impact performance, reliability, and cost as more time and resources are required to debug and evolve the pipeline.

This chapter is about helping you design codebases that will be resilient to the shifting sands of data pipeline design, with a focus on developing code that is ETC.

To start, I'll discuss some common coding environments you encounter in data pipelines and show you how to effectively manage code in each situation based on my experience developing across all these tools.

Then I'll show you techniques for creating modular codebases, using best practices from software engineering applied to common scenarios when working with data pipelines. To set the stage, I'll share an experience of working with a codebase that became difficult to change as a product evolved.

---

1 Topic 8, *The Pragmatic Programmer, 20th Anniversary Edition*. If you don't have this book, order it now from your local bookstore.

Building on these earlier topics, the last technique is configurable design, which consists of a modular codebase that can be dynamically configured. This is a powerful technique that can help you deploy new features quickly without the risk of adding bugs to your codebase.

The code examples in this chapter are primarily to show you how to structure code. Unless otherwise specified, these are not intended to be examples that you would run. You can find many of these code examples in the GitHub repo (*https://oreil.ly/B0D_1*).

Managing Different Coding Environments

Data pipeline code can be developed in a variety of ways. While software developers may be more accustomed to thinking about code developed in an IDE, data analysts, data scientists, and machine learning (ML) scientists may be more familiar with notebook interfaces, such as Jupyter (*https://jupyter.org*). There are also web UIs available for some cloud services, such as with AWS Lambda and AWS Glue, which give you the ability to write code and manage connections with other services in the browser.

It can be challenging to manage code across these different environments. From a reliability perspective, code should be source controlled and tested following software development best practices. That can be tricky or impossible for notebooks and web UIs, which can open the door for mistakes and bugs.

To give you a sense of some of these challenges and remediation strategies, I'll walk you through a real-world example in which I've dealt with multiple coding environments in the past. You'll get a sense of the pros and cons of each, and I'll share some advice for how to use them effectively.

Example: A Multimodal Pipeline

As it turns out, one of the data pipeline projects I worked on (detailed in "A Lifeline for Medicaid Beneficiaries" (*https://oreil.ly/wdL_S*)) used all three of the environments I just mentioned: notebooks, an IDE, and the AWS Lambda web UI. The pipeline architecture is depicted in Figure 6-1.

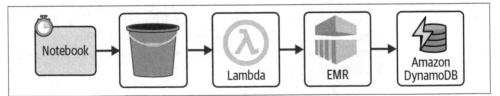

Figure 6-1. Pipeline architecture with different coding environments

A team of analysts developed the transformation logic for the pipeline, which ran against a data warehouse (not pictured). This portion of the pipeline was written in SQL using a Databricks notebook (*https://databricks.com*).

The notebook ran on a schedule and saved the transformation results to S3, which triggered a Lambda function on the creation of new objects. The Lambda function, written in Python, launched an EMR cluster that performed a second data transformation step before loading the data into DynamoDB.[2]

The following sections detail opportunities, challenges, and strategies for working with notebooks and web UIs, using the ETL process in Figure 6-1 as an example.

Notebooks

This example is a nice use case for notebooks, where we were collaborating with another team with the expertise to develop the transformation logic. The analysts could express the transformation code in a language they were familiar with (SQL) in an environment that allowed them to get immediate feedback while testing queries. This also helped us quickly test updates the analysts made without the overhead of a more traditional build and deploy process.

Notebooks are also great for prototyping and sharing ideas early in the design process. The ability to combine code, visualization, and notes is fantastic for conducting exploratory data analysis and figuring out data transformation logic, while also providing context to others for collaboration.

On the drawbacks side, there wasn't a great way to test the notebook code, which is a downside of using notebooks in general. If you're working with notebooks, factoring out critical code into a package that can be tested is preferable. Source control for notebooks is evolving, but there are still some shortcomings in this space. This is yet another reason to favor packaging code to import into a notebook.

While packaging code is a good option for languages that support it, you also need a way to deploy packages for this method to work. If packaging isn't an option, you can consider separating code into another notebook. This gives you some insulation from accidentally introducing a bug when editing the notebook, and you can run some tests like this as well. Jupyter notebooks support importing code from other notebooks (*https://oreil.ly/m2TD1*), and if you're working with Databricks notebooks, you can achieve this same behavior with workflows (*https://oreil.ly/8Qu_7*).

Another way you can guard against introducing bugs in notebooks is by using *widgets*, which are UI elements that you can add to the notebook to parameterize values,

---

2 See the lifeline ingestion architecture image in the Medium article "A zero-downtime serverless ingestion architecture for Medicaid's first cross-agency API" (*https://oreil.ly/pSSjZ*).

similar to how you have parameters for a function. These UI elements, such as text boxes and radio buttons, provide a place to specify values without touching the code within the notebook and enable you to run a notebook for different inputs. Widgets are supported in both Jupyter (*https://oreil.ly/C3Lro*) and Databricks (*https://oreil.ly/RmU0_*) notebooks.

The widgets notebook (*https://oreil.ly/wd83h*) shows a simple widget example, illustrated in Figure 6-2. Instead of changing the name in the notebook code, you can type a different name in the Text widget.

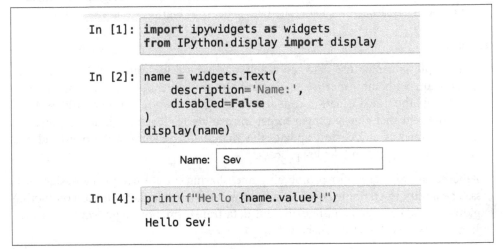

Figure 6-2. Widget example

One place I've used widgets is in a notebook that ran query performance analysis, which you'll see in Chapter 11. The widgets allowed users to specify a time frame and query name to inspect, which enabled the notebook to be used across various use cases without modifying the code.

Web UIs

Services with web UIs, such as AWS Lambda, give you the ability to write code directly in the browser, which can be very powerful for getting things up and running quickly. You can also see the impact of code changes immediately as opposed to waiting on a release cycle, which can be both good and bad. In the best case, you immediately update your system with a fix. In the worst case, you immediately deploy a bug.

Web UIs sometimes keep a short history of the last few code edits, allowing you to roll back to a prior version, but if you overrun this history, you'll find yourself trying to re-create what was without the benefit of source control. I can tell you from experience that this is not how you want to spend your time.

In the case of AWS Lambda, you have the option to specify test events to validate the Lambda code. While convenient, keep in mind that using this mechanism executes the Lambda function, incurring costs. A better approach is to create a test event and download it for local development, including it as test collateral with your codebase. This gives you the benefit of having the event structure to test code against, without incurring the cost of running the Lambda.

Web UIs also let you specify relationships between different services. For example, in the Lambda UI, you can click an SNS trigger (*https://oreil.ly/Be8CC*) and write the name of the SNS topic that should trigger the Lambda function.

Maybe I'm just anxious, but I see every point-and-click connection in a web UI as a dependency that I won't remember and my teammates won't be aware of, creating an opportunity for bugs that are especially hard to track down. If you must use a web UI, my advice is to extract as much configuration and code as you can and put it into source control for better testing, versioning, and visibility.

Infrastructure as Code

The ability to deploy cloud infrastructure like storage buckets, serverless functions, and clusters with web UIs is a great usability feature that helps you get things up and running. This approach quickly becomes unwieldy as you set up more components—permissions, networking, and multiple environments, to name a few.

Infrastructure as code (IaC) encapsulates these settings and operations in configuration files, resulting in a more consistent, repeatable, and time-effective approach to cloud infrastructure deployment. A good IaC practice can quickly deploy multiple environments with a few variables changed from DEV to TEST to PROD, spin up new environments for disaster recovery (DR), and roll out infrastructure changes smoothly.

You may need to put in additional effort to set up deployment processes to make this a reality, as you saw in the example I shared earlier. Use management tools such as AWS Serverless Application Model (*https://oreil.ly/iEExt*) (SAM) where you can, and keep in mind that when you're looking for information on how to do this you will likely come across documentation from your CSP suggesting that you pay for more of their services to do it; the AWS article "How to unit test and deploy AWS Glue jobs using AWS CodePipeline" (*https://oreil.ly/B8P28*) is a case in point. Another option for Lambda specifically is to use GitHub actions (*https://oreil.ly/TK9Ti*) to deploy code. This is a lighter-weight solution than using SAM, but it requires that you give GitHub permission to interact with your AWS account (*https://oreil.ly/n_UdL*).

Along these lines, rather than using the Lambda UI to host our code, we created a Python module. Using SAM, we were able to source-control, test, and deploy the

Lambda code as part of our regular build and deploy process. SAM uploaded our code artifacts to S3, which is a supported option for deploying AWS Lambda code (*https://oreil.ly/V5HTA*).

The last piece of code is the EMR-based data transformation and load into Dyna-moDB. This code was developed in an IDE. To deploy this code, we zipped it into the same file as the Lambda function so that both the EMR transformation code and the Lambda function were deployed to S3 by SAM. Our team had a strong IaC practice,[3] so when a new version of the Lambda Python code was deployed, the corresponding template was updated with the link to the latest artifacts.

The remaining sections focus on code development strategies you can use in any environment where you are using languages such as Python, Scala, or Java. To begin, let's look at an example of how code can become difficult to change.

Example: How Code Becomes Difficult to Change

To motivate the development strategies in the following sections, let's look at an example scenario of how code becomes difficult to change. This example is based on experiences I've had in the field, which I've fictionalized to relate to the HoD example running throughout this book.

With all the data the HoD social media platform has collected, Lou and Sylvia have been able to design a very clever ML engine, kind of like a Magic 8 Ball (*https://oreil.ly/xju2y*) for birds, where you ask a question and get an answer, though a lot more sophisticated.

At first, HoD users could submit their questions directly to the ML engine. Over time, the HoD team got a sense of the questions users typically asked, such as "How long is a night heron's neck?" and "What species of heron are present in Fort Lauder-dale, Florida?" In response, the team created a handful of stock questions and bolted on some logic to execute the questions to the ML engine. This piece of code became known as the execution engine. Once the questions were processed, the execution engine stored the results in a database, as depicted in Figure 6-3.

---

3 IaC is beyond the scope of this book, but if you're interested, check out *Infrastructure as Code, 2nd Edition*, by Kief Morris (O'Reilly).

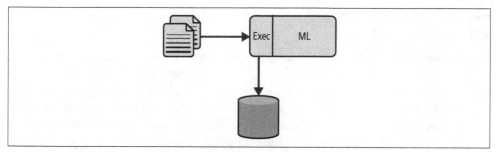

Figure 6-3. ML engine with execution layer to process stock questions

You'll notice that the execution engine directly abuts the ML engine in Figure 6-3. I've done this to communicate that these are tightly coupled at the code level. The stock questions were an experimental feature, offered as a sideline to the main HoD product, so it was preferential to get something up and running just to try it out versus spending a lot of time designing a separate system.

The stock questions feature turned out to be very popular, so the HoD team decided to do a fast-pivot to making stock questions the main feature of their platform. They developed an automation that created thousands of questions that were stored in a database. They had some other data that users wanted to incorporate into the ML results, so they added another data source as well. With more questions and more users, it became necessary to diversify how the results were stored, so an additional data sink to the cloud was added. This resulted in the system depicted in Figure 6-4.

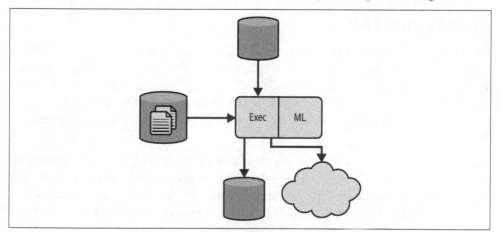

Figure 6-4. Evolution of greater execution responsibility and interfaces

You can see that the execution engine is still tightly coupled to the ML engine, but it has grown due to the architectural changes. There are also many more dependencies; instead of a single connection to a database, there are now three database connections to deal with, and cloud storage as well. These dependencies represent more potential points of failure and performance impacts in production, and more interfaces to manage when testing.

In addition, the exponential increase in the number of stock questions put more load on the system, resulting in performance and reliability issues. The tight coupling between the execution and ML engines meant debugging and testing became time consuming and laborious. Anytime changes were made on the ML side, there was a potential to break in the execution engine. When bugs arose, the HoD team had to replicate failures by rerunning the failed questions, adding monitoring and logging after the fact.

If you've worked on data pipelines, there's likely something in this story that you can relate to. In the following sections, I'll show you some techniques for handling these kinds of changes in your codebases.

Modular Design

One way to develop code that is easy to change is by thinking of code as reusable building blocks. Consider the different aspects of a LEGO brick (*https://oreil.ly/ JF2yT*). LEGOs have a standard connection interface that lets you build stable, interlocking structures. LEGO bricks also come in a variety of shapes, sizes, and colors that you can swap in as you like because of this standardized interface. Many software development principles are fundamentally about designing code to be more modular, like a LEGO brick.

Single Responsibility

Data processing tends to involve a variety of distinct operations: data acquisition, storage, and transformation. The single-responsibility principle (*https://oreil.ly/ T09z7*) encourages keeping the operations of a given bit of code within a well-defined scope. This helps you isolate different functions to improve modularity, testability, and readability. It also protects code from bugs and reduces your maintenance burden.

Think about this as the different shapes and sizes of LEGO bricks. If you want to build a car out of LEGOs, you can create whatever size, shape, and color of car you like by using individual bricks. If instead of these discrete pieces, LEGO supplied a single car-shaped LEGO, you would be much more limited in how you could customize it.

To get a sense of how to use single responsibility, let's consider one of the stock questions in the example: "What species of heron are present in Fort Lauderdale, Florida?" The ML engine would provide a set of data that is pretty likely to contain herons near Fort Lauderdale, leaving the execution engine to filter and aggregate the results with the `create_aggregate_data` method, which you can find in *storage_example.py* (*https://oreil.ly/waj46*). Don't worry about the internals of `aggre` `gate_by_species` for now; just know that it returns a dictionary representation of the aggregated data:

```
def create_aggregate_data(data):
    bird_agg  = aggregate_by_species(data)
    key = f"aggregate_data_{datetime.utcnow().isoformat()}.json"
    ...
    s3.put_object(Bucket="bucket_name", Key=key, Body=bytes(json.dumps(bird_agg)))
```

In the preceding code, `create_aggregate_data` performs two functions: aggregating data based on species and storing the result in an S3 bucket. An important thing to note is the different interfaces present in this method. You have the data passed in as a variable, which minimizes the dependency on how the data is created, but you also have the interface to S3. There is also a dependency on Boto3 (*https://oreil.ly/nH7Qx*), which is the AWS SDK for Python.

Every time you touch a piece of code, there is a potential for creating bugs. With these different interfaces and dependencies, there are a lot of reasons why the `create_aggregate_data` method as it is currently written would need to be modified. If you need to change the region the data is stored in, you will have to update this method. There's also the possibility that you may want to put the aggregated data in another place, such as a database, which will again lead you to modify this code. Finally, when testing, you'll be writing data to S3, which is undesirable; it incurs unnecessary costs and requires authenticating to create a client in your test environment.

One step you can take to loosen the coupling between the data aggregation and the storage code is to refactor them into separate functions:

```
def write_to_s3(data, key):
    s3 = boto3.client('s3', region_name='us-east-1')
    s3.put_object(Bucket="bucket_name", Key=key, Body=data)

def create_species_agg(data):
    bird_agg  = aggregate_by_species(data)
    key = f"aggregate_data_{datetime.utcnow().isoformat()}.json"
    write_to_s3(bytes(json.dumps(bird_agg)), key)
```

 When trying to understand whether your code is doing a good job of following single responsibility, try to state in a sentence what the code is doing. For example, before refactoring `create_aggre` `gate_data`, you would have stated "create_aggregate_data aggregates data *and* writes it to S3." That *and* in the sentence is a sign that you might consider factoring out those different actions into separate methods. Compare this with `write_to_s3`, which has the sole action of writing to S3.

By encapsulating the Boto3 code in the `write_to_s3` method, `create_aggre`
`gate_data` is now insulated from changes in the implementation details of how the
data is uploaded to S3. For example, as more bird data becomes available, it could be
desirable to compress the aggregated data to reduce its size, which you can now do
without modifying `create_aggregate_data`:

```
def write_to_s3(data, key):
    s3 = boto3.client('s3', region_name='us-east-1')
    s3.put_object(Bucket="bucket_name", Key=key, Body=gzip.compress(data))
```

In addition, you can use this generic function to store other results in S3. For example, in the HoD survey data pipeline in Chapter 1, the bird survey data is enriched
with the social media data and stored to S3. You can reuse `write_to_s3` to perform
this operation as well:

```
with_social = enrich_with_social(data)
write_to_s3(with_social, "with_social")
```

Something you should be conscientious about is *overengineering
your code*, where you try to make code overly generic and flexible
in anticipation of future changes. Modular, extensible code is
something you should strive for, but there are trade-offs with trying to do too much too early.

Understanding the priorities of the moment and the project phase
(from prototype to MVP to production) will help you determine
this. For example, if you're working on a proof of concept or trying
to get an idea out in the world, you might be prioritizing getting
the system up and running quickly. I've worked on pipelines that
started as a notebook that enabled us to quickly test out different
ideas, in which case we weren't focused on code design because we
didn't know what we needed yet.

In this same vein, keep in mind that the software principles I refer
to in this chapter are guidelines, not rules to be blindly followed.
It's important for you to determine when it makes sense to put
these into practice and to what extent.

Dependency Inversion

Implementation details in data pipelines can change considerably in terms of how
data is being transformed, how it is being acquired, and how it is being stored. You
may have to incorporate new data sources and sinks, or modify or remove existing
ones as you saw in the example earlier in this chapter.

If you're familiar with object-oriented design, you may have heard of dependency
inversion (*https://oreil.ly/DKzIq*), which can be summarized as "depend on abstractions, not concretions." This means that rather than writing your code depending on

a specific implementation, you should write it so that you can depend on an abstract version of what you need. This allows the implementation details to fluctuate without impacting the surrounding logic.

Think about dependency inversion as keeping your options open. To use an analogy, let's say you're in the mood for pizza. If you will only accept pizza from Pizza Shack, that's a concrete dependency. You have more options if pizza from a variety of purveyors is acceptable, be they Pizza Shack, Short King's Pizza, or Pepperoni Palace. This is an abstract dependency, where your pizza desires can be fulfilled by multiple restaurants, so long as pizza is on the menu.

In Java this abstraction is an interface (*https://oreil.ly/Pt-5i*), and in Scala this would be a trait (*https://oreil.ly/mivLd*). Python has abstract base classes (*https://oreil.ly/ SfRzB*) (ABCs). An ABC has no implementation details, but it can be used to enforce that specific entities exist in subclasses. Continuing with the storage example, I've defined an abstract base class, denoted by the decorator @abc, which you can see in *storage_example.py* (*https://oreil.ly/fRMpn*):

```
@abc
class AbstractStorage:
    def add(data, id):
        raise NotImplementedError
```

This defines an expected interface, namely that an add method is available, which you can then customize based on the storage medium. You can create an implementation of AbstractStorage for S3 by subclassing AbstractStorage, as shown in S3Storage in *cloud_storage.py* (*https://oreil.ly/lPMjA*):

```
class S3Storage(AbstractStorage):
    def __init__(self, bucket):
        self.s3 = boto3.client('s3', region_name='us-east-1')
        self.bucket = bucket

    def add(self, data, id):
        self.s3.put_object(Bucket=self.bucket, Key=id, Body=data)
```

Going back to the create_aggregate_data example, you can encapsulate this method in a class where you can also specify the storage method:

```
class ProcessBirdData:
    def __init__(self, storage -> AbstractStorage):
        self.storage = storage

    def create_aggregate_data(self, data):
        bird_agg = aggregate_by_species(data)
        self.storage.add(bytes(json.dumps(bird_agg)), "species_data")
```

You may be wondering what's the point of creating this extra class scaffolding around create_aggregate_data, as it just seems like more lines of code to do the same thing.

At this point, you would be correct! Let's take a look at what this class structure and dependency inversion can give you.

Supporting multicloud

You can use this approach to deploy a single codebase across multiple cloud providers. This kind of flexibility is nice to have if you aren't sure what provider you plan to choose long term, or if you want to keep your codebase cloud agnostic.

Consider a pipeline deployment that can run on both AWS and GCS. You can add another implementation of AbstractStorage specifically for GCS:

```
class GCSStorage(AbstractStorage):
    def __init__(self, bucket):
        self.gcs = storage.Client()
        self.bucket = self.gcs.bucket(bucket)

    def add(self, data, id):
        blob = self.bucket.blob(id)
        blob.upload_from_string(json.dumps(data))
```

Notice that the interface is the same as S3Storage, but the implementation is different.

With classes implementing the GCS and AWS storage, you can create another implementation of AbstractStorage that chooses the correct storage mechanism based on where the code is deployed:

```
class CloudStorage(AbstractStorage):
    def __init__(self, deploy):
        if deploy == 'gcs':
            self.cloud_storage = GCSStorage()
        elif deploy == 'aws':
            self.cloud_storage = S3Storage()

    def add(self, data, id):
        self.cloud_storage(data, id)
```

Let's put all these pieces together. Assuming you use an environment variable DEPLOYMENT to denote what CSP you've deployed the code to, you can run the bird data processing with:

```
storage_platform = CloudStorage(os.getenv('DEPLOYMENT'))
data = acquire_data()
bird_data_process = ProcessBirdData(storage_platform)
bird_data_process.create_aggregate_data(data)
```

In the preceding code, storage_platform will be chosen based on where the code is deployed.

Plugging in other data sinks

AbstractStorage provides a predictable interface for the rest of your codebase to work with, which you can use to plug in new data sinks. For example, you can add another subclass that stores data to a database:

```python
class DatabaseStorage(AbstractStorage):
    def __init__(self, connection_string, model_cls):
        self.engine = create_engine(connection_string)
        self.model_cls = model_cls
    def add(self, data, id):
        data['id'] = id
        with Session(self.engine) as session:
            model_inst = self.model_cls(**data)
            session.add(model_inst)
            session.commit()
```

In this case, model_cls would be the object model that translates the dictionary to a given table in the database:

```python
from sqlalchemy import Column, Integer, String
from sqlalchemy.orm import declarative_base

Base = declarative_base()
class AggData(Base):
    __tablename__ = "aggregate_data"

    id = Column(Integer, primary_key=True)
    description = Column(String)
    species = Column(String)
```

In this implementation of AbstractStorage, the __init__ method creates a database connection and the add method inserts the data using the supplied model. This is a very simple example where the keys in the data dictionary match the attribute names in the model, allowing you to use ** to unpack the values. For more on database mapping, see the SQLAlchemy ORM Quick Start guide (*https://oreil.ly/GK-IU*).

If you wanted to store the aggregate data to a database instead of the cloud, you would pass DatabaseStorage to the ProcessBirdData constructor:

```python
bird_data_process = ProcessBirdData(DatabaseStorage(connection_string, AggData))
bird_data_process.create_aggregate_data(data)
```

You can see how, with a different connection_string and implementation of the add method, you could create different implementations of AbstractStorage for different types of relational databases.

Testing

I'll get into testing in depth in Chapter 7, but another benefit of dependency inversion I want to discuss before leaving this topic is testing. In addition to using the `AbstractStorage` abstract base class as an interface to create different storage solutions across CSPs and data sinks, you can create a subclass for testing as with the `MockStorage` class in *cloud_storage.py* (*https://oreil.ly/J0eZX*):

```python
class MockStorage(AbstractStorage):
    def __init__(self, bucket):
        self.bucket = bucket

    def add(self, data, id):
        print(f"Would have written {data} to {self.bucket} at {id}")
        return (data, f"{self.bucket}/{id}")
```

With a mock for the storage layer, you don't have to set up credentials to create an AWS or GCS client locally. Instead, you can implement `MockStorage`; however, you need to support your tests. In this example, `MockStorage` prints some information and returns the data and the path, giving you the opportunity to write tests like the following:

```python
def test_bird_data_process(test_data, expected_data, expected_path):
    storage = MockStorage("bucket_name")
    bird_data_process = ProcessBirdData(storage)
    result, object_path = bird_data_process.create_aggregate_data(test_data)
    assert result == expected_data
    assert object_path == expected_path
```

Knowing When to Refactor

As the opening example illustrates, it's not hard for a data pipeline codebase to get into a place where it becomes difficult to work with. Here are some things I've experienced as clues that it might be time to refactor your pipeline:

Working around the existing code

A codebase I worked on had a message-processing module that initiated a pipeline job based on the message contents. To communicate the message contents to the pipeline, this code set properties on a pipeline object. This was done in a rush to get something up and running on a deadline, but it created tight coupling that resulted in any updates to the message processing requiring updates to the pipeline class as well. Thinking back to the single-responsibility principle, clearly there was some leakage of responsibility between the pipeline module and the message module. Really, the dependencies between these two modules were reversed: the message module was attempting to set pipeline properties, whereas a better design would have been to provide an instance of the message class as a parameter to the pipeline constructor.

Leaky data structures

Generic data structures like dictionaries and tuples can be really helpful when you're working with semistructured and unstructured data and when you're prototyping. A pitfall of this approach is that you can hide leaky data structures. If you find that your Python methods are relying a lot on **kwargs to pass an ever-increasing number of things to a method, it could be time to refactor. This is something that contributed to the tight coupling between the execution and ML engines in the example story in this chapter. Using Data Classes (*https://oreil.ly/ 5ZzID*) is a lightweight approach that retains flexibility while making the data structure explicit, offering a way to continue using schemas throughout the code. This is good documentation for other developers and can help enforce a clear interface between different parts of the codebase.

Inability to unit-test, or relying heavily on connecting to live services to run unit tests

I've worked on several codebases that were tangled up to a point that most testing had to be run as an integration test. This is definitely a sign to revisit your design and look for opportunities to modularize.

Modular Design with DataFrames

DataFrames both illustrate some of the modular principles I've discussed so far and present some challenges. The functional interface of a DataFrame allows you to chain discrete operations, which provides a lot of nice flexibility. You can add, remove, or modify transformations easily, and the read and write functions allow for a lot of customization that you can do without modifying the transformation methods. The code in this section can be found in *dataframes.py* (*https://oreil.ly/BvLbn*).

This example is a possible implementation of `create_aggregate_data`, where a lowercase copy of the `description` field is searched with a regular expression that will match any of the names in the `species_list`. The matched species, or empty if no match, will be represented in a new column, `species`. This data is grouped by the `species` column with the `count` field summed, resulting in a count of each species found in input data:

```
r_species = f".*({'|'.join(species_list)}).*"
df = (spark
      .read.json('s3://bird_bucket/bird_data.json')
      .withColumn("description_lower", f.lower('description'))
      .withColumn("species", f.regexp_extract('description_lower', r_species, 1))
      .drop("description_lower")
      .groupBy("species")
      .agg({"count":"sum"})
      .write.mode("overwrite").json("s3://bird_bucket/result.json")
)
```

In this example, discrete read, write, and transformation functions are applied to some JSON data. The ability to chain these methods mimics the logical process you walk through when working with data, but the result is not modular. You'll have to interact with S3 to test this code, and the chained data transformations can make it difficult to isolate bugs. In addition, if you add more transformation logic, you'll have to touch all the code, from reading the data through writing it out.

Something you can do to improve modularity is to factor out the data transformation code into discrete methods that operate on a DataFrame:

```python
def apply_species_label(species_list, df):
    r_species = f".*({'|'.join(species_list)}).*"
    return (df
        .withColumn("description_lower", f.lower('description'))
        .withColumn("species", f.regexp_extract('description_lower', r_species, 1))
        .drop("description_lower")
    )

def create_aggregate_data(df):
    return (df
        .groupBy("species")
        .agg({"count":"sum"})
        )
```

These methods take a DataFrame as input and return the updated DataFrame, which is the same interface the PySpark DataFrame provides. You can use the transform method to chain the discrete methods:

```python
df = (spark
        .read.json('s3://bird_bucket/bird_data.json')
        .transform(partial(apply_species_label, species_list))
        .transform(create_aggregate_data)
        .write.mode("overwrite").json("s3://bird_bucket/result.json"))
```

You'll notice that I've used partial (*https://oreil.ly/2RG2m*) here, as the apply_species_label method takes both the DataFrame and the species_list as inputs.

One of the biggest improvements that comes from this refactoring is the ability to test each part of a complex data transformation by breaking it into smaller methods. Consider if you had to test the original version of create_aggregate_data prior to factoring out apply_species_label and create_aggregate_data. In this case, the test cases would have to cover both species extraction and aggregation, as shown in Table 6-1.

Table 6-1. Test cases covering both species extraction and aggregation

Test case row	Description value	Count value
0	""	2
1	"Nothing to see here"	4

Test case row	Description value	Count value
2	"Night hEron is very cool"	1
3	"Saw a night heron"	2
4	"Many hummingbirds"	0
5	"A blue heron on the lake"	1

You then have to think about two vectors simultaneously: test cases for extracting the species and test cases for aggregating the results. You also have to create expected results, as shown in Table 6-2. How do you know which rows in Table 6-1 contribute to expected result row 0, where species is an empty string? It's difficult to know with the aggregation.

Table 6-2. Expected results for combined species extraction and aggregation

Expected result row	Species	Sum
0	""	
1	"night heron"	3
2	"blue heron"	1

On the other hand, factoring out `apply_species_label` and `create_aggregate_data` enables you to focus on these test cases independently. Without the aggregation, you can define test cases and expected results in the same table for `apply_species_label`, as shown in Table 6-3. It's now abundantly clear which cases match a given species name and which do not.

Table 6-3. Test cases and expected results for `apply_species_label`

Description value	Expected value for species
""	""
"Nothing to see here"	""
"Night hEron is very cool"	"night heron"
"Saw a night heron"	"night heron"
"Many hummingbirds"	""
"A blue heron on the lake"	"blue heron"

Here's an example of testing `apply_species_label` with one of the test cases shown in Table 6-3:

```
def test_species_label(spark_context):
    data = [{'description': "Saw a night heron"}]
    data_df = spark_context.parallelize(data).toDF()
    species_list = ['night heron']
    result_df = apply_species_label(species_list, data_df)
```

```
result = result_df.toPandas().to_dict('list')
assert result['species'][0] == 'night heron'
```

While this example is trivial, consider that production data transformations often include multiple transformations and aggregations, which can quickly balloon into complex testing needs where it's easy to miss important cases.

Another advantage of modularization is being able to change the transformation logic on its own, without impacting the top-level code that calls `apply_species_label`.

Let's say the ML engine is updated to export a species identification guess in the column `ml_species`. A confidence rating is provided in the `species_conf` column. If the confidence rating is greater than 0.8, you want to use the identification from the ML engine. Otherwise, you will use the previous implementation with the regular expression search:

```
def apply_species_label(species_list, df):
    return df.withColumn(
            "species",
                f.when(f.col("species_conf")) > 0.8, f.col("ml_species")
                f.otherwise(<previous implementation>)
```

Configurable Design

At this point, you've seen techniques to help you create modular codebases. While these practices on their own will improve your design, you can take this further by leveraging modularity to create dynamic codebases. By using configurations to direct how the pipeline operates, you can add functionality without touching or deploying any code. This shows up in *The Pragmatic Programmer* as Tip 55: Parameterize Your App Using External Configurations (make sure to also check out the end-of-chapter tip on not overdoing it).[4]

One of the projects I worked on had the "configuration as a service" concept really nailed down.[5] To add a new data source for the pipeline, we just had to add a new configuration. No code updates for the pipeline code were required at all. We could bring a new source online in under an hour.

Configurable code can really supercharge your development process if you get the abstractions right. You can use this technique to dynamically generate Airflow DAGs, which can include dynamically generating tasks at runtime. The Airflow documentation includes examples of using configurations to create DAGs (*https://oreil.ly/1QXrc*) and using dynamic task mapping (*https://oreil.ly/VcvQK*) to create tasks at runtime.

---

4 *The Pragmatic Programmer, 20th Anniversary Edition*: Chapter 5, Section 33

5 *The Pragmatic Programmer, 20th Anniversary Edition*: p. 167

There are two conditions you need to satisfy to use this technique successfully:

- The target process you want to parameterize can be expressed as a configuration.
- The code can support the level of configuration required.

I'll take you through an example to show you how to evaluate these conditions and create a configurable pipeline.

Recall the system in Figure 6-4, where thousands of automatically generated stock questions are run using the execution and ML engine. The success of this offering has resulted in numerous groups coming to HoD asking for help with bird identification. Since there seems to be fairly healthy demand, the HoD team decides to start offering heron identification as a service (HIaaS) in which companies bring their own data to be processed by the HoD species extraction and then stored in the customer's database of choice. The pipeline for this process is depicted in Figure 6-5.

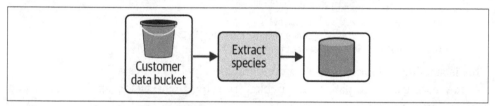

Figure 6-5. Heron identification as a service

When I'm looking for opportunities to use configuration, I find it helpful to ask whether there is something in the pipeline that could be modeled as a function. The parameters to the function are the elements I can configure.

In the case of the HIaaS pipeline in Figure 6-5, you can see this potential with the "Extract species" step, where the source data and output database are configured based on the customer. The first thing to notice here is that we have some quantities that vary from customer to customer: the source bucket and the destination database. The following is not a real method, but rather a high-level thought experiment of how you could factor out these quantities:

```
def run_extract_species(bucket, database):
    source_data = read_from_bucket(bucket)
    extracted = extract_species(source_data)
    store_data(extracted, database)
```

The next step is to determine whether you can build a codebase that can be configured based on the bucket and database information. You've seen from "Modular Design with DataFrames" on page 125 how you can create different implementations of `AbstractStorage` for different cloud storage providers and different database types, so it seems pretty likely that, given a bucket name and a database connection string, you can configure these elements.

You don't want to keep any secret information, such as database connection parameters, in the config, so you'll need a way to create the database connection string at runtime. One option would be to create a method that generates a database connection string given a database type and `customer_id`, where the `customer_id` is used to fetch the database credentials from a secret store. Here's a possible configuration that would give you the parameters you need:

```
{
    "customer_id": "1235",
    "bucket": "gs://bestco/bird_data",
    "db": "postgres"
}
```

You can now rewrite `run_extract_species` to directly consume the config, with a new method, `get_connection`, that creates the connection string:

```
def run_extract_species(bucket, db, customer_id):
    raw = get_data(bucket)
    extracted = extract_species(raw)
    connection_string = get_connection(customer_id, db)
    store_data(extracted, connection_string)
```

This is starting to look more like a configurable pipeline process. You are retrieving the raw data using the path to the bucket, running the `extract_species` step, and handing off the result to `store_data`.

Now, to bring new customers on board, HoD simply has to add a new configuration:

```
configs = [
    {"customer_id": "1235", "bucket": "gs://bestco/bird_data", "db": "postgres"},
    {"customer_id": "3423", "bucket": "gs://for_the_birds", "db": "mysql"},
    {"customer_id": "0953", "bucket": "s3://dtop324", "db": "postgres"},
]
```

To run the pipeline for these customers, you can simply call `run_extract_species` for each line in the config:

```
for config in configs:
    run_extract_species(**config)
```

An important note about this code if you're not familiar with Airflow or other orchestration tools: each call to `run_extract_species` generates a new DAG run. This means each customer extraction runs independently, as opposed to a batch job that runs all customers at once.

Make sure your configuration isn't making promises your infrastructure can't deliver on. When you've got a configurable setup, it can be easy to forget that each new configuration, while more trivial to add from the development side, will have impacts on the resources in your system. It might be a good idea for the HoD team to do some evaluation of the size of the customer source data before adding a configuration. You can also use the scalable techniques you saw in Chapter 3 to increase capacity as needed.

This example illustrates how to run a method based on a configuration, but this approach is supported in orchestration tools as well. I've implemented DAG factories in Airflow using a similar approach. An Astronomer article about dynamic DAG generation in Airflow (*https://oreil.ly/DjfR3*), while a bit dated, will give you a general idea of different ways you can create dynamic DAGs based on a configuration.

Summary

In this chapter, you saw how to best work with different coding environments you encounter when building data pipelines, and how to create modular, configurable codebases to bring features online quickly. This knowledge will help you design pipelines that adapt quickly to changes in data, transformation needs, and external services.

Starting out by looking at different coding environments, you saw how to improve notebook testability by packaging code. This enables you to test and modify important logic using software development best practices, and it insulates this code from being accidentally modified. Even if you're working with code that is not packageable, like SQL, you can use widgets and multiple notebooks to isolate code from undesirable changes.

When working with code in the browser, such as the web interface provided by AWS Lambda, you can save cloud service costs by packaging code and infrastructure configurations. Rather than using these services in the process of testing and development, you can develop and test code locally, as well as integrate with your CI/CD pipelines. Keeping this code in source control will help you roll back to prior states that can be lost in the short history kept by these interfaces. In addition, your present and future teammates will know exactly where this code is and what it does.

When it comes to how you code, favoring design that creates discrete building blocks will help you build code that is extensible, easy to test, and easy to debug. While you're coding, think about the single-responsibility principle. If you find code that is trying to do several different things, consider refactoring to narrow the scope. Another advantage of this approach is that it minimizes bugs that can be introduced when modifying code. If you've structured code so that each entity has a single responsibility, you need only touch that part of the codebase when making changes, without exposing unrelated code to modification.

This same approach can be applied to DataFrames by factoring out transformation logic into separate methods. You don't lose the ability to chain these transformations, and you gain more modular and testable code.

Apart from the Magic 8 Ball, no one can predict the future. While modular code is an ideal to strive for, it's important to gauge when to spend time building reusable code versus when you need to get something glued together quickly.

Developing abstract representations of data sources and sinks results in nimble codebases that can support a variety of implementations. You saw how to use dependency inversion to provide a consistent interface while insulating dependent code from the details. This technique gives you the opportunity to swap in different storage and retrieval mechanisms, support multicloud with a single codebase, and create mock interfaces for testing.

With these modular building blocks, you now have a codebase that can be configured, enabling you to create a variety of topologies without making any code modifications. This can greatly reduce your code maintenance burden and increase the speed with which you can bring new customers, features, and data online.

When evaluating how to parameterize a design, you need to make sure the underlying codebase can be configured as needed and that this configurability can be expressed in a form your code can understand. From here, you saw how configurability can be used to create new pipeline instances and layouts using a single codebase.

Throughout this chapter, I've mentioned testability as an essential consideration when developing data pipeline code. The unit-testing examples in this chapter were a warmup for the main event in Chapter 7, where you'll see how the code structure advice from this chapter enables you to use low-cost, high-coverage unit tests instead of depending on costly system-level tests.

Recommended Readings

- The Medium article "Bring your Jupyter Notebook to life with interactive widgets" (*https://oreil.ly/qyaY7*)
- The Python.org (*http://python.org*) proposal "PEP 3119—Introducing Abstract Base Classes" (*https://oreil.ly/DJX8K*)
- Astronomer's "Dynamically generate DAGs in Airflow" (*https://oreil.ly/SKMZy*)
- The "Encapsulation" entry on Wikipedia (*https://oreil.ly/loFdd*)

CHAPTER 7

Unit Testing

Hayao Miyazaki's movie *The Wind Rises* chronicles the life of Jiro, an aeronautical engineer who designs airplanes during World War II. While he sketches planes at his drafting desk, he imagines these ideas coming to life. As a plane soars into the sky, Jiro probes the design for failure points. He sees that his wing design is inadequate, watching as the wing rips off and the plane crashes to the ground.

From a spark of creativity to a ball of flames, perhaps you can relate to Jiro's thought process. It's important to consider the ways your design could fail and to correct bugs before they happen, which is why testing is a cornerstone of software development best practices. Fortunately, software is a lot easier to test than airplanes.

Data pipelines present a particular challenge for unit testing, with a multitude of interfaces, dependencies, and data needs to consider. This complexity often leads to heavy reliance on end-to-end testing, where a pipeline is run from start to finish using many of the cloud services, data sources, and sinks required for production operation. Not only is this approach costly in terms of cloud bills, it also wastes engineering resources by increasing the amount of time it takes to run tests, fix bugs, and develop new features.

In my experience, there are two primary drivers of an "end-to-end testing to rule them all" strategy. In Chapter 6 you saw one of these drivers, code design, and how to structure data pipeline code to be modular and testable. The other driver is the challenge of unit-testing data pipelines, which is covered over the next two chapters: this chapter covers how to create a unit-testing plan, and in Chapter 8 you'll see how to create test doubles to reduce dependencies on data sources, sinks, and cloud services when testing.

The Role of Unit Testing in Data Pipelines

Much like any other software system, data pipelines need to be tested. As an example, consider the HoD bird survey pipeline introduced in Chapter 2 and pictured in Figure 7-1. You may notice that this pipeline has evolved from its earlier state.

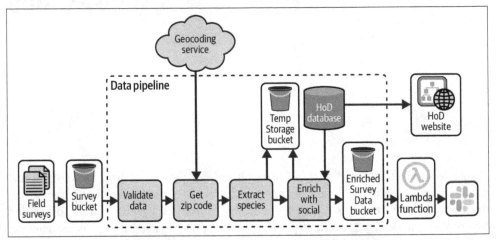

Figure 7-1. HoD batch survey pipeline, augmented with additional features

The first change is the addition of a data validation step, "Validate data." This makes sure the survey data is formatted as expected by the rest of the pipeline.

Another augmentation is the "Get zip code" step, which does reverse geocoding to get a zip code given the latitude and longitude associated with the bird survey data. The HoD social media database ("HoD database" in Figure 7-1) includes the zip code for each user. The HoD team is hoping that adding the zip code to the bird survey data will help find more matches in the HoD database, as opposed to finding an exact latitude, longitude match.

A new "Extract species" step has been added to support a new staff member at the university, Marsha, whose research focuses exclusively on night herons. Labeling the raw survey data with the specific heron species will enable Marsha to search within the Enriched Survey Data bucket for night heron content.

With the added "Validate data," "Get zip code," and "Extract species" steps, the HoD team felt it was a good idea to add retry capabilities at the "Enrich with social" step. Storing the results from "Extract species" in the Temp Storage bucket means "Enrich with social" has a place to get the "Extract species" data if a failure occurs within the "Enrich with social" step. The alternative would be to restart the pipeline from the beginning. When "Enrich with social" completes successfully, the intermediate data is deleted.

Marsha has a doctoral student who is sweating their dissertation deadline and wants to know immediately when new night heron data is available. To enable this, the HoD team sets up an AWS Lambda function to fire whenever new data is written to the Enriched Survey Data bucket. If the data contains night heron content, an alert will be sent to a Slack channel.

Take a few moments to think about some of the things that could go wrong with this pipeline. If you were on the HoD team, what would you have as part of your test plan?

Unit Testing Overview

Unit tests exercise code functionality at a fine-grained level, such as a method or class, referred to as a *unit*. In Figure 7-1, a unit would be the code that extracts the species label from the survey data in the "Extract species" step, which you saw in Chapter 6 as `apply_species_label`.

To help identify a suite of test cases for a given unit, ask yourself: what is the domain of possible inputs, outputs, and states for this code, and how should it behave in each case?

Ideally, a unit test takes less than one second to run. This helps you quickly iterate as you are developing or fixing code, minimizing the length of time between writing code and verifying whether it works.

Unit tests should run with a minimum of dependencies. A dependency can be a data source, sink, or other service the pipeline connects to. Dependencies also include adjacent pipeline stages. For example, let's say you want to unit-test the "Get zip code" step in Figure 7-1. "Get zip code" has a dependency on "Geocoding service" to get the zip code and a dependency on the previous pipeline stage, "Validate data," to provide the input data.

Minimizing dependencies has several advantages. For one thing, it takes time to interact with a dependency, such as waiting for the Geocoding service to respond. This increases test runtime.

There's also the possibility that a dependency is unavailable when running tests. Say the Geocoding service experienced a temporary outage. If your tests depend on reaching this service while it's down, they will fail. The failure wouldn't be about the code under test, it would be due to a failure in the dependency. This illustrates two issues with dependencies: they can muddy the waters, making it difficult to discern whether a test failure is a real issue or a dependency problem, and they can make tests unreliable.

In my experience, dealing with dependencies is one of the biggest barriers to unit testing data pipelines. You have two choices: rely on the dependency when unit testing, or create a mock of it. This is where the lines blur between integration and unit testing data pipelines. While some would argue it's technically not unit testing if you have to connect to a database, for example, there are times when this is unavoidable. That's just the reality of working with data pipelines. Later in this chapter you'll see how to identify dependencies and evaluate this trade-off.

Connection issues like this can be a real pain for the team that manages your continuous integration (CI) process. In addition, any connection you need to make outside the CI server represents privileges that must be provided to another point in the system, with potential security implications. Altogether, unit-test dependencies provide more points of failure, resulting in more overhead for an Ops team to manage.

I mention this because one of the biggest values of unit tests is being able to run tests automatically as part of CI. Referred to as *regression testing*, this helps prevent changes from breaking existing functionality, thus regressing the functional state of the product. I can't overstate the importance of automated regression testing to help prevent bugs. Maybe you're on your last brain cell trying to get a fix in before an important release and you (and the reviewer of your merge request) forget to run unit tests. The robots in your CI pipeline will not forget to run the tests.

As an example of the issues unit-test dependencies can cause, I was in a situation where unit testing part of a data pipeline required several database connections, making it a no-go for adding to CI. Several times code was modified and unit tests were not run locally before a merge, breaking the data pipeline. Because we didn't have unit tests in CI, we didn't know until after the code deployed and the pipeline failed.

Other Types of Data Pipeline Testing

While unit testing validates individual components, *integration testing* validates that interactions across components and with external services, such as databases and APIs, are functioning as expected.

You would use integration testing to test the retry of the "Enrich with social" step in Figure 7-1. Unit testing would validate that "Enrich with social" reads from the Temp Data bucket and merges the data, while integration testing would validate that "Enrich with social" retries when that step of the pipeline fails.

End-to-end testing is a type of integration testing that involves running a pipeline from start to finish. This tests both the integrations and the data processing steps by using sample data to run the pipeline and validating the output. End-to-end testing is also useful for testing observability, ensuring that events are monitored as expected.

You can see the attraction of end-to-end testing as a primary testing strategy. There are no mocks to create to emulate databases or cloud service interactions; you just use these services, and their data, directly. The trade-off is lengthy test times and inferior test coverage of lower-level components.

Lastly, *load testing* can show you how your infrastructure performs when working with data at scale, helping you identify potential resourcing shortfalls before you encounter them in your production environment.

Some bugs in data pipelines only appear in the presence of large data. As an example, I worked on a pipeline that processed customer data of various sizes. The system operated as expected, until we got a new, large customer and one of our pipelines broke when processing their data. It turned out that there were characteristics in the data of this new customer that we hadn't seen before, and it exposed a data transformation that had to be rethought to work at scale.

 A project I worked on deployed and ran an end-to-end test for every merge request. To run the pipeline, an AWS EMR cluster had to be launched. If we were in an out-of-capacity event, as discussed in Chapter 2, these tests would fail as no resources were available to run the tests, blocking merges. Even if resources were available, these tests took 30 minutes to an hour to run, slowing development velocity and racking up cloud bills.

Example: Identifying Unit Testing Needs

Before getting into different aspects of data pipeline unit testing, let's walk through an example of figuring out what to unit-test. This will get you thinking about different trade-offs involved in testing data pipelines.

Figure 7-2 shows part of the data pipeline in Figure 7-1, where the Temp Storage bucket is used to facilitate retries. Recall that the Temp Storage bucket should be emptied when "Enrich with social" completes successfully. Let's consider what would happen if the temporary data removal step failed in production, resulting in data accumulating in the bucket for each ingestion job.

When evaluating whether you want to set up unit tests, consider the following:

- What is the impact of this code not operating as expected?
- Can this be adequately tested in an integration test?
- Is it possible to meaningfully test the function of this unit?
- What is the likelihood of a later code update creating a bug?

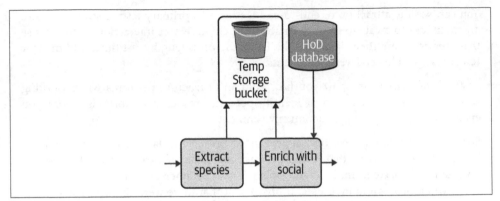

Figure 7-2. Temporary data use in survey pipeline

The temporary data is used in the event of a retry of the "Enrich with social" step, which joins data from the Social Media database with the results from "Extract species." Given that the intent of this step is to augment the survey data with matching information from the database, you're likely to implement this as a left join, capturing all the data from the "Extract species" step and only the matching data in the database.

Is this something worth testing?

In my opinion, if you've written code to do something, such as delete data from a bucket, it is worth testing if you want it to work. The criticality of the testing depends on the impact of the accumulated data.

For instance, if "Extract species" writes to the Temp Storage bucket partitioned by the ingestion time, and the "Enrich with social" step only reads the partition relevant for the current ingestion job, there won't be any impact to the data processing. The impact of the delete step failing is storing a lot of unused data, which you can clean up with a lifecycle policy, as you saw in Chapter 3. In this case, if someone updated the code and introduced a bug into the delete operation, the lifecycle policy and code operation would prevent bugs and data accumulation.

On the other hand, if "Enrich with social" reads all data in the Temp Storage bucket to perform the merge, you will have more problems resulting from a failed delete operation. If you keep running a left join with the Temp Storage bucket, you will re-ingest old data with new matches from the database, creating duplicate records for survey data with different database data, resulting in a data-quality issue. There's also the compute cost of running increasingly larger joins as the Temp Storage data grows. In this scenario, a code update that breaks the delete function would have serious consequences.

In terms of how you would test the delete operation, you can write an assertion that the Temp Storage bucket is empty when the pipeline completes in an integration test.

You can also test this by mocking cloud service operations, which will result in faster test times, less use of cloud resources, and the ability to integrate this test into CI, which would prevent code updates from breaking the delete operation.

Ideally you would use both: the unit test coverage will help you test the delete function in isolation and maintain code correctness, while the integration test coverage will help surface issues at an infrastructure level, such as an inadequate IAM policy that prevents deleting data from the bucket.

Pipeline Areas to Unit-Test

Pipelines perform a variety of operations, including operating on data; transforming, validating, querying, and connecting to services; creating, modifying, or deleting data; working with cloud components; and surfacing observability information and alerts. When you're coming up with a unit-testing plan, it's helpful to think about these different areas to help you pinpoint candidates for unit testing.

Data Logic

Any code that operates on data as it moves through the pipeline is a good candidate for unit testing. This includes data validation, such as "Validate data" in Figure 7-1, and data transformation code, such as "Extract species" and "Enrich with social." The code in the Lambda function that identifies night heron data is another piece of data logic to unit-test.

For data transformation code, you want to test different input data possibilities and validate the results. Typically when developing data logic you're working with an ideal sample that lets you work out the correct code. This sample data emulates the "happy path," that is, the data you expect to be working with. While this is one case of data you will encounter in production, there could be many others. For example, could there be nulls in the dataset? If so, how should your code handle this? Corrupt data can be another consideration.

Keep in mind that testing is one aspect of your overall strategy that includes monitoring and validation. It can be tempting to try to model every single corner case in unit testing, which can lead to overdesign or pulling your hair out trying to model esoteric data. Remember that you have other strategies to surface pipeline issues.

For example, perhaps you can't come up with every potential test case that would fail data validation because the data is not well understood. You could handle this by raising an exception when bad data causes a downstream step in the pipeline to fail, logging the bad data and triggering an alert that gives you the heads-up and debug information to know what you need to change.

With data validation code, your considerations are similar. Your test cases should cover data that fails and passes the validation check.

Having a suite of data logic tests makes it easy to add a new test case when you find a bug.[1] This makes your testing more robust and helps communicate expectations to other developers. As you accumulate test cases, you may start to notice patterns that lead you to refactor the underlying code.

Connections

Connections to databases, APIs, cloud services, and other external services are potential failure points in a system. While integration testing will help you validate the connections to these services in a test environment, in production a lot can go wrong.

When it comes to connections, think about the assumptions you make and what happens if they no longer hold. For example, think about the "Get zip code" step in Figure 7-1. This step involves making a request to the Geocoding service and processing the response, as depicted in Figure 7-3.

Figure 7-3. Internal process for "Get zip code" step

What is the expected behavior if the Geocoding service is unreachable? What happens if the service returns an error code, or a 429 indicating you've made too many requests? Is it possible the zip code might not be in the response? If so, how should this be handled?

Asking these questions will help you determine what kinds of unit tests you need to build for this connection. Think about the different states the connection could be in: healthy; unreachable; slow to respond. Test the handling of different error responses, retry logic, and in the case of the API, decoding the result data.

---

1 Pragmatic Programmer Tip 31: Failing Test Before Fixing Code—Create a test focused on a bug before you try to fix it.

Observability

Unit tests can also be used to validate the information you send to logging and monitoring tools. While an integration test would verify the connections between the pipeline and monitoring services, you can unit-test pipeline code that creates monitoring information.

For example, I worked on a pipeline that created Prometheus (*https://prometheus.io*) metrics for different failure cases. This gave our Ops team visibility into both when the pipeline failed and what component caused the failure, helping them quickly root-cause the issue. My unit tests included verifying that the correct metrics were generated given the different failure scenarios that should create them.

Another aspect of observability you can include in your unit tests is checking log messages using the caplog *pytest* fixture (*https://oreil.ly/89Yu-*). I've used this to ensure that log messages have important debugging information and to create tests that will fail if the information isn't found. This is another example of communicating expectations to other developers with your test cases.

Data Modification Processes

In addition to data transformation, the primary operations of a data pipeline include creating, deleting, and modifying data. Unit testing these operations requires having data to modify or delete and having access to the service that would be used for these operations, or a mock.

Consider unit testing the actions you expect this code to perform. For example, the "Extract species" step in Figure 7-1 saves data to the Temp Storage bucket. A unit test for this can include verifying that an object is created in the Temp Storage bucket, by either using a test bucket or creating a mock. In Chapter 8, you'll see how to create cloud storage mocks and test databases to unit-test this kind of interaction.

Cloud Components

Operations that are running entirely in the cloud present an interesting challenge for unit testing. Consider the Lambda function from the survey pipeline shown in Figure 7-4.

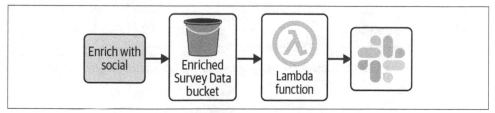

Figure 7-4. Survey pipeline Slack messaging

"Enrich with social" is the last code in the pipeline. The rest is done entirely by cloud services. When the "Enrich with social" data is written to the Enriched Survey Data bucket, an object creation event occurs, which triggers the Lambda function. The Lambda function inspects the new object for night heron content and sends a Slack alert if any exists.

As you saw in Chapter 6, you can extract the code in the Lambda function to a module, which is how you can test this component in "Data Logic" on page 139. Apart from this, you're likely better served using an integration test to validate the part of this process that goes from object creation to Lambda execution to Slack message.

This is not to say that you cannot unit-test code that interacts with cloud components. I worked on a batch pipeline that supported an API with a zero-downtime requirement (*https://oreil.ly/9xzAY*), meaning the API had to stay online and provide accurate responses while new data was ingested.

Part of the architecture involved creating a new table in DynamoDB (*https://aws.amazon.com/dynamodb*) for every ingestion event. Once the ingestion completed, the pipeline updated a parameter in AWS Systems Manager Parameter Store (*https://oreil.ly/Qzw8K*) to point to the new table. The API determined which DynamoDB table to query based on the value of this parameter. Once the parameter was updated, we could retire older tables to save costs. This process is depicted in Figure 7-5, where Ingest_01 refers to the prior ingestion and Ingest_02 is a new ingestion job. You can see how a new table is created in the "Store" step, the parameter value is changed in the "Update pointer" step, and the table from the prior ingestion event is removed in the "Retire" step.

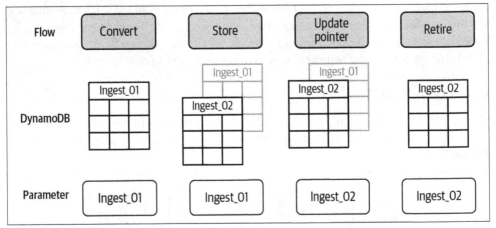

Figure 7-5. DynamoDB table creation and parameter update during Ingest_02 job

In this situation, we had to create, modify, and delete entities in cloud components as part of a core process of the pipeline. At first, we tried using integration testing to test this behavior. To do this we had to create old tables to test the retirement process. We also had to set the parameter to an initial value and validate that it changed in the "Update pointer" step. Besides the setup involved, it also took a long time to test since we needed to spin up an EMR cluster to run the job.

To reduce overhead and speed up the process, I created mocks of DynamoDB and the Parameter Store. This method gave me the ability to unit-test, reducing test runtime from half an hour to a few seconds. I could create whatever state I needed in the mock and validate that the code created, modified, or deleted DynamoDB tables and the Parameter Store as expected.

Working with Dependencies

As I mentioned earlier, there's a conundrum in data pipeline testing where you want to minimize dependencies but there are many to manage. You got an introduction to this trade-off with the architecture in Figure 7-5: our team tried using DynamoDB for testing but ultimately decided that replacing this dependency with a mock was the right approach.

When you break a pipeline down into individual units for testing, you want to be cognizant of the environment in which each unit will need to be tested. The environment includes anything the unit interacts with, such as cloud services, data sources and sinks, and the data you need for testing. Thinking this through up front will make you aware of the dependencies you need to use or replace with test doubles, which you'll see in Chapter 8.

Let's consider the "Enrich with social" step from the survey pipeline, as pictured in Figure 7-6.

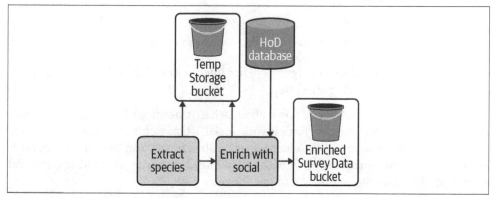

Figure 7-6. "Enrich with social" dependencies

"Enrich with social" has the following steps:

- Receive data from "Extract species."
- Join this with data from the HoD database.
- Store the result in the Enriched Survey Data bucket.

If there is an error, "Enrich with social" should retry the computation using data from the Temp Storage bucket:

- Read data from the Temp Storage bucket.
- Join this with data from the HoD database.
- Store the result in the Enriched Survey Data bucket.
- Remove files from the Temp Storage bucket.

There are a lot of dependencies to consider when unit testing "Enrich with social." You need source data, either from the prior pipeline step or from the Temp Storage bucket, as well as from the HoD database. There's also storing the result in the Enriched Survey Data bucket.

When evaluating dependencies, I find it helpful to break them down into two parts: interfaces and data.

Interfaces

Interfaces highlight the components you need to mock or connect with to run unit tests. Interfaces include:

- Where you get data
- Where you put data
- What services you use
- Where you transition from one pipeline stage to another

The "Enrich with social" step in Figure 7-6 has interfaces with cloud storage, the HoD database, and the "Extract species" step.

When you identify an interface, think about what it needs and provides. The HoD database provides data for the "Enrich with social" step, so for unit testing this code you need to either connect to the database or create a mock. You have similar considerations for cloud storage; "Enrich with social" needs to write to cloud storage and read from the Temp Storage bucket to test the retry path.

To access cloud storage and the database, you need permissions, credentials, and networking capabilities. These are requirements for anyone to run the unit tests, including your CI server, if you connect to these resources for unit testing.

Data

Considering the data a given unit interacts with will help you discern how to test and what kind of test data you need to create. The "Enrich with social" step in Figure 7-6 uses data from the "Extract species" step and the HoD database. While "Enrich with social" *connects* to the Temp Storage bucket, the data it uses for this step is the same as the data produced by "Extract species."

When you think about data dependencies for testing, think about the data you need to exercise the code under test. For example, in "Enrich with social," the HoD database information is joined with the "Extract species" data. To test this join, you need common data between both of these data dependencies. Do these data sources have this kind of data that you can use for testing, or do you have to create mock data to test this case?

Another consideration for data dependencies is cost and quotas. There's a cost to using cloud databases and storage. You might be working with a data source that implements quotas, such as number of API calls per billing period. In this case, unit tests using the API would eat into this quota.

If you are connecting to resources in a shared environment, be cognizant of what else is using those resources. I worked on a project where we shared a test environment with QA. Sometimes testing would impact database performance, making it appear to QA that our website was lagging.

Example: Unit Testing Plan

Now that you've got a sense of what aspects of data pipelines to unit-test and how to identify dependencies, let's apply this process to the survey pipeline in Figure 7-1.

Identifying Components to Test

First, let's determine what aspects of the pipeline to unit-test, referring back to "Pipeline Areas to Unit-Test" on page 139:

Data logic
> Any code that modifies data as it moves through the pipeline:
>
> - "Validate data": check that validation flags bad data and passes good data.
> - "Get zip code": test the ability to extract the zip code from the API response and add the zip code to the data.

- "Extract species": test the ability to extract the species label.

- "Enrich with social": test the merge with "Extract species."

- Lambda function: test code that identifies night heron data.

Connections
Connections to databases, APIs, cloud services, and other external services. In all these cases, you would want to test the ability to handle service issues such as retries and handling different error codes:

- Cloud storage

- HoD database

- Geocoding service

Observability
Information you send to logging and monitoring tools. This is not shown in Figure 7-1, but here are some examples:

- Metric generation on connection failures to the database, cloud storage, or Geocoding service

- Metric generation for bad data flagged by "Validate data"

- Log messages if any step fails, noting the batch ID

Data modification processes
Code that creates, deletes, or modifies data:

- "Extract species" creating temp data

- "Enrich with social" deleting temp data and creating enriched survey data

Cloud components
For unit testing, the Lambda function code is tested as part of data logic.

Identifying Dependencies

With these tests in mind, now think through dependencies. I find it helpful to do this part as a table where you can look at each unit you want to test and note the related dependencies. Table 7-1 shows the dependencies for the data logic and data modification processes, with a column for notes about the tests to perform.

Table 7-1. Identifying dependencies for data logic and data modification tests

Unit	Interfaces	Data	Notes
Data logic			
Validate data	Survey bucket	Survey data	Passing and failing cases
Get zip code	Geocoding service	Geocoding API response	Extract zip code, add to data
Extract species		Valid survey data	Cases with and without species
Enrich with social	Extract species, HoD database, Temp Data bucket	Extract species, HoD database	Cases with and without matches in HoD database
Lambda: night heron identification	Enrich with social bucket	Enrich with social	Content with and without night herons
Data modification processes			
Extract species, create temp data	Temp Data bucket	Extract species	Validate that data is stored in cloud
Enrich with social, delete temp data	Temp Data bucket	Enrich with social	In retry case, validate that temp data is deleted
Enrich with social, create result data	Enrich with social bucket	Enrich with social	Validate that result data is stored in cloud

The connection tests don't have data dependencies and are themselves the interfaces they depend on. The observability tests can be performed as part of the associated tests in the relevant areas.

With this plan, you're ready to move on to creating mocks to run these tests.

Summary

While Jiro had only a slide rule and his imagination to test his airplane designs, you have a lot of tools to help you test data pipelines, reducing the chance of flameouts. Keep your imagination handy while considering what could go wrong to help identify test cases, and use your critical thinking as a foil to keep you from going too far down the rabbit hole.

When it comes to testing data logic, connections, and processes that create, modify, and delete data, unit testing puts these areas under a microscope, enabling you to quickly evaluate code validity at a low level. Unit testing can also help you verify that monitoring and logging events are created as expected, and can include interactions with cloud components when the trade-off between mock complexity and criticality makes sense.

When you want to test how data pipeline steps interact with one another and connections with external services such as databases, APIs, and cloud services, integration tests give you a system-level view. End-to-end tests provide confidence that the pipeline operates as expected, and they can be used to supplement unit tests when mocking dependencies doesn't make sense.

With dependencies on data sources, sinks, and external services, unit-testing data pipelines can be a bit of a hybrid between pure unit testing and integration testing. Focusing on interfaces and data will help you determine where you can replace these dependencies.

Replacing dependencies can improve test validity and speed up the development process. Fewer dependencies means easier integration with CI, enabling you to run unit tests automatically and helping to surface-test failures before code is updated.

Now that you've seen the benefits of dependency replacement, let's jump into Chapter 8 where you'll see how to do it.

Mocks

As illustrated in Chapter 7, it's desirable to replace data pipeline dependencies when unit testing. This helps reduce cloud costs, as you aren't using resources or quotas while testing, and it expands test coverage. In addition to making it easier to run tests in CI, this approach can provide better test coverage versus using live services.

With the different types of dependencies in data pipelines, creating mocks can feel like peeling an onion. Maybe you just created a mock for unit-testing code that acquires data from an API, and now you are back on Stack Overflow looking for advice on how to mock interactions with cloud storage. It's not that mocking is difficult; it's the variety of interfaces data pipelines interact with that can make this endeavor challenging.

This chapter eliminates the onion peeling by consolidating techniques for replacing common data pipeline dependencies in one place. Starting with advice on how to evaluate test double placement and efficacy, you'll see how to build mocks for generic interfaces and cloud services using common Python modules and CSP client mock libraries. The last technique is to use test databases for situations where you need to test code that manipulates database objects.

The code examples in this chapter can be found in the *testing* directory (*https://oreil.ly/SST4N*) in GitHub. To run these examples, follow the setup instructions in the README (*https://oreil.ly/1azGp*). The Spark dependencies are not required for running the examples in this chapter.

For a deeper dive into these techniques, "Further Exploration" on page 170 has some derivative mocking techniques you can try out.

Considerations for Replacing Dependencies

A good test double can save time, lower costs, and improve test coverage. A bad test double can be ineffective or, worse, hide broken code. In this section, you'll see how to assess where dependency replacement makes sense and how to position a test double to be most effective.

Placement

Test doubles involve a trade-off of being able to test without a dependency at the expense of not having a live service to work with. Live services provide feedback, such as via HTTP error codes with an API. These behaviors need to be mimicked by a mock that replaces this service.

When creating a test double, apply it as close as possible to the interface with the dependency you are replacing. I'm pointing this out explicitly because it is often possible to place a test double at several places along the code path of a dependency. Let's take a look at an example to see how this can occur and the consequences when it does.

The `lat_long_to_pop` method in *geocoding.py* (*https://oreil.ly/tANO2*) gets the population of an area given a latitude and longitude. The lookup is performed by the methods `get_zip` and `get_population`, which make requests to a fictitious API:

```
def lat_long_to_pop(lat_long):
    zipcode = get_zip(lat_long)
    pop = get_population(zipcode)
    return {zipcode: pop}
```

To test *geocoding.py* without querying the API, you may be tempted to stub the `get_zip` and `get_population` methods. These stubs enable testing of `lat_long_to_pop`, as shown in *test_geocoding.py* (*https://oreil.ly/fQiOL*), without hitting the API endpoint. Don't get too caught up on the mock decorators in this code; you'll see how to use these shortly. For now, just know that the `get_zip` and `get_popu` `lation` methods are not actually called during the test. Instead, a fake response is provided, denoted by the `return_value`:

```
@mock.patch('geocoding.get_zip', mock.Mock(return_value='95472'))
@mock.patch('geocoding.get_population', mock.Mock(return_value='1000'))
def test_lat_long_to_pop():
    assert lat_long_to_pop((38.4021, 122.8239)) == {'95472':'1000'}
```

While this test validates that `lat_long_to_pop` returns the expected values in the expected format, you need more than this test to have adequate test coverage. There's no coverage for error conditions that could occur when querying the API or verifying that the API response is parsed as expected.

This is a gap between the stub and the interface to the API, which is the `requests.get` methods in `get_zip` and `get_population`. Without additional testing, these stubs effectively hide the code in `get_zip` and `get_population` from testing.

A former colleague shared that a situation like this led to deploying a broken service, despite thousands of passing unit tests. It turned out that a gap between where a mock was applied and the interface to the dependency hid some broken code.

Dependency Stability

When working with a dependency that can change, such as a beta product feature, building a test double may not be feasible or reasonable. On a project for which my team was evaluating an experimental Druid feature, an engineer built the code in an integration test environment, where he ran a Druid instance locally instead of trying to mock the Druid interactions.

Because the Druid feature was experimental, it didn't make sense to try to mock the interactions, as they were likely to change. This can also happen if dependencies roll out backward-incompatible changes. In this case, the mock would need to be updated to reflect the changed dependency. If the dependency was modeled with a client library, using `autospec` will alert you to this change (more on this later). This is another reason to mock close to a dependency interface.

Complexity Versus Criticality

It's important to keep in mind that a test double is another piece of code that needs to be maintained. Similar to being judicious with corner cases in unit tests, consider the trade-off of creating and maintaining test doubles against the importance of the test coverage they provide.

In "Cloud Components" on page 141, you saw how to evaluate whether to test cloud service interactions. I mentioned that our team unit-tested DynamoDB interactions, which required setting up a few layers of cloud service mocks. This was a bit more complex on the mocking side, but it was worth the investment due to both the criticality of the code and the cost in cloud resources and time to test by running the entire pipeline.

On the other hand, the AWS Lambda function in the HoD pipeline was created to alert on the presence of night heron content. This is an important function of the system, but trying to mock a cloud event, the Lambda function invocation, and the Slack message would not be worth the time to run this as a unit test. This was not as critical as the DynamoDB process, and it was also something that could be checked with an integration test.

Reducing gaps between dependency interfaces and test doubles, assessing dependency stability, and evaluating the complexity versus criticality trade-off will pinpoint where test doubles make sense in your test suites. With this in mind, let's move on to different techniques for replacing common data pipeline dependencies.

Mocking Generic Interfaces

To get started building mocks, consider the interfaces in Figure 8-1, which shows the "Validate data" and "Get zip code" steps of the HoD survey data pipeline.

Internal interfaces, such as the one between "Validate data" and "Get zip code," can often be unit-tested by providing fake data, which is the topic of Chapter 9. For example, to test "Get zip code," you need data that has passed the "Validate data" step.

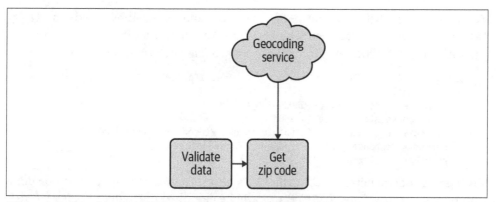

Figure 8-1. Interfaces for "Validate data" and "Get zip code" steps

When it comes to external dependencies, such as the interface between the "Get zip code" step and the Geocoding service, mocks may be needed to test interactions. Interacting with external interfaces often involves the following actions:

- Making a request
- Handling a response
- Detecting and handling connectivity issues

There are a few ways to replace a dependency with a mock. One approach is dependency injection, which was covered in Chapter 6. Instead of using the module that connects to the dependency, pass in a module that provides a mock response for testing.

More often, I've seen codebases where the ability to inject dependencies is limited, either due to code design or because the method that needs to be mocked is in a library. In these cases, you can apply a patch to swap in a mock, as illustrated in the next section.

Responses

External interfaces often return something in response to a request, such as a job identifier, data, or the status of a running job. On the surface, unit testing the logic that handles this response is similar to testing data transformation logic: provide input data and test that the output is as expected. The difference is that often the data and the mechanism for acquiring it are tightly coupled, requiring you to mock the behavior of the interface in addition to providing fake data.

Recall the gap between the API interface and the stubs used in test_lat_long_to_pop in "Placement" on page 150. Let's take a look at how to close this gap with a mock for the get_zip method in *geocoding.py* (*https://oreil.ly/zSjxF*):

```
GEOCODING_API = "http://www.geocoding.com/get_zipcode"
def get_zip(lat_long):
    response = requests.get(GEOCODING_API)
    if response.status_code != 200:
        raise GeocodingError(f"Unable to get zipcode for {lat_long}")
    result = response.json()
    return result["zipcode"]
```

Testing this code requires mocking the geocoding API interactions. This can be done with *responses* (*https://oreil.ly/5PYPc*), as will be described in "Requests" on page 155. Rather than starting with *responses*, I'll illustrate how to set up mocks from scratch. This will help you generalize the techniques to other types of interfaces besides APIs. As it turns out, *responses* uses some of the approaches described in this section.

The test_get_zip_404 test in *test_geocoding.py* (*https://oreil.ly/X2jYN*) is an example of mocking an API response by patching the requests module using unittest.mock (*https://oreil.ly/sqEB8*):

```
@mock.patch('geocoding.requests', autospec=True)
def test_get_zip_404(mock_requests):
    mock_requests.get.return_value.status_code = 404
    mock_requests.get.return_value.json.return_value = {}

    with pytest.raises(GeocodingError):
        get_zip((38.4021, 122.8239))
```

In this test, the *requests* library is replaced with a mock, mock_requests. When requests.get(GEOCODING_API) is executed in the get_zip method during the test, the mock is called instead of the requests module. Rather than sending the request to the Geocoding service, the mock_requests patch is configured to return a 404 status code and an empty JSON value.

Notice that mock.patch is applied to geocoding.requests. This applies the mock only to requests methods called in the geocoding module. If instead the test was decorated with @mock.patch('requests', . . .), all calls to the *requests* library would use the mock. The *unittest* documentation (*https://oreil.ly/0C3Qt*) has some helpful advice on where to apply patches.

Beware that misspellings in mocks can result in tests passing silently while the mocks are not getting called, as described in the autospeccing documentation (*https://oreil.ly/WOFF2*). This occurs because any attribute can be added to a mock object, so something that looks to you like a typo looks to a mock like a new attribute. The recommended mitigation for this issue is to use `autospec`, which creates mock objects that have the same attributes and methods as the objects they're replacing. An additional advantage of using `autospec` is that if the class being spec'd changes, your mocks will break instead of silently allowing code to pass while doing nothing.

In addition, pay particular attention when working with semistructured formats like JSON and dynamically typed languages. It's easier to make mistakes representing data and data structures in mocks without the benefit of type checking.

Using the same approach, here is a test to validate a successful API call. In this case, a successful response results in providing a JSON payload with the zip code:

```
@mock.patch('geocoding.requests', autospec=True)
def test_get_zip_ok(mock_requests):
    mock_requests.get.return_value.status_code = 200
    mock_requests.get.return_value.json.return_value = {"zipcode": "95472"}

    assert get_zip((38.4021, 122.8239)) == "95472"
```

Requests

Another aspect of testing interfaces is checking the information sent when issuing a request; *unittest* provides a variety of assertion methods (*https://oreil.ly/Pki6D*) for performing this kind of validation.

As an example, you can assert that the Geocoding service is called exactly once with the expected parameters, as illustrated in `test_get_zip_ok` in *test_geocoding.py* (*https://oreil.ly/SYK-p*):

```
@mock.patch('geocoding.requests', autospec=True)
def test_get_zip_ok(mock_requests):
    . . .
    assert get_zip((38.4021, 122.8239)) == "95472"
    mock_requests.get.assert_called_once_with(
            url=geocoding.GEOCODING_API,
            params={"lat_long": (38.4021, 122.8239)}
        )
```

Now that I've covered how to create a few mocks for APIs created from scratch, let's take a look at how to validate request parameters with *responses*.

The `test_get_zip_ok_resp` method in *test_geocoding.py* (*https://oreil.ly/ZoNpd*) performs the same test as `test_get_zip_ok` but uses *responses* to mock the API behavior:

```python
@responses.activate()
def test_get_zip_ok_resp():
    zip_resp = responses.get(
        geocoding.GEOCODING_API, status=200,
        json={"zipcode": "95472"})
    assert get_zip((38.4021, 122.8239)) == "95472"
    assert zip_resp.call_count == 1
```

The line `responses.get(. . .)` creates the mock response, similar to the `mock_requests` object. Here, a `requests.get` call with the specified parameters is registered in the *responses* environment. When a call to `requests.get` occurs, *responses* checks to see whether a similar signature was registered, and if so, it returns the registered values. If not, the test will fail.

To see how this works, modify the `responses.get` signature, such as by replacing the URL:

```python
def test_get_zip_ok_resp():
    zip_resp = responses.get(
        # geocoding.GEOCODING_API,
        "www.python.org",
```

Now run the test and observe what happens:

```
$ cd testing
$ pytest -v test_geocoding.py::test_get_zip_ok_resp
. . .
test_geocoding.py::test_get_zip_ok_resp FAILED
. . .
- GET www.python.org Next 'Response' in the order doesn't match due to the
        following reason: URL does not match
```

Because the API call in `get_zip` was made with a different URL than what was registered with `responses.get`, *responses* throws an error because it can't find a `get` method with the corresponding URL in the registry. Comparing this code to `test_get_zip_ok` you can appreciate the work *responses* saves when testing API interactions.

Connectivity

The `test_get_zip_404` test validated how `get_zip` would handle an error response from the API. In addition to testing the handling of known error responses from an external interface, consider testing logic that deals with connectivity issues. For example, an external dependency could be offline or temporarily overloaded, or you may need to periodically check back on a job status. Often these scenarios can be handled with retry logic.

When thinking about how to test retry logic, consider the potential failure scenarios and how the code should respond. Thinking back to "Automatic Retries" on page 67, you wouldn't want to retry a database query if the reason it failed was because the underlying table didn't exist, but you would want to retry on a connectivity error that could be a temporary networking blip.

Another thing to consider when testing retries is limiting tests to the failure conditions that exercise specific code paths. For example, there are more than 20 HTTP response status codes (*https://oreil.ly/HiRBg*), but that doesn't mean all of them should be tested. Logging errors that occur when interacting with interfaces will help track down error cases not handled in testing. If a particular error type starts showing up regularly in the logs, you can add logic to handle that case and add a unit test to cover it.

To see how to test connectivity issues, let's add retries to `get_zip` using the *tenacity* library (*https://oreil.ly/r07JP*) in this new method, `get_zip_retry`:

```
@tenacity.retry(retry=tenacity.retry_if_exception_type(GeocodingRetryException),
        stop=tenacity.stop_after_attempt(5),
        wait=tenacity.wait_exponential(multiplier=1, min=4, max=10),
        reraise=True)
def get_zip_retry(lat_long):
    response = requests.get(GEOCODING_API, {"lat_long": lat_long})
    if response.status_code == 429:
        raise GeocodingRetryException()
    . . .
```

The `get_zip_retry` method includes an additional check for `status_code == 429` that typically is used to signify too many requests. In this case, retries are made using an exponential backoff defined by `wait_exponential` and are stopped after five retry attempts. If at this point the API returns another 429, the `GeocodingRetryException` will be reraised by *tenacity*. An important note for testing: using `stop_after_attempt` allows the retry delay to be eliminated in testing, as you'll see shortly.

When retrying, multiple calls are being made to the same resource. To test retries you need to mock different responses every time `requests.get` is called. One way to approach this is to continue using `mock.patch`, using the `side_effect` parameter to supply different responses for every call to `geocoding.requests`:

```
@mock.patch('geocoding.requests', autospec=True)
def test_get_zip_retry_mock(mock_requests):
    . . .
    responses = [resp_429, resp_429, resp_200]
    mock_requests.get.side_effect = responses
    zip = get_zip((38.4021, 122.8239))
```

The order of the responses dictates the order in which the mock response will be provided. In this example, the mock will return two 429 events followed by one 200 event.

Another option is to use *responses* to handle the retries. The OrderedRegistry guarantees that the API calls will be performed in the order they are added to the registry with responses.get:

```
from responses.registries import OrderedRegistry

@responses.activate(registry=OrderedRegistry)
def test_get_zip_retry():
    responses.get(geocoding.GEOCODING_API, status=429, json={})
    responses.get(geocoding.GEOCODING_API, status=429, json={})
    responses.get(geocoding.GEOCODING_API, status=200, json={"zipcode": "95472"})
    zip = get_zip_retry((38.4021, 122.8239))
    assert zip == "95472"
```

One final line of code needed for both of the get_zip_retry tests is get_zip_retry.retry.sleep = mock.Mock(). This sets the *tenacity* delay between retries to zero. Because the retry logic uses stop_after_attempt, setting the delay to zero eliminates waiting for the retry loop.

Something else you can test is the number of retries using *tenacity* statistics, which can be accessed by the calling method via the get_zip_retry.retry.statistics property. After a run of test_get_zip_retry, get_zip_retry.retry.statistics returns the following:

```
'attempt_number': 3,
'delay_since_first_attempt': 0.00052,
'idle_for': 8,
'start_time': 1.546632987
```

This can be handy to ensure that a specific number of retries are attempted. For example, this method tests that the code retries five times before raising a Geocoding RetryException:

```
def test_get_zip_retries_exhausted():
    resp_429 = MockResponse({}, 429)
    get_zip_retry.retry.sleep = mock.Mock()
    with mock.patch('geocoding.requests.get', side_effect=[resp_429]*6):
        with pytest.raises(GeocodingRetryException):
            get_zip_retry((38.4021, 122.8239))
    assert get_zip_retry.retry.statistics.get('attempt_number') == 5
```

 Not only can it take a few attempts to connect to an external resource, it can also take a few tries to get retry logic right. This is especially true if you are using a CSP client library to handle retries, where there isn't a lot of visibility or control over how the retries are done.

The techniques in this section illustrated how to use `unittest.mock` and *responses* to set up mocks at a dependency interface, helping to reduce the gap between a dependency and its mock. This enables you to test the responses, requests, and connectivity interactions with an external resource. I've used these approaches for testing API interactions and database reads, connectivity, and exception handling.

Mocking Cloud Services

Cloud service interactions can be a bit different than the API interactions described in the previous section. When working with major CSPs like Azure, AWS, or Google, you often have access to a client library to interact with services, instead of making an API request. In the case of AWS there is also a mocking library, *moto* (*https://oreil.ly/RgUbl*), that can be used with the official AWS Python client, *boto* (*https://oreil.ly/MOCOD*).

Building on "Mocking Generic Interfaces" on page 152, this section covers how to combine *unittest* mocks and patches with *pytest* fixtures to set up cloud service mocks, as well as some examples of *moto* for AWS.

Recall the retry mechanism for the HoD survey data pipeline, as shown in Figure 8-2. When "Extract species" completes, it writes data to the Temp Storage bucket to provide a state to retry from if "Enrich with social" fails. Once "Enrich with social" has succeeded, the Temp Storage data should be removed.

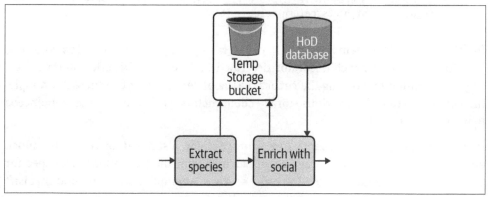

Figure 8-2. Temporary storage of "Extract species" data

This section describes a few ways to approach testing the code that deletes the temporary data by creating mocks for cloud storage.

Building Your Own Mocks

While AWS users have the luxury of the *moto* library, Google users presently have to create their own mocks, as a mock library is out of scope for the Google cloud storage library (*https://oreil.ly/ba_Fd*). Interestingly, the contributor responding to this issue recommends using `mock` with `autospec`, which should sound familiar.

Following is the `delete_temp` method from *cloud_examples.py* (*https://oreil.ly/3ooQl*) that performs the temporary data deletion using GCS. Given a `bucket_name` and `prefix`, the `delete_temp` method will remove all objects under *gs://bucket_name/prefix*:

```python
from google.cloud import storage

def delete_temp(bucket_name, prefix):
    storage_client = storage.Client()
    bucket = storage_client.get_bucket(bucket_name)

    blobs = bucket.list_blobs(prefix)
    for blob in blobs:
        blob.delete()
```

To test that `delete_temp` removes all objects in the specified location, you can create a mock of the Google storage client and create some mock objects to delete, as in `test_delete_temp` from *test_cloud_services.py* (*https://oreil.ly/oCGgn*):

```python
@mock.patch('cloud_examples.storage', autospec=True)
def test_delete_temp(storage):
    blob = mock.Mock(Blob)
    Blob.delete.return_value = None
    mock_bucket = storage.Client.return_value.get_bucket.return_value
    mock_bucket.list_blobs.return_value = [blob, blob]
    . . .
```

In this test, the GCS client imported in *cloud_examples.py*, `cloud_examples.storage`, uses the same `mock.patch` decorator described in "Mocking Generic Interfaces" on page 152. Similar to mocking the `return_value` of `requests.get` in the API example, the `return_value` of the various storage client methods called in `delete_temp` needs to be mocked as well.

In addition to setting `autospec` for the storage client, a spec can be set for the mock objects returned from the storage client, such as with the `blob` mock. The spec for `blob` is set to the cloud storage `Blob` class, so if you attempt to add a method that isn't in the spec, an `AttributeError` will be raised:

```python
from google.cloud.storage import Blob
def test_delete_temp(storage):
    blob = mock.Mock(Blob)
```

It can be a little hard to follow the chain of mocks from the `storage` client down to the list of blobs returned by the `list_blobs` method. I find it helpful to think backward when building mocks like this. Start with what you need the mock to produce, in this case a `blob` that has a `delete` method, and begin by creating those mocks, `blob` in this case. The next level from here is mocking a `bucket` that has a `list_blobs` method that returns the list of `blob`.

To help you visualize this, here's the `delete_temp` method commented with the corresponding mock for each storage client method call:

```python
def delete_temp(bucket_name, prefix):
    storage_client = storage.Client() # @mock.patch('cloud_examples.storage' . . .)
    bucket = storage_client.get_bucket(bucket_name)
            # storage...get_bucket.return_value

    blobs = bucket.list_blobs(prefix) # mock_bucket.list_blobs.return_value
    for blob in blobs: # [blob, blob]
        blob.delete() # blob = mock.Mock(Blob); blob.delete.return_value = None
```

With the mock in place, consider what cloud component operations to validate. You can start by validating that the blobs returned from the `list_blobs` have been deleted, which can be done by checking the `call_count` of the `blob.delete` mock. Since there are two blobs in the list, `delete` should be called twice:

```python
@mock.patch('cloud_examples.storage', autospec=True)
def test_delete_temp(storage):
                . . . mock setup code . . .
    mock_bucket.list_blobs.return_value = [blob, blob]
    cloud_examples.delete_temp("fake_bucket", "fake_prefix")
    assert blob.delete.call_count == 2
```

In addition to verifying that something is getting deleted, check that the items getting deleted are the ones specified in the call to `delete_temp`:

```python
cloud_examples.delete_temp("fake_bucket", "fake_prefix")
client_mock = storage.Client.return_value
client_mock.get_bucket.assert_called_with("fake_bucket")
client_mock.get_bucket.return_value.list_blobs.assert_called_with("fake_prefix")
```

If you run the test, it should pass, which is not terribly interesting:

```
$ cd testing
$ pytest -v test_cloud_services.py::test_delete_temp

test_cloud_services.py::test_delete_temp PASSED
```

To simulate a code bug, comment out the delete loop in `delete_temp` in *cloud_examples.py* (*https://oreil.ly/2u7_j*):

```python
    blobs = bucket.list_blobs(prefix)
    # for blob in blobs:
    #     blob.delete()
```

Now the test will fail because nothing is getting deleted:

```
test_cloud_services.py::test_delete_temp FAILED
. . .
FAILED test_cloud_services.py::test_delete_temp - AssertionError: assert 0 == 2
```

You'll notice that there are no GCS authentication credentials in place for this test—the mock enables this behavior to be tested without connecting to GCS. There's no need to set up authentication and no risk that objects could be unintentionally deleted or modified, which could happen if you were testing while connected to GCS. This unit test is entirely self-contained.

Mocking with Moto

If you're working in AWS, you have a leg up on this mocking business thanks to the *moto* (*https://oreil.ly/F9vsq*) library. Unlike the GCS scenario, it's not necessary to create the storage client mock from scratch. To see how this works, let's take a look at an AWS version of the `delete_temp_aws` function from *cloud_examples.py* (*https://oreil.ly/L9bg3*), which uses the *boto3* AWS client library:

```
def delete_temp_aws(bucket_name, prefix):
    s3 = boto3.client('s3', region_name='us-east-1')
    objects = s3.list_objects_v2(Bucket=bucket_name, Prefix=prefix)
    object_keys = [{'Key':item['Key']} for item in objects['Contents']]
    s3.delete_objects(Bucket=bucket_name, Delete={'Objects':object_keys})
```

Fundamentally it's pretty similar to the GCS version: create a client, list the objects at the specified bucket/prefix, and delete the objects.

The difference between these approaches is more pronounced when you see how to set up mocks with *moto*. With the GCS client, the mock needs to be set up to return a list of objects so that `delete_temp` has objects to delete. With *moto*, the objects to be deleted need to be created. Keep in mind that these objects aren't created in the cloud but rather in the mock environment created by *moto*.

Here, *moto* is mocking the environment, whereas the GCS mock in the previous section mocks the results of method calls. Where the GCS mock used `mock.patch` for the GCS client, *moto* provides a *pytest* fixture for the S3 client:

```
def test_delete_temp_aws(s3):
    s3.create_bucket(Bucket="fake_bucket")
    s3.put_object(Bucket="fake_bucket", Key="fake_prefix/something",
                  Body=b'Some info')
```

With the bucket and object created in the mock environment, `delete_temp_aws` has something to delete. Rather than asserting that mock calls occurred as in the GCS case, you can check that there are no objects in the bucket when `delete_temp_aws` returns:

```
delete_temp_aws("fake_bucket", "fake_prefix")
obj_response = s3.list_objects_v2(Bucket="fake_bucket", Prefix="fake_prefix")
assert obj_response['KeyCount'] == 0
```

Where does the mock environment for *moto* come from? The `s3` and `aws_creden tials` fixtures in *conftest.py* (*https://oreil.ly/y7rXz*) provide some clues:

```
@pytest.fixture(scope="function")
def aws_credentials():
    os.environ['AWS_ACCESS_KEY_ID'] = 'testing'
    . . .

@pytest.fixture(scope="function")
def s3(aws_credentials):
    with mock_s3():
        yield boto3.client('s3', region_name='us-east-1')
```

The *moto* library works by intercepting calls to the AWS API. Notice that the s3 mock is creating a *boto* S3 client, but within a *moto* mock_s3 context. The *boto* library expects to find credentials in the environment, which is why the aws_credentials fixture is present, but these credentials are bogus. They never get used because the *boto* client is created within the mock context.

Another thing to notice is that the scope on the *moto* fixtures is set to function. scope (*https://oreil.ly/5SEbt*) refers to how often a *pytest* fixture is invoked during a test run. function is the default scope, but I wanted to make it explicit here to talk about state.

Remember that in the unit test, you're creating a bucket and some objects. These are created in the *moto* mock_s3 environment. If instead I used a session scoped fixture, the objects created in test_delete_temp_aws would become part of the mock environment for other tests. It's important to avoid accumulating state in this way with test fixtures as it leads to inaccurate unit-test results.

Another thing about the s3 fixture is the use of yield. By yielding the s3 client, the fixture provides the test with access to the context where the s3 client has been set up with the credentials. If instead I returned the s3 client, the context would be closed and this setup information would be lost.

To see the *moto* mocks in action, first try commenting out the code that creates and tests the bucket and object:

```
def test_delete_temp_aws(s3):
    # s3.create_bucket(Bucket="fake_bucket")
    # s3.put_object(Bucket="fake_bucket", Key="fake_prefix/something",
    #               Body=b'Some info')

    # obj_response = s3.list_objects_v2(Bucket="fake_bucket",
    #                                   Prefix="fake_prefix")
    # assert len(obj_response['Contents']) == 1
```

You should see the following error when running the test:

```
pytest -v test_cloud_services.py::test_delete_temp_aws
. . .
botocore.errorfactory.NoSuchBucket: An error occurred (NoSuchBucket)
when calling the ListObjectsV2 operation: The specified bucket does
not exist
```

Because the bucket wasn't created in the s3 mock environment, the `list_objects_v2` call failed. You might want to write a unit test for this case explicitly; what should `delete_temp_aws` do if it can't find the bucket?

While the next section moves on from mocking, you'll notice a lot of similarities between setting up mocks and working with a test database. Although a test database is not a mock, it is still necessary to manage state across tests, using fixtures to set up and tear down between tests.

Testing with Databases

When testing code that stores, modifies, or deletes data in a database, it can be preferable to create a test database instead of attempting to mock these interactions. Using a test database also prevents accidental corruption of data in a live system, in addition to removing the database as a testing dependency. This helps reduce the cost of testing by using a small, local database instead of connecting to a hosted instance, where you would incur cloud costs.

Sometimes, using a test database is not an option given the database infrastructure. For example, one pipeline I worked on interacted with Druid, which was not conducive to using as a local test database. In this case, the database interactions were limited to storing and retrieving data, so our team used mocks and fake data instead. In "Further Exploration" on page 170, you'll have an opportunity to try out this technique of using mocks with databases.

This section illustrates how to set up a test database and where this can be helpful. In this situation, a test database is a local database, either in a local development environment or in CI, as opposed to a database hosted in a test tier, as described in Chapter 6.

 One caveat to consider with test databases is that, ideally, you want to use the same type of database for testing as is used in production. For example, if production uses an AWS RDS instance running Postgres, you would want to use Postgres for the test database.

If you choose to use a different database type, such as SQLite for a smaller footprint, be sure that the operations being tested behave consistently between the test database and production database types.

Test Database Example

To set up the code examples and give you a sense of where a test database can be helpful, I'll walk you through a project where I used a test database for testing a medical data management system. The input data had to be normalized for use by dashboards and search mechanisms. As a result, the process involved a lot of database interactions. A subset of the ETL process is depicted in Figure 8-3.

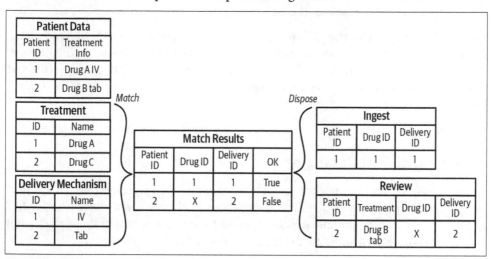

Figure 8-3. ETL process for medical data management system

Starting with the Patient Data table in the upper left, the ETL process parsed the Treatment Info field to find matches in the Treatment and Delivery Mechanism lookup tables. A Match Results table was updated with the results, setting OK to true if both treatment and delivery mechanism had a match.

You can see the results of this process in the Match Results table; for Patient ID 2, "Drug B" is not found in the Treatment table, but for Patient ID 1, both the Drug ID and Delivery ID are present.

A later step in the process was to separate out records that needed review, shown in the Dispose step in Figure 8-3. Any records with OK=False in the Match Results table would be set aside for review by a medical data steward in the Review table. Records that were matched successfully across all lookups were moved to the Ingest table.

Because this was a medical data system, our team had to follow strict requirements for retaining data at every step of the ETL process. Where you might perform a lot of these steps in memory, writing out only the Ingest and Review tables, our team had to persist the results for each step in the pipeline. This information was also helpful for the data steward to assess where issues occurred in the process. As a result, we needed to test that intermediate tables such as Match Results were getting populated correctly.

Throughout this process, the ETL pipeline was manipulating data in the database—adding and updating records in the Match Results table and creating new records in the Ingest and Review tables. To unit-test this logic, our team needed to verify that these changes were happening as expected. With a test database, we could populate the Delivery Mechanism and Treatment lookup tables and the Patient Data table with the cases we wanted to test, run the ETL steps, and set assertions for each case.

As an interesting aside, the ETL process was written using SQL stored procedures, meaning we didn't have access to the kinds of mocking tools described in this chapter. For unit testing, I wrote a configurable test framework in Python to execute the stored procedures against a test database, which you can find on GitHub (*https://oreil.ly/oGliM*).

With this system in mind, let's take a look at how to set up and use a test database.

Working with Test Databases

There are test database packages, such as the pytest-postgresql plug-in (*https://oreil.ly/Syht7*) for *pytest*. Under the hood, these packages use a database installed locally or in a Docker container. Keep in mind these are not mocks of databases but rather are fakes that encapsulate the techniques illustrated in this section.

To run the code referenced in this section, you need a local Postgres installation, or you need to use containers as described in Chapter 5. If you have another local database that is supported by SQLAlchemy (*https://oreil.ly/TPV8_*), you can change the connection string in the `test_conn` fixture in *conftest.py* (*https://oreil.ly/lFHmU*).

Linking test database creation and destruction closely to the testing process will ensure that the test database is always starting from scratch, preventing state from accumulating and causing unreliable test results. This can be done with a similar approach to the AWS example in "Mocking with Moto" on page 162 by using *pytest* fixtures, as shown with the `test_db` fixture in *conftest.py* (*https://oreil.ly/Em6me*):

```
@pytest.fixture(scope="session")
def test_db():
    engine = setup_test_db()
    yield engine
    teardown_test_db(engine)
```

Using `yield` in the `test_db` fixture ensures that the database engine will be torn down when tests that use this fixture have completed, which is the recommended approach (*https://oreil.ly/FaG61*) for teardown in *pytest*. In the `teardown_test_db` method, the test database is deleted. While not strictly necessary since the `setup_test_db` method removes the database if it exists, if a lot of data is accumulating in the test database, you can save resources by tearing it down when the test concludes. On the other hand, to retain the test database for debugging test failures, you would not want to execute `teardown_test_db` in the `test_db` fixture.

If not much data is accumulating during the test session, omitting `teardown_test_db` from the `test_db` fixture is fine. `setup_test_db` will drop the database if it exists at the beginning of the next test session. To have the choice to do either, add a command-line flag to *pytest* to selectively persist the database:

```
def pytest_addoption(parser):
    parser.addoption(
        "--persist-db", action="store_true",
        help="Do not teardown the test db at the end of the session",
    )
@pytest.fixture(scope="session")
def test_db(request):
    engine = setup_test_db()
    yield engine
    if request.config.getoption("--persist-db"):
        return
    teardown_test_db(engine)
```

Use this flag when you want to keep the test database, such as when debugging a test failure:

```
pytest -v test_medical_etl.py --persist-db
```

Notice that the fixture scope for `test_db` is `session`. This means that, once created, the `yield` will not be returned until the end of the testing session. Creating a database can be a resource-intensive activity, similar to the `spark_context` fixture in Chapter 7. `session` scoping amortizes this cost over the entire test session.

It's important to note that while the `session` scope reduces overhead, it can mean you need to carefully manage state versus using a `function` scope. Similar to the cloud service mocks, the scope of fixtures for test databases is important to ensure that tests are idempotent.

For example, in *conftest.py* (*https://oreil.ly/TN4-9*), the lookup tables Treatment and Delivery Mechanism are created as part of the `session` scoped fixture `test_conn`, but they are not torn down after the `yield`. This makes sense, as these are static tables that are not modified during the ETL process. The final teardown that deletes the test database in the `test_db` fixture will remove these tables:

```
def create_tables(conn):
    conn.execute("""
        CREATE TABLE treatment
        . . .
        INSERT INTO treatment VALUES(1, 'Drug A');
        . . .
        CREATE TABLE delivery_mechanism
        . . .
        INSERT INTO treatment VALUES(1, 'tablet');
        . . ."""")
```

```
@pytest.fixture(scope="session")
def test_conn(test_db):
    . . .
    test_engine = create_engine(f"postgresql://{creds}@{host}/test_db")
    test_conn = test_engine.connect()
    create_tables(test_conn)
    yield test_conn
    test_conn.close()
    test_engine.dispose()
```

On the other hand, the Patient Data and Match Results tables have a `function` scope and are cleaned up after each test. This makes sense because each test case of Patient Data records will be unique, having a unique Match Result:

```
@pytest.fixture(scope="function")
def patient_table(test_conn):
    test_conn.execute("""
        CREATE TABLE patient_data (
        . . . )
    yield
    test_conn.execute("DROP TABLE patient_data")
```

Notice that the `patient_table` fixture creates the `patient_data` table but does not populate it. This enables you to insert whatever data is relevant within the test method, as shown in *test_medical_etl.py* (*https://oreil.ly/mu3OP*):

```
def test_match_success(test_conn, match_table, patient_table):
    test_conn.execute("""
        INSERT INTO patient_data VALUES (1, 'Drug A tablet 0.25mg')
    """)
```

When using a test database, it can be necessary to inspect the database state to debug a failing test. You've already seen one approach to doing this with the custom `-persist-db` command-line option.

When using a debugger, setting a breakpoint before and after database calls provides an opportunity to query the test database.

Another approach is the time-honored practice of adding `print` statements, as illustrated in the tests in *test_medical_etl.py* (*https://oreil.ly/wS6kL*).

By default, *pytest* won't print the `print` statements for passing tests, but it will if the test fails. To see `print` messages for passing tests as well, use the `-s` flag, which turns off the `stdout` and `stderr` capture mechanism in *pytest* (*https://oreil.ly/0v83e*).

In terms of how to use the db_engine fixture in unit tests, there are a few options. Chapter 6 covered how to use abstractions to have different possibilities for object storage, including a MockStorage class that could be used for testing. Similarly, if the code accepts the database engine as a parameter, you could use a TestDatabase class to connect to the test database, or pass the engine as a parameter to a method. Another possibility is to use mock.patch for the database connection, where the engine or conn objects are patched.

As mentioned earlier, test databases allow you to avoid the cost of testing with cloud databases. For example, the official Google Cloud SQL Python examples (*https://oreil.ly/jxse7*) show how to use Google's connector library with the sqlalchemy .create_engine method to create the database connection. When testing, substitute the engine for the test database instead of the Cloud SQL engine.

Using a test database doesn't preclude you from running unit tests in a CI pipeline. The Docker Compose techniques covered in Chapter 5 can be used to include a test database container for CI testing. I've used this technique with Google Cloud Build (*https://oreil.ly/GpGPq*) by adding a test database container to the build config (*https://oreil.ly/g27OA*).

Summary

This chapter illustrated how to replace data pipeline dependencies for testing, reducing test time, complexity, and cost and improving test coverage.

It's not always practical to replace a dependency with a test double. Dependencies that are stable, are well understood, and play a critical role in pipeline operation are good candidates for replacement. On the other hand, if dependencies are immature, complex, or not critical, it may not be worthwhile or even possible to create quality test doubles.

You've seen several different approaches to creating and working with mocks. The *responses* and *moto* libraries provide ready-to-use mocks for APIs and AWS services, respectively. Python's standard *unittest* library (which is used in both *responses* and *moto*) provides tools to patch, mock, and validate a wide variety of conditions. Combining these approaches with *pytest* fixtures helps streamline test code and manage state across a test suite.

Across these different techniques, there are common threads for creating good test doubles:

- Place test doubles at the interface between the dependency and your codebase.
- Focus mock behavior on critical interactions and log unexpected or rare cases.

- Pay attention to state accumulation in mocks and fakes shared across multiple tests.

- Use specs, such as `autospec`, to ensure that mocks accurately represent dependencies.

- When testing against a mock, validate request and response payloads, error handling, and retries.

When testing code that modifies database objects, a test database provides the ability to test without connecting to an external database. This enables CI testing, reduces complexity in managing shared test tier databases, and does not incur cloud costs or risk data corruption.

Test databases are another case where *pytest* fixtures are a great help, enabling you to create test databases at test time and manage database state throughout testing. Creating static tables once per session, while creating and tearing down dynamic entities on a per-function basis, will streamline test fixtures and limit state accumulation.

Peeling onions is an unpleasant experience. I hope the collection of techniques and code examples in this chapter have peeled back some of the layers of mocking, helping you quickly replace dependencies without too much crying.

Recall from Chapter 7 that cost-effective testing involves minimizing dependencies, one part of which is mocking interfaces and using test databases as you saw in this chapter. The second part is reducing data dependencies through judicious use of live resources and creating robust fake datasets, which we will discuss in the next chapter.

Further Exploration

To build on the techniques described in this chapter, the following examples provide an opportunity to try them out for yourself. Possible solutions are provided as a guide.

More Moto Mocks

In *cloud_examples.py* (*https://oreil.ly/6bacA*), the `hod_has_night_heron_data` method is the code used by the AWS Lambda function to check whether night heron content is available. This method is called with a prefix to a location of the latest ingested data in `env.ENRICHED_DATA_BUCKET`. For example, if the latest data is stored at *s3://{ENRICHED_DATA_BUCKET}/20220530T112300*, the method call would be `hod_has_night_heron_data("20220530T112300")`.

Using what you've seen about creating mocks with *moto*, write unit tests that validate the case where data at the specified prefix has night heron content as well as the case where there is no night heron content.

You can find a possible solution to this exercise in *test_exercises.py* (*https://oreil.ly/ fxlfa*).

Mock Placement

Earlier I talked about the "Enrich with social" step of the survey data pipeline in Figure 8-2, where relevant data from the HoD social media database would be matched back to the survey data based on the extracted species and zip code information. I've provided an implementation of a few methods in *database_example.py* (*https://oreil.ly/f4C-E*) that look up this information.

Given a species and zip code, `get_hod_matches` will return a DataFrame of IDs and content from the HoD database that matches on both parameters. Without rewriting the SQL, come up with an approach for testing `get_hod_matches` for the cases where there are no results from `get_species_matches` that occur in the results of `get_zip code_matches`, meaning there are no rows in the DataFrame returned from `get_hod_matches`, and the case where you have one or more results returned from `get_hod_matches`.

Another thing to keep in mind when you are building mocks is that the fewer assumptions you need to make, the less likely you will be to have mistakes in your mocks. There is one very simple way to solve this problem, and one more involved way that results in better test coverage. For a hint, review the content for the `get_zip` tests earlier in this chapter.

A possible solution to this exercise is provided in *test_database.py* (*https://oreil.ly/ x9Foq*).

CHAPTER 9

Data for Testing

In the preceding chapter, you saw how to replace one of the two dependencies in data pipeline testing: interfaces to external services. This gets you part of the way to cost-effective testing. This chapter covers how to replace the second dependency mentioned in Chapter 7: external data sources. Instead of using a live data source for testing, you'll see how to replace it with synthetic data.

There are a lot of neat techniques in this chapter for creating synthetic data, but before you fire up your IDE, it's important to assess whether replacing a data dependency with synthetic data is the right move. This chapter opens with guidance on how to make the choice between live and synthetic data for testing and the benefits and challenges with each approach.

After this, the remainder of the chapter focuses on different approaches to synthetic data generation. The approach I'll cover first, manual data generation, is likely one you've done when creating a few rows of fake data for unit testing.

The learnings from creating manual data will help you build accurate models for automated data generation, the approach I'll cover next. You'll also see how to use data generation libraries to customize data generators so that they provide the data characteristics needed for testing.

Finally, you'll see how to keep automated data generation models up to date with source data changes by linking data schemas with test generation code. This is a powerful approach that can catch breaking changes as soon as they hit the repo.

The code examples throughout this chapter can be found in the *testing* directory (*https://oreil.ly/9JLbb*) of the GitHub repo (*https://oreil.ly/aJWLC*), where you will also find the instructions for setting up a virtual environment and dependencies for running the code.

Working with Live Data

Before getting into creating and working with synthetic data, it's important to keep in mind that there are times when connecting to live data is a better option. Remember, the goal of testing is to accurately identify bugs. While it is desirable to reduce data dependencies for testing, you don't want to sacrifice test quality to this goal.

Benefits

Live data, such as from a production environment, can be a rich source that is large in scale and contains a variety of data characteristics. If tests pass using production data, at a minimum you can expect that code changes won't break production. That's pretty good.

When working with data where features change unpredictably or with complex data structures that are difficult to create synthetically, working with live data is likely to give you more accurate test results.

Challenges

Corrupting production data with testing activities is a risk you absolutely must avoid when using live data. A former colleague shared a story in which some well-meaning developers at her company added production credentials to unit-test some data pipeline code locally. As a result of running the unit tests, the developers accidentally deleted all the production data in the most important table, in the product's most central service, resulting in a total outage and major reputational damage.

For this reason, I recommend limiting live data use to read-only. If tests need to create, modify, or delete data, you're better off using a fake, such as a test database, or a mock.

When testing with live data, additional steps are needed to connect to and authenticate with data sources. Depending on company policies and the type of data involved, it can take time to get access approval and, potentially, additional time to anonymize data for testing purposes. You'll also need to configure local development environments to access these resources and make sure test code can authenticate and connect.

As an example, I was running a test suite that connected to an Elastic instance in a test environment. If the Elastic connection was down, the code under test would retry for five minutes. Several times I wondered why my *pytest* session was hanging, ultimately realizing it was retrying the Elastic connection because I forgot to connect or the tunnel went down while testing. In another case, when working with Medicaid data, getting approval to access data could be an endeavor that took weeks or months.

With only live data as a testing option, I wouldn't have been able to meaningfully contribute during that time.

Data privacy is a significant concern when working with production data. Throughout this book, I've shared some examples where I've worked with medical data, including the ephemeral test environment approach in Chapter 5, which our team used to test against production data due to the strict privacy rules.

Testing with Live Data

I worked on a product that had two databases: one that stored query configurations and another that stored the source data the queries ran against. New query configurations, which were added daily, could reference any items in the source data; perhaps the query configurations added today referenced a new table in the source data that was added yesterday.

Because both the query configurations and the source data were constantly in flux, our team couldn't replace the live data with a synthetic version and still have thorough code coverage. Instead, we created a copy of the configuration database, which had a small footprint, for local development. For the source data, we connected to a database in our test environment. With this setup, we could run unit tests in a local environment against the live data.

This approach provided the test coverage we needed, but we couldn't automate unit tests in CI as a result of using these live services. To cover testing all the query configurations, we ran an end-to-end test daily in our test environment before we promoted code to production. We had a longer loop for finding potential bugs, but it was a reasonable trade-off given the complexity of the data.

In some cases, data may need to be anonymized for testing, where sensitive information such as PII or PHI is removed or obfuscated. If you find yourself in this situation, stop and consult your company's legal and security teams.

In some cases, the process of anonymizing data removes essential data characteristics needed for accurate testing. If you need to test with anonymized data, compare it to production to ensure that data characteristics are consistent before betting test results on it.

When testing with live data, another thing to consider are the impacts of testing on the resource serving or storing the data. For example, in Figure 8-2 the HoD social media database is processing and serving content for the HoD website. Performance for the website could be impacted with additional load on the database for testing. In these cases, having dedicated read replicas or snapshots available for testing is a good alternative.

A lower-cost alternative to replicas or full snapshots are partial data dumps, providing only the subset of data used for testing over a shortened time period. You can use the test database technique from Chapter 8 and load the database dump using test fixtures.

I've worked with systems in which a job is set up to periodically refresh test data, storing a compressed object in cloud storage that is limited to the tables and fields that are of interest for testing. This approach has a smaller storage footprint than a full database dump and does not require database replicas or managing database connections in your unit-testing code. In addition, the refresh cycle kept data up to date with the current state of production.

Working with live data when testing can also increase your bills. Keep this in mind especially when testing data extraction logic. Data pulled from cloud storage will incur costs for egress and object access. When working with third-party data sources, keep in mind how test loads could impact quotas, limits, and costs. For example, I worked on a system that synced data from a content management system (CMS). The CMS had pretty paltry API quotas, so when making code changes, we had to be careful not to exhaust our daily allotment.

Finally, your software development lifecycle may not support live data use. Consider whether you are developing a pipeline that ingests data from a data source maintained by another team at your company. This is an issue I've dealt with in the past, where the data source team was trying to meet a deliverable that changed the data schema before the pipeline team had time to implement the schema changes on the ingestion side. The pipeline team was accustomed to using the live data source, but they had to use synthetic data in the interim while adapting to the schema changes. Building in a plan for synthetic data creation can be a good backup strategy so that you won't be scrambling if a situation like this occurs.

Working with Synthetic Data

I don't think I've ever worked on a data pipeline that didn't use some form of synthetic data in testing. When I talk about *synthetic data*, I mean data that has been created manually or through an automated process, as opposed to data that comes directly from a data source such as an API. You'll have a lot of opportunity to work with synthetic data generation in this chapter.

Benefits

One of the superpowers of synthetic data is that you aren't limited to the data available in production. That may sound sort of odd: limited by production data? Production data doesn't always include all the possible cases pipeline code is designed to operate against. With synthetic data, you can ensure that all the important data code paths are tested.

As an example, I worked on a project that got permission from a customer to use their production dataset for testing. While the dataset was large, it didn't contain the right data characteristics to trigger a performance issue we were debugging in our database queries. This highlights another benefit of synthetic data in that you don't have to get customer permission.

Another benefit of synthetic data is it can help communicate important data characteristics to other developers. With synthetic data included in your test suite, a new developer can quickly come up to speed without having to gain access to remote systems where live data is stored. You also bypass the kinds of connectivity and authentication issues I mentioned in "Working with Live Data" on page 174.

Eliminating connections to data sources saves costs, as you aren't running queries against a database or accessing cloud storage, and it enables unit tests to be easily added in CI. Later in this chapter, you'll see how schema-driven data generation and CI testing catch a data pipeline bug before it hits production.

 Generating test data in JSON format will help you share that data across different tools, libraries, and languages. In addition, a lot of data sources provide JSON either natively, in the case of many APIs, or as an export format, such as from a database client.

One of my favorite uses of synthetic data is regression testing, where tests are added to ensure that prior functionality hasn't been lost. When a data-related bug arises in production, you can reproduce the failure in testing by adding test data that emulates the data that caused the failure. As an aside, if you aren't already in the practice of reproducing bugs in tests before fixing them, I *highly* recommend it. Not only will you feel like Sherlock Holmes for isolating the root cause and reproducing the failure, you will be incrementally making your testing more robust.

Finally, the more you can test with synthetic data and unit tests, the less cost and complexity will be associated with testing. Depending on live data or snapshots of live data requires additional cost and overhead for accessing these systems and maintaining snapshots. Even if you can cheaply create a snapshot of data to load into a local database for testing, consider the additional work involved in keeping that development database up to date. In my experience, this often leads to inadvertently testing against stale data and the "it works on my machine" conundrum.

Challenges

While you may find it straightforward to create synthetic data for small-size, low-complexity data sources, this process can become difficult or impossible as data gets larger and more complicated.

It is very easy to go down a rabbit hole[1] when creating synthetic data. Fundamentally, you are trying to come up with a model of the source data. When getting started, you'll naturally gravitate to modeling the most straightforward cases, but things can get complicated as corner cases are encountered that don't fit the model.

I don't know about you, but for me, when I've gotten most of the way through a problem and uncovered some thorny corner cases, I can easily become enamored with finding a solution. As a matter of fact, this happened to me while trying to come up with examples for this chapter. As a result, I created a model that I wouldn't use for development but that was very intellectually satisfying to figure out.

I encourage you to resist this temptation. If you find yourself creating a lot of one-off special cases or spending more than a day trying to model a data source, stop and reevaluate whether synthetic data is the right choice. The next section will provide some guidance for this.

Another challenge can be overdoing it on the data model and creating cases that either aren't relevant or overexercise the code under test. When creating synthetic data, do this side by side with the logic the data will exercise. This will help you home in on the data cases that are relevant to the code under test, keeping you from going overboard with test data generation.

 Be cautious about spending too much time creating synthetic data for data sources that are poorly understood. At worst, you can create invalid data that results in passing tests when the actual data would cause them to fail.

There's an excellent chance synthetic data will quickly become obsolete and unusable if it requires constant maintenance to stay up to date. Keep in mind the maintenance required when developing synthetic data. You'll see some techniques in this chapter to automate the data generation process, which will help reduce maintenance needs.

---

1 Carroll, Lewis. *Alice's Adventures in Wonderland*, Chapter 1.

Is Synthetic Data the Right Approach?

Synthetic data can be a real boon to your testing process, but it can be disastrous if it is applied in the wrong situations. In my experience, synthetic data is most valuable when one or more of the following is true:

- It models well-characterized, stable data sources.
- It is kept up to date automatically or with a minimum of effort.
- It is used to test well-bounded logic.

To get a sense of whether synthetic data is right for a given data dependency, consider these questions:

What are the consequences of inaccuracies in the synthetic data?
> Consider the role synthetic data plays in pipeline fidelity and data quality. The more critical testing is in this process, the greater the risk of issues arising from mistakes in synthetic data.
>
> For example, when working with an API data source for a pipeline project, I used both synthetic data and JSON schemas together to ensure that the data was transformed correctly. I used the synthetic data in unit tests to verify handling of different API responses, while the JSON schema was used during runtime to validate that the API response was as expected.
>
> At some point, the API response changed. The unit tests did not catch this change because the synthetic data was not up to date, but the pipeline validation did catch it. Because I was using both unit tests and data validation, as you saw in Chapter 6, the out-of-date synthetic data did not result in a data-quality issue in the pipeline. This is also a good example of how data validation and unit testing complement each other in ensuring pipeline fidelity.
>
> If instead you have a situation where tests are the primary mechanism for ensuring data quality, be absolutely sure that any synthetic data used is accurate. It can be a better idea to use real data in this case.

How complex is the data source you want to model? How stable is the data format?
> Continuing with the API example, this was a good candidate for synthetic data for the following reasons:
>
> - There were only a handful of potential responses.
> - The data structure was consistent across responses.
> - The API was developed internally.

With a limited number of distinct values to model and a consistent data structure, the API response was low effort to create and maintain. An additional benefit was that the API was developed by another team at the company, so it was possible to share API response schema information. By linking the schema with the synthetic data generation, I could guarantee that the test data was an accurate model.

What is involved in maintaining the synthetic data? Is the benefit worth the time investment?

If synthetic data is high maintenance, consider how likely it is that it will be kept up over time. Based on my experience, I suspect there is a vast graveyard of well-intentioned synthetic data that fell by the wayside due to lack of maintenance.

For the rest of the chapter, you'll see different techniques for creating synthetic data to test parts of the HoD survey pipeline from Chapter 7, repeated here in Figure 9-1.

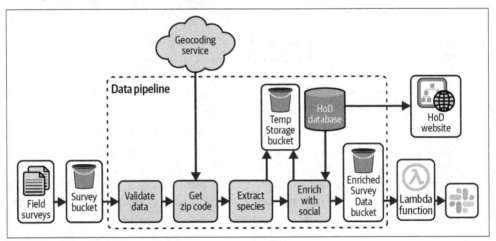

Figure 9-1. HoD batch survey pipeline

The synthetic data approaches presented are based on building some simple models of live data samples. There are more advanced techniques that I won't cover, such as creating data through statistical processes, artificial intelligence, or other algorithmic means. There are entire products and services that focus on creating synthetic data, as well as books and journal articles on the topic.

The data you'll see modeled in the rest of the chapter is the source data for the survey pipeline, the Field survey data stored in the Survey bucket in Figure 9-1. An example of the survey data is shown in Table 9-1 to provide a sense of the data characteristics.

Table 9-1. Field survey data

User	Location	Image files	Description	Count
pc@cats.xyz	(45.2341, 121.2351)		Several lesser goldfinches in the yard today.	5
sylvia@srlp.org	(27.9659, 82.8001)	*s3://bird-2345/34541.jpeg*	Breezy morning, overcast. Saw a black-crowned night heron on the intercoastal waterway.	1
birdlover124@email.com	(45.4348, 123.9460)	*s3://bird-1243/09731.jpeg, s3://bird-1243/48195.jpeg*	Walked over to the heron rookery this afternoon and saw some great blue herons.	3

The survey dataset contains a row for each sighting recorded by a user of the bird survey app. This includes the user's email and location and a freeform description. Users can attach pictures to each sighting, which are stored by the survey app in a cloud storage bucket, the links to which are listed in the "Image files" column. Users can also provide an approximate count of the number of birds sighted.

The survey data is transformed in the "Extract species" step in Figure 9-1. The transformation looks for specific heron species within the Description field and creates a new column, Species, that contains the matching species, or null if no match is found. Table 9-2 shows the results of the survey data in Table 9-1 after it is transformed by the "Extract species" step.

Table 9-2. "Extract species" output

User	Location	Image files	Description	Species	Count
pc@cats.xyz	(45.2341, 121.2351)		Several lesser goldfinches in the yard today.		5
sylvia@srlp.org	(27.9659, 82.8001)	*s3://bird-2345/34541.jpeg*	Breezy morning, overcast. Saw a black-crowned night heron on the intercoastal waterway.	night heron	1
birdlover124@email.com	(45.4348, 123.9460)	*s3://bird-1243/09731.jpeg, s3://bird-1243/48195.jpeg*	Walked over to the heron rookery this afternoon and saw some great blue herons.	great blue heron	3

This transformation is performed by the `apply_species_label` method, as depicted in the following code, which you can find in *transform.py* (*https://oreil.ly/iqocA*). You'll run this code later as part of the unit test; for now, just get a sense of how it works:

```
species_list = ["night heron", "great blue heron", "gray heron",
                "whistling heron"]

def apply_species_label(species_list, df):
    species_regex = f".*('|'.join(species_list)}).*"
    return (df
        .withColumn("description_lower", f.lower('description'))
        .withColumn("species", f.regexp_extract('description_lower',
                                                species_regex, 1))
        .drop("description_lower")
    )
```

To extract the species label, a list of species, `species_list`, is combined into a regular expression (regex). This regex is applied to a lowercase version of the description column, `description_lower`. The first substring to match an element in `species_list` is extracted as the `species` column. Once the species has been determined, the `description_lower` column is dropped as it is not needed anymore.

Manual Data Generation

When you've decided to use synthetic data, manual data generation is the place to start. It may also be the place to end depending on the data you are modeling and the tests that use it.

In general, manual data generation is best suited when the scope of both the test and the data is small and well defined. Anytime you have to modify code or test collateral, there are opportunities for bugs, in addition to the staleness problem I mentioned earlier. Keeping the scope limited when using manual data will minimize these undesirable states.

Manual data is a good approach if the following statements describe your intentions:

- The tests you need to run are limited in scope, such as validating a handful of possible API responses.
- The data you are modeling changes infrequently.
- You need a small number (let's say 10 or fewer) of attributes.
- You aren't trying to validate the handling of wide, sparse datasets.

Even if an automated data generation process is the end goal, curating a small dataset by hand will help you get to know the data characteristics and think through the cases that need to be modeled.

Let's dive into creating some test data for testing the `apply_species_label`. This is a good place to use manual data generation; you need a few rows of data to validate that the transformation is working properly, but because it's early in the development process, bugs are likely. Rather than investing the time to set up synthetic data generation at this point, it's better to focus on iterating quickly with simple tests.

Before moving on, think about some test cases you'd want to create for `apply_species_label`. Notice how you start building a mental model of possible values for the `description` field and how you expect `apply_species_label` to perform in those cases. Oftentimes I find bugs in my code just thinking through different possible test cases before writing any test code.

Here is a snippet of some manually generated test data for `apply_species_label`, showing just the `description` field for brevity. The full code is in the `create_test_data` function in *manual_example.py* (*https://oreil.ly/qbbU_*):

```
fake_data = [
    {"description": "there was a night heron", . . . },
    {"description": "", . . .},
    {"description": "there was a heron", . . .}
]
```

There are a few cases represented in this test data. There's a case where an entry in the `species_list` is part of the `description`, `"there was a night heron"`, as well as some edge cases of an empty `description` and a `description` that partially matches entries in the `species_list`.

This provides the input data for the unit test, but you also need to create the expected output for each case. When testing `apply_species_label`, make sure the `species` field is accurately extracted and that no other fields are modified. For now, let's focus on validating the `species` field using the following expected results:

```
expected = [
        {"user": "something@email.com", "species": "night heron"},
        {"user": "anotherthing@email.com", "species": ""},
        {"user": "third@email.com", "species": ""},
    ]
```

To see these test cases run, set up a local development environment, as described in the *testing* README (*https://oreil.ly/H58qA*). To activate the virtual environment, try running the test as follows:

```
(my_venv)$ cd testing
(my_venv)$ pytest -v test_transform.py::test_transform_manual
```

You may notice that the test takes several seconds to run. This is due to setting up the fixture `spark_context`, which creates a new Spark session when the testing session begins. Once the test completes, you should see something like the following:

```
collected 1 item
test_transform.py::test_transform_manual PASSED
```

To see what a failing test looks like, set `description=None` for this line of synthetic data in *manual_example.py* (*https://oreil.ly/MB0Rz*):

```
"user": "anotherthing@email.com",
"location": "45.12431, 121.12453",
"img_files": [],
"description": None,
"count": 10,
```

When you run the test again, you'll see a failing case:

```
>           assert result_case[0]['species'] == species
E           AssertionError: assert None == ''
```

The test code has some print statements to help debug which test cases failed. Here you can see the case where `description` in the input data is set to `None`, causing the test failure:

```
Result: [{. . . 'description': None, 'user': 'anotherthing@email.com',
                 'species': None}]
Expected: {'user': 'anotherthing@email.com', 'species': ''}
```

Manual data generation doesn't necessarily mean you have to handcode test cases. For example, one of the synthetic datasets I've used was manually curated by gathering a few representative rows of data from a test environment database. You may also be able to use free datasets as a source of test data, such as those from NASA (*https://data.nasa.gov*).

Automated Data Generation

If all data was well defined, small in scope, and static, you probably wouldn't be reading this book because there would be little need for data pipelines. When you have more sophisticated testing needs, automated data generation can be a better choice than trying to manually curate test data. Consider automation when you need the following:

- A significant number of fields for testing (wide datasets)
- A large dataset (i.e., load testing)
- A desire and ability to tie data generation to specs, such as data models or schemas
- Data generation based on a distribution of values

Consider that the pipeline in Figure 9-1 operates on a batch of survey data. While some enthusiasts may be surveying birds year-round, it's likely that there will be larger batches at certain times of the year. In addition to batch size, there is also variation in the `description` field contents. Some users may rarely use the `description` field, while others may use it extensively but never mention any particular species. This section illustrates a few ways to automate data creation for these examples.

Synthetic Data Libraries

One approach to creating synthetic data is to use a library. *Faker* (*https://faker.readthe docs.io*) is a Python library that generates synthetic data, from primitive types such as boolean and integer to more sophisticated data such as sentences, color, and phone numbers, to name a few. If you don't find what you need among the standard and community providers, try creating your own. A *provider* is the *Faker* term for a fake data generator.

The method `basic_fake_data` in *faker_example.py* (*https://oreil.ly/TdiUr*) shows how to use *Faker* to create synthetic data to test `apply_species_label`. This example uses several *Faker* built-in providers, including email, latitude and longitude, filepath, and words:

```python
def basic_fake_data():
    fake = Faker()
    fake_data = {
        "user": fake.email(),
        "location": fake.local_latlng(),
        "img_files": [f"s3://bucket-name{fake.file_path(depth=2)}"],
        "description": f"{' '.join(fake.words(nb=10))}",
        "count": random.randint(0, 20),
    }
    for k,v in fake_data.items():
        print(k, ":", v)
```

Try running this code by opening a Python terminal in the virtual environment in the *testing* directory. Keep in mind that the results are random; the results printed here will be different from what you see when running the fake data generators:

```
(my_venv)$ cd testing
(my_venv)$ python
. . .
>>> from faker_example import basic_fake_data
>>> basic_fake_data()
user : lindseyanderson@example.org
location : ('41.47892', '-87.45476', 'Schererville', 'US', 'America/Chicago')
img_files : ['s3://bucket-name/quality/today/activity.txt']
description : another voice represent work authority daughter best dream name
              meeting
count : 13
```

While developing test data with a generator, it's a good idea to log the test cases so that you can review them for unexpected results.

Looking at basic_fake_data, notice that there isn't a list of different test cases, as there is with the manual data generation approach. Instead, fake_data is a dictionary that can be created any number of times to generate new test cases. In the terminal, call basic_fake_data again and you'll see that a new set of synthetic data is created:

```
>>> basic_fake_data()
user : wilsonbront@example.net
location : ('39.78504', '-85.76942', 'Greenfield', 'US',
            'America/Indiana/Indianapolis')
img_files : ['s3://bucket-name/sure/ground/establish.pptx']
description : budget panda animal act visit agent important half respond stuff
count : 8
```

Another benefit of this automated approach is that you don't need to manually update all the test cases if there is a change to the data schema. Instead, you just update the *Faker* definitions. For example, let's say the user field changes from an email address to a UUID. In the basic_fake_data function, change fake.email() to fake.uuid4(). To see this change in the terminal, you'll need to quit and restart Python and then reimport the module. Now when you run basic_fake_data, you can see the UUID instead of the email for the user field:

```
(my_venv)$ python
>>> from faker_example import basic_fake_data
>>> basic_fake_data()
user : b7e61421-b7e5-4266-bc3f-2e3575358d32
location : ('41.47892', '-87.45476', 'Schererville', 'US', 'America/Chicago')
img_files : ['s3://bucket-name/quality/today/activity.txt']
description : another voice represent work authority daughter best dream name
              meeting
count : 13
```

When using a library to help generate synthetic data, make sure to validate your assumptions about the data being created.

For example, while working on this chapter, I realized the *Faker* email provider does not generate unique results when creating more than 1,000 test cases. While libraries like *Faker* can help streamline your code, make sure to validate the data they produce.

Customizing generated data

When using synthetic data providers such as *Faker*, it may be necessary to tweak the values they provide out of the box to match the data you need to create. In this example, the description field needs to occasionally include elements from the species_list.

The `DescriptionProvider` class in *faker_example.py* (*https://oreil.ly/og-GG*) implements a customer *Faker* provider, with a `description` method that adds this functionality:

```python
def description(self):
    species = fake.words(ext_word_list=util.species_list, nb=randint(0,1))
    word_list = fake.words(nb=10)
    index = randint(0, len(word_list)-1)
    description = ' '.join(word_list[0:index] + species + word_list[index+1:])
```

`species` will be either an entry from `species_list` or an empty list. Note that in this case, `word` refers to a single entry in the list provided to `ext_word_list`. `species` is concatenated with additional words to create a sentence, emulating what a user might submit in the bird survey.

Continuing with the Python terminal opened earlier, you can generate some descriptions using this new provider:

```python
>>> from faker_example import DescriptionProvider
>>> from faker import Faker
>>> fake = Faker()
>>> fake.add_provider(DescriptionProvider)
>>> fake.description()
'leave your stop fast sport can company turn degree'
>>> fake.description()
'card base environmental very computer seek view skin assume'
>>> fake.description()
'choose sense night student night heron two it item mouth clearly'
```

Something to keep in mind about this approach is the use of `randint(0,1)` for choosing whether to include the species in the `description`. You could call `fake.description()` several times and never get a description that has a species.

 To use *Faker* in a unit-testing scenario where you want to create the same data each time, provide a seed to the generator (*https://oreil.ly/qw9lD*). In the description generator from this example, make sure to seed the random number generator (*https://oreil.ly/hjqg9*) as well. Consider logging the seed; if a test is flaky, you can re-create the test case with the logged seed.

Assuming you are generating a large number of cases, this shouldn't be a problem.[2] If there are specific cases that must be included in a test suite and you cannot guarantee

---

2 Determining the number of times to generate data to cover a specific number of cases is the topic of the Coupon collector's problem (*https://oreil.ly/LDQa6*). Refer to this to determine how many times you need to sample to hit all cases.

the data generator will be called enough times to exercise all the cases, you would be better served by adding some manual cases:

```
def create_test_data_with_manual(length):
    data, expected = manual_example.create_test_data()
    auto_data, auto_expected = create_test_data(length)
    return (data+auto_data, expected+auto_expected)
```

Distributing cases in test data

If you have multiple cases to represent and want to control their distribution in the test data, apply weights when generating test data. In Spark, RandomRDDs (*https:// oreil.ly/vzeON*) can be used to generate randomly distributed data. Continuing the *Faker* example, try combining a customized `description` provider with `ran dom.choices` to choose how the cases should be distributed.

At this point, the `description` provider provides two cases: a description with a species and a description without a species. There is no empty string, there are no partial species matches, and there is no string that has a full or partial species name without any other text.

These cases are included in the *Faker* provider, as shown in `description_distribu tion` in *faker_example.py* (*https://oreil.ly/3caYu*):

```
def description_distribution(self):
    . . .
    cases = ['', species, species_part, words_only, with_species, with_part]
    weights = [10, 2, 3, 5, 6, 7]
    return choices(cases, weights=weights)
```

In this provider, there are cases representing the possible description values, which include an empty description and the cases in Table 9-3.

Table 9-3. Possible cases for `description_distribution` provider

Case	Description example
species	"night heron"
species_part	"heron"
words_only	"participant statement suggest country guess book science"
with_species	"night heron participant statement suggest country guess book science"
with_part	"heron participant statement suggest country guess book science"

The `weights` in `description_distribution` indicate how frequently a given case occurs. In this example, the most common occurrence is an empty string. This might reflect the actual survey data, since many users could choose to include images instead of a description. You could also intentionally skew the weights to stress certain scenarios. For example, the bird survey app could add a speech-to-text feature that populates the `description` field. With the overhead of typing removed, users might start adding more descriptions.

At this point, you have a `description` provider that will provide a distribution of all possible cases. Just as in the manual case, generate the expected results for testing at the time the test data is generated. The `description_distribution_expected` method in *faker_example.py* (*https://oreil.ly/evZje*) returns both the generated description and the expected values of the `species` field. I'm omitting the code here for brevity, but when reviewing it, consider how to write generator code to return the expected results along with the generated test data.

Better Testing with Automated Test Data

I worked on a project where a data model with about 100 different attributes was tested with manually generated test cases for each attribute. In fact, I think the test data was already out of date when I joined the project.

Following several failed data ingestions, our customers were sufficiently annoyed that the team was given development cycles to correct this issue. A colleague fixed the test data by creating an automated process based on our data model schemas, an approach described later in this chapter. With the test data generated based on production data models, our team didn't have to worry about test data becoming stale.

If the time it takes to generate test data bloats test time, consider generating the test data in another process. Depending on how often the test data needs to be refreshed, this could run as a scheduled process that checks test data into source control. Another option is a commit hook that generates new test data every time a *Faker* provider change is checked in or a schema change is made, as you'll see in the next section.

If you're generating test data outside the test suite, be sure to also provide an on-demand way to update the data during unit testing.

While synthetic data libraries can be handy, there are times when they can be overkill too. You can create data generators using Python standard libraries.

For example, let's say there is a unique ID attached to every Survey Data record with the format `bird-surv-`*DDDDD* where *D* is a digit. Using Python's *string* and *random* libraries, it's possible to create a data generator for this, as shown in `generate_id` in *faker_example.py* (*https://oreil.ly/_3rVQ*):

```
from string import digits
def generate_id():
    id_values = random.sample(digits, 5)
    return f"bird-surv-{''.join(id_values)}"
```

`create_test_data_ids` illustrates using this function to generate IDs, similar to how the *Faker* providers are called:

```
def create_test_data_ids(length=10):
    mock_data = []
    for _ in range(length):
        mock_data.append(
            {
                "id": generate_id(),
                "user": fake.email(),
            . . .
```

To give this a test drive, return to the terminal where you loaded `Description Provider`:

```
>> import util
>> from faker_example import create_test_data_ids
>> create_test_data_ids()
[{'id': 'bird-surv-26378', 'user': 'iperry@example.com', 'location': ...
```

Schema-Driven Generation

So far, you've seen how to create a synthetic data generator that can mimic the size and distribution of values from a source dataset. The data generation happens at test time, so there is no data to maintain or store. While this provides some benefits over manual data, there's an outstanding question of what happens when the source dataset changes. How will you know the synthetic data generator is out of date?

As described in Chapter 4, schemas are a powerful tool for data validation. Schemas are also useful when creating test data; linking the data generation process to schemas will help you track changes in source data. In this section, you'll see how to link the automated data generation techniques in "Synthetic Data Libraries" on page 185 to a schema to further automate test data generation.

Ideally you have access to explicit *data schemas*, meaning definitions that are used as part of the data pipeline to describe the data being processed. These could be represented as JSON or Spark schemas. If explicit schemas aren't available, you can extract schemas from a data sample for testing. *mock_from_schema.py* (*https://oreil.ly/I-YoO*) provides an example of how to do this for a Spark DataFrame:

```
def create_schema_and_mock_spark(filename, length=1):
    with open(filename) as f:
        sample_data = json.load(f)
    df = spark.sparkContextparallelize(sample_data).toDF()
    return generate_data(df.schema, length)
```

With the DataFrame loaded, `df.schema` gives you the schema, which can be used for the data generation technique in this section:

```
StructType(List(
    StructField(count,LongType,true)
    StructField(description,StringType,true)
    StructField(img_files,ArrayType(StringType,true),true)
    StructField(location,ArrayType(StringType,true),true)
    StructField(user,StringType,true)))
```

A JSON version of the schema can be obtained by calling df.schema.json().

When working with Pandas, you can extract a JSON schema using build_table_schema (*https://oreil.ly/E_wts*), but keep in mind that the schema inference provided by Spark gives a richer view of the underlying data types. Consider this Pandas schema generated from the same sample data as that used for the preceding Spark schema:

```
'fields': [{'name': 'index', 'type': 'integer'},
    {'name': 'user', 'type': 'string'},
    {'name': 'location', 'type': 'string'},
    {'name': 'img_files', 'type': 'string'},
    {'name': 'description', 'type': 'string'},
    {'name': 'count', 'type': 'integer'}],
```

Notice that img_files and location are listed as string types, while their contents are an array of strings. There is also no nullable information.

Mapping data generation to schemas

The way to drive synthetic data generation from schemas is to map the schema columns and data types to data generators (such as *Faker* providers) that represent the types described in the schema.[3]

For fields where you just want to create data that is of the data type defined in the schema, you can create a map from the field type to a data generator, as illustrated in *mock_from_schema.py* (*https://oreil.ly/puZCg*) in DYNAMIC_GENERAL_FIELDS:

```
DYNAMIC_GENERAL_FIELDS = {
    StringType(): lambda: fake.word(),
    LongType(): lambda: fake.random.randint(),
    ArrayType(StringType()): lambda: [fake.word()
                                for i in range(fake.random.randint(0,5))]
}
```

For cases where you want to create more specific values than just the data type, you can create a separate map that considers both the column type and the name, as with the DYNAMIC_NAMED_FIELDS map:

```
DYNAMIC_NAMED_FIELDS = {
    ("count", LongType()): lambda: fake.random.randint(0, 20),
```

---

3 The approach in this section is based on a Scala solution (*https://oreil.ly/5GpSM*).

```
        ("description", StringType()): lambda: fake.description_only(),
        ("user",StringType()): lambda: fake.email(),
    }
```

 The column-based data generation approach in this section is really helpful for wide datasets. You can simply add new entries to the DYNAMIC_GENERAL_FIELDS map or the DYNAMIC_NAMED_FIELDS map for the columns you want to generate data for.

Using these maps, you can set up a data generator based on the Spark schema. First, determine which data generator to return for a given column name and data type. Raising an exception if a column isn't found in the maps will highlight when the data generation code needs to be updated:

```
def get_value(name, datatype):
    if name in [t[0] for t in DYNAMIC_NAMED_FIELDS]:
        value = DYNAMIC_NAMED_FIELDS[(name, datatype)]()
        return value

    if datatype in DYNAMIC_GENERAL_FIELDS:
        return DYNAMIC_GENERAL_FIELDS.get(datatype)()

    raise DataGenerationError(f"No match for {name}, {datatype}")
```

Another note about get_value is that the DYNAMIC_NAMED_FIELDS map is searched for a name match. If there is a name match but the data type does not match, value = DYNAMIC_NAMED_FIELDS[(name, datatype)]() will throw a KeyError. This is intentional; if the test fails due to this exception, it will help you track breaking schema changes. With the ability to get a generated data value for each column, you can create a DataFrame of test data by running a map over the fields specified in the schema:

```
def generate_data(schema, length=1):
    gen_samples = []
    for _ in range(length):
        gen_samples.append(tuple(map(lambda field: get_value(field.name, field.dataType),
                            schema.fields)))

    return spark.createDataFrame(gen_samples, schema)
```

Let's take a look at what the schema-based data generation looks like. A schema for the survey data is available in *schemas.py* (*https://oreil.ly/7xib4*):

```
$ cd testing
$ python
>>> from schemas import survey_data
>>> from mock_from_schema import generate_data
>>> df = generate_data(survey_data, 10)
>>> df.show(10, False)
```

Table 9-4 illustrates some of the generated data for the description and user fields.

Table 9-4. Sample-generated description and user fields

Count	Description	User
13		`"jamesshannon@example.net"`
5	`"heron"`	
6	`"sure and same culture design gray heron fire use whom sell last"`	`"ewilliams@example.com"`
0	`"cold beat threat keep money speech worker reach everyone brother"`	`"aflores@example.net"`

Now that schema-based mock generation is working, you can add the expected data generation. This is a bit trickier than the earlier *Faker* case in "Synthetic Data Libraries" on page 185. In that case, the entire row of data is being generated at once. With the schema-based generation, you're creating each column of data individually. To keep track of the expected values, you can add some state that persists over the course of generating each row. `generate_data_expected` in *mock_from_schema.py* (*https://oreil.ly/4jFMw*) shows this updated approach.

To see the schema-driven data generation in action you can run the test from the virtualenv:

```
(my_venv)$ cd testing
(my_venv)$ pytest -v -k test_transform_schema -s
```

Table 9-5 shows example description and species values returned by `apply_species_label` during the test with the schema-generated data.

Table 9-5. Sample `apply_species_label` result printed during the unit test

User	Description	Species
`"wanglisa@example.net"`		
`"vclements@example.net"`	`"change you bag among protect executive play none machine spring night heron"`	`"night heron"`
`"brian30@example.net"`	`"heron"`	
`"margaret92@example.org"`	`"himself suddenly industry chance sister whistling heron economic teacher early run name"`	`"whistling heron"`

Example: catching schema change impacts with CI tests

To really get a sense of how much more coverage you get by linking synthetic data generation to production schemas, let's take a look at what happens if there is a schema change.

Let's assume that the `description` field changes from a string to an array of strings. The `survey_data` schema gets updated to reflect the change:

```
T.StructField("description",T.ArrayType(T.StringType(), True), True)
```

A merge request is created for the updated schema, kicking off CI testing. Because you've replaced the Survey Data bucket dependency in Figure 9-1 with synthetic data, `test_transform_schema` can be included in a CI test suite. This test fails with the following error:

```
mock_from_schema.DataGenerationError: No field mapping found for description,
    ArrayType(StringType,true)
```

This failure highlights that the synthetic data is broken as a result of this schema change. The code for `apply_species_label` will also be broken, but the manual and *Faker*-generated data tests would not have caught this because the schema wasn't applied to the test data.

Had this test not caught this failure, the next place it would have shown up is in a pipeline fault, ideally a validation error that halted the pipeline, preventing bad data from being ingested. Instead of identifying the error in a controlled environment like unit tests, this schema change could have resulted in an incident.

Property-Based Testing

A data generation and testing methodology wrapped in one, *property-based testing* starts from the assertions in a test and works backward to generate data inputs that break those assertions. The *Hypothesis* library (*https://oreil.ly/qq6zh*) provides different data generation strategies that you can apply when running unit tests. There is some similarity here to how *Faker* providers generate data.

Property-based testing is really a different way of thinking about tests. Your test assertions serve the functions of both validating the code under test and providing property-based testing frameworks with criteria for coming up with test cases. Done well, test assertions are also great documentation for other developers.

For example, *Hypothesis* will generate new test cases in an attempt to cause the test to fail and then present the minimum version of that test case for inspection. If you're new to property-based testing, the Hypothesis team provides *a nice introduction* (*https://oreil.ly/sili-*) to the topic.

Property-based testing is a specialized approach you can use when a method's requirements can be expressed in mathematical terms. It's not likely to be a go-to approach for most of your data pipeline tests, but when it's relevant it is really effective. Giving a property-based testing framework the job of coming up with the data corner cases frees you up to focus on the big picture.

Recall the "Validate data" step in the survey data pipeline in Figure 9-1. Part of this data validation is checking that the user field is a valid email address. Now, there are already a lot of ways to validate an email address (*https://oreil.ly/sqEzI*), but for the sake of illustration, let's suppose the HoD team started with this method in *test_validation.py* (*https://oreil.ly/RbyEz*):

```
def is_valid_email(sample):
    try:
        assert '@' in sample
        assert sample.endswith(".com")
        return True
    except AssertionError:
        return False
```

Here is a test using the hypothesis email strategy for is_valid_email:

```
from hypothesis import given
from hypothesis import strategies as st

@given(st.emails())
def test_is_valid_email(emails):
    assert is_valid_email(emails)
```

The given decorator marks a test as using hypothesis, and the arguments to this decorator are the strategies to use as the fixtures to the test. The emails strategy generates valid email addresses.

Try running this test and you'll see how quickly *Hypothesis* comes up with a failing case:

```
(my_env)$ pytest -v -k test_is_valid_email

>       assert is_valid_email(emails)
E       AssertionError: assert False
E        +  where False = is_valid_email('0@A.ac')

test_validation.py:17: AssertionError
------------ Hypothesis -------------
Falsifying example: test_is_valid_email(
    emails='0@A.ac',
)
```

hypothesis prints the test case it generated that failed the check, providing important information that you can use to either fix the underlying code or modify the *Hypothesis* strategy if the falsifying example is not valid. In this case, the assertion that an email address needs to end in *.com* is what caused the failure.

Spending a lot of time customizing a strategy to provide the right test cases can be a sign that property-based testing isn't the right approach. Similar to how you can end up down a rabbit hole when creating synthetic data models, keep an eye on the complexity of property-based strategies.

Summary

There are a lot of advantages to using synthetic data when testing data pipelines: reducing cost and test environment complexity by eliminating data dependencies, enabling CI testing, improving team velocity by baking important data characteristics directly into the codebase, and empowering you to tailor test data to testing needs.

Remember, accurate testing and minimal maintenance is the goal. While there are many benefits of synthetic data, it's not always the right choice, particularly if data is poorly understood, variable, or complex. You may be able to assess this right off the bat, or you may uncover complexities as you start trying to model the source data.

If you need to use live data for testing, consider read replicas or snapshots to reduce load on shared resources. You can also use the test database method covered in Chapter 8 to load partial database dumps for testing. If sensitive information is a concern when using live data, get in touch with the security and legal teams at your company to determine how to proceed.

Manual data is the place to start when creating synthetic data for testing, even if you plan to use an automated approach. Handcrafting a few rows of data to test logic and data transformations will help you iterate quickly to refine code and will provide a sense of the contours of the data and your testing needs. This will help you come up with good models when creating automated data generation processes.

For small amounts of relatively static data, manual data generation may be all you need. When you need synthetic data at scale, automated techniques can generate any number of rows or columns of data while minimizing the maintenance burden with data generators.

You may find that Python's standard library has the tools needed for creating synthetic data models, as you saw with the *strings* and *random* libraries. Another option is data generation libraries like *Faker*, which give you a large selection of off-the-shelf data providers.

A powerful way to keep synthetic data models up to date with source data is by linking data schemas to data generation. As you saw in the example, this approach can help detect breaking schema changes as soon as they trigger CI tests. In addition, the map-based generation technique can be easily extended to include various data types and shapes.

If you have methods that lend themselves to property-based testing, it can be a helpful tool to offload test data generation responsibilities. Be sure the property-based strategies create test cases that accurately represent your data to avoid under- or over-testing code.

The last pillar of cost-effective design is observability, starting with logging in Chapter 10 and monitoring in Chapter 11. Without good logging and monitoring, the work you've put into design resources, code, and testing will fall short of giving you the best bang for your buck. Observability is such a critical part of cost-effective practices that I nearly made it the first chapter in the book!

Logging

In his book *In Defense of Food* (*https://oreil.ly/QT8M8*) (Penguin Press), Michael Pollan explores the evolution of food chains in the United States, from garden-grown vegetables to processed foods created by food scientists. Encouraging readers to return to a focus on nutrition, not nutrients, Pollan distills the 205 pages of this book into the short phrase "Eat food, not too much, mostly plants."

This phrase came to mind when I was thinking about this chapter. Logging is a distillation of software execution state, ideally striking a balance in which you log just enough information, but not too much, especially in large-scale environments. When it comes to cost-effective logging, I think of a similar phrase: "Write logs, not too much, never sensitive information."

Done well, logging can provide you with invaluable information about the state and operation of complex systems such as data pipelines. It's a relief to come across a well-considered log message telling you exactly what went wrong when debugging a problem.

In addition to debugging issues and observing execution, the ability to export log data to query tools like Google BigQuery (*https://oreil.ly/Tzh_x*) can turn well-formatted logs into a database. Analyzing logs at scale can give you further insight into performance and system health, in addition to generating metrics.

Done not so well, logging can be a pit of despair. Excessive logging drags down performance and racks up cloud costs. Noisy or poorly considered logging can ruin the ability to use logs for debug and analysis. Accidentally logging secrets and other sensitive information can create security incidents and, in some cases, violate the law.

In this short chapter, you'll see advice for logging that is effective across debug, analysis, and cost. To start, you'll see how cloud data pipelines can lead to a lot of log data that not only is costly in terms of cloud billing but also impacts performance and is difficult to navigate.

From here, the focus turns to cost mitigation, with techniques spanning cloud services to code design to reigning in logging costs. Finally, I'll share some tips for creating informative logs for debugging and analysis in distributed environments.

Logging Costs

The scale of data processing coupled with the elasticity of cloud storage can create a perfect storm for data pipelines to generate massive amounts of log data.

I encountered this in a pipeline where logging *doubled* execution time and racked up thousands of dollars per month in cloud costs. The logging approach was developed for debugging single processes over a small dataset in a local environment. In this setting, there was no need to provide identifying information with the log messages, as there was only a single process running in debug. At scale, the logs were incomprehensible, having lost the context of which process was generating a given log message.

This was a worst-of-all-worlds situation; the abundance of logs severely impacted performance, driving up cloud costs due to both log data volume and increased execution time. On top of that, the logs weren't created with scale in mind, so they not only were useless for debugging but also crowded out important log messages with all the noise.

Impact of Scale

One of the issues is that logging practices designed for smaller scales can become problematic at larger scales. This is especially true for more verbose log settings, such as those set for debugging.

Sometimes this occurs when code designed for a smaller scale finds its way into a large-scale data processing pipeline. A volume of logging that provides helpful information when running in a centralized environment can turn into huge amounts of contextless messages when deployed in parallel. Code used for development or added for debugging can cause these issues as well. You'll see advice on crafting a logging approach that scales in "Effective Logging" on page 203.

Besides the number of log messages, it's also possible that the log messages themselves increase in size. A modest amount of data logged for debug purposes can balloon in size as the data grows. In the worst case, a combination of log volume and data size increases can rapidly multiply the size of log data.

Impact of Cloud Storage Elasticity

If you've worked on laptops with smaller hard drives or in containers that have a limited amount of disk space, you may have experienced overenthusiastic logging causing an out-of-space error of some sort. Consider yourself lucky that you were warned about log size because that doesn't happen when using cloud logging.

When working in the cloud, oftentimes logs will be forwarded to cloud storage. As you saw in Chapter 3, there are frequently no limits for sending data to cloud storage, unless you impose them yourself.

Sometimes log forwarding happens automatically, such as AWS EMR automatically forwarding logs to S3 (*https://oreil.ly/Pq1cB*). Other times you may have explicitly requested log forwarding, as with setting up cloud logging for Google Kubernetes Engine (GKE) (*https://oreil.ly/UUZZm*). Frankly, cloud logging is a great thing, giving you the ability to go back and introspect logs after a pod or cluster spins down. The drawback is that you're unlikely to realize that a lot of log data is generated, until the cloud bill shows up.

In "Managing Retention in CloudWatch" (*https://oreil.ly/sIXD6*), the FinOps Foundation reported that over $1,400 per month was attributed to unnecessary debug logs.[1] An interesting thing to note about this situation is that in the cloud bill, the costs were presented as the cost of a specific object action, `PutLogEvents`. Recall from Chapter 3 that when objects are saved to cloud storage, you incur multiple costs: the cost of storing data at rest and the cost of operations performed on the object. When using cloud logging, there can also be costs for ingesting the logs in addition to storing the logs, as you can see in the Google Cloud Logging pricing summary (*https://oreil.ly/Eh_pZ*).

Another thing to note about this example is that the log message contained a few hundred kilobytes of data. Thinking back to the preceding section on the impact of scale, this turns into hundreds of gigabytes at the scale of millions of events.

Reducing Logging Costs

There are a variety of things you can do to reap the benefits of cloud logging while keeping costs in check, ranging from manipulating cloud service settings to utilizing logging techniques and tools for handling logs at scale.

Let's start on the cloud services side. When you use cloud logging, typically the logs will be kept forever unless you configure a log retention period, such as described in the AWS article "Altering CloudWatch log retention" (*https://oreil.ly/xn912*).

---

1 FinOps Framework by FinOps Foundation (*https://www.finops.org*).

Establishing a retention period will result in logs being removed after a specific duration, ensuring that you aren't holding on to logs that are no longer of use.

Similar to the lifecycle policies you saw in Chapter 3, retention periods will vary across services and environments. For instance, retaining production logs for a week could be worthwhile for debug and monitoring. In a test environment, you'll likely debug failures over a smaller window, making it cost-effective to use a shorter retention period.

In addition to the retention period, you can configure which logs to forward to the logging service and which to ignore. This can further reduce your logging footprint by homing in on just the logs of interest. For example, Google Cloud Logging gives you the ability to set exclusion and inclusion filters (*https://oreil.ly/IzoLi*) to this end.

In terms of logging techniques, making use of different log levels helps you tune log verbosity. The Python logging documentation (*https://oreil.ly/Uyw0-*) includes an overview of when to use different log levels depending on the types of messages you want to convey. You can then select the level of logging in different environments. In a production environment, you may use the default level of WARNING to surface informational messages, warnings, and errors while suppressing debug messages. In a development or test environment, you can set the log level lower to DEBUG to get additional information.

For especially noisy modules, consider more granular control over logging. For example, in a test environment with a log level of DEBUG, you can introduce an additional flag to set the log level for a module that has verbose DEBUG logging. By default, you could set the module log level flag to INFO to reduce log messages. If circumstances warrant the additional logging, you can change the level, rather than constantly dealing with a flood of log messages that may not be useful.

Using configurations lets you change the log level without code changes. This approach also enables different logging levels across various environments. I've seen this done with environment variables, where a DEBUG flag was turned on for the test environment but disabled for production. If an issue came up in production, our team could enable debug logs with just a flip of an environment variable.

For Python in particular, you can reduce the performance impact of logging by delaying the creation of log messages. You can see in the Python logging flow (*https://oreil.ly/dxMWJ*) that a logging record is created only if the logger is enabled for the log level of the logging call. If not, the log record doesn't get created.

For example, here are two different approaches for logging a message with variables, one using % formatting and the other using f-strings:

```
logger.debug("Finished extracting species for user %s. Species extracted: %s",
              user_id, species)

logger.debug(f"Finished extracting species for user {user_id}.
              Species extracted: {species}")
```

Let's consider what happens in an environment where the log level is set above DEBUG. In the f-strings case, the log message is interpolated before the call is made to `logger.debug`. Regardless of whether the logger actually creates the log record, this string will be created.

In the %s case, you're passing the `user_id` and `species` as arguments to the `logger.debug` method. Instead of the string creation happening before the logger method is called, the string interpolation will be performed by the logging handler, only if the log level warrants it.

This may seem like small potatoes, but remember that these little things can add up at scale.

Another optimization from the Python logging cookbook is conditional logging (*https://oreil.ly/NRux3*). In this technique, logs are only emitted if a certain condition is met. This is a great way to limit logs that are primarily intended to help debug failures; if the failure doesn't occur, the would-be log messages are pass:[dumped rather than written to the log. In the scenario I shared earlier where logging doubled pipeline runtime, conditional logging that emitted the diagnostic messages only if an error occurred would have eliminated most of the logs.

As with the example in the Python documentation, setting the capacity for the log buffer is a good practice to use memory judiciously. This will prevent wasting memory on buffered log messages.

The techniques you've seen in this section will help reduce log volume and help you surface only those log messages that are relevant in a given environment and situation. This both reduces costs and cuts down on log noise.

The next section switches the focus from log costs to creating logs that are effective at scale and can be leveraged by aggregation tools for analysis.

Effective Logging

When it comes to building for parallel execution, whether in a distributed system or in a parallel processing environment, it's important to reconsider how to approach logging versus a centralized environment.

For example, when you have multiple processes or workers executing in parallel, your log messages need to contain some identifying information to help you determine what a log event refers to. Returning to the earlier Python logging example, notice that I included the user_id in this log message about species extraction:

```
logger.debug("Finished extracting species for user %s. Species extracted: %s",
             user_id, species)
```

This log message would produce something like the following:

```
[DEBUG] Finished extracting species for user abc. Species extracted: night heron
```

Contrast this with the following messages, which lack this context. You can imagine how unhelpful a string of log messages such as these would be for root-causing an issue:

```
[INFO] Start extracting species
[INFO] Start extracting species
[ERROR] Failed extracting species
[INFO] Finish extracting species
[INFO] Finish extracting species
```

This was the state of the logs in the situation I shared in "Logging Costs" on page 200; without identifying information, the log messages couldn't be correlated to the relevant process.

When crafting log messages, think about information you would want when debugging an issue, such as:

- The environment where the job is running
- The service or process executing the code
- Data identifiers, including IDs for the related batch, row, or event

Some of this information might be available as a consequence of how your infrastructure is set up. For example, a data platform I worked on that ran in Kubernetes used separate projects for each environment, so it wasn't necessary to log this information. I could also get the service information from the name of the pods. If I wanted to look at logs in the Spark deployment on production, I opened the Logs Explorer in the production project and filtered by pod names matching "spark."

If your source data does not include batch, event, or row identifiers, it's advisable to create them—the earlier in the pipeline, the better. I worked on a streaming pipeline that created IDs for each row of data processed. As data passed through various parts of the pipeline, the ID was propagated as part of the Kafka payload. If malformed or missing data was identified, our team could inspect the Kafka messages to trace where the error occurred.

Returning to the species extraction example, what if there were multiple rows of data for user abc?

```
[DEBUG] Finished extracting species for user abc. Species extracted: night heron
[DEBUG] Finished extracting species for user abc.  Species extracted: None
```

In this case, you don't know what the description field looked like, so it's hard to say whether the extraction is correct. Including row, batch, and event IDs in your logs can help disambiguate issues like this:

```
[DEBUG] Finished extracting species for user abc, batch 1, record 1-1.
        Species extracted: night heron
[DEBUG] Finished extracting species for user abc, batch 1, record 1-2.
        Species extracted: None
```

Keeping sensitive information out of logs can be tricky when working with data. While best practices like "Don't log the password to the production Postgres server" are straightforward, variations in data privacy laws alongside changes in data sources can make it difficult to be sure you aren't logging sensitive information.

There are approaches for masking sensitive data, but they mostly rely on your ability to model what sensitive data looks like. My advice if you are working with sensitive data is to not log any data, and to work with your company's security or legal teams when in doubt.

If you need data for debugging, consider writing it to a secure environment, such as a database or private cloud storage. To keep costs in check, couple this technique with automated expiration to remove old data. You'll also want to check database log settings to ensure that sensitive information passed in transactions isn't getting logged.

In addition to what you log, how you structure log information is important. Logging data in a JSON format gives you the ability to query logs using tools such as Google BigQuery, giving you another window into system behavior. This also gives you an opportunity to create metrics and alerts from log information. Schemas can be a great help to this end—a schema for log messages will keep your log format consistent across different teams and services. This makes analysis a lot simpler than having to accommodate different log format styles.

One of the pipelines I've worked on used logs as a cheap way to record and analyze profiling data, something you'll see in Chapter 11, which covers monitoring. When execution of the profiled tasks finished, the results were written to the log in JSON. Our team could later query the logs to acquire and analyze the profiling data.

For example, you could capture the earlier debug messages in JSON to see which species were extracted for a given batch of bird survey data:

```
extract_info = {"user": user_id, "species": species}
logger.debug('Finished extracting species: %s', extract_info)
```

The preceding code would produce log messages like the following:

```
[DEBUG] Finished extracting species: {'user': 'user1', 'species': 'night heron'}
[DEBUG] Finished extracting species: {'user': 'user2',
                                    'species': 'great blue heron'}
[DEBUG] Finished extracting species: {'user': 'user3', 'species':
                                    'great blue heron'}
```

With the log data in JSON format, you can extract attributes:

```
SELECT
    JSON_VALUE(log_data_json,'$.user) AS user,
    JSON_VALUE(log_data_json,'$.species) AS species
    . . .
```

In the preceding code, `log_data_json` can be extracted from the log messages using REGEXP_EXTRACT (*https://oreil.ly/zLpvG*) to capture the data following "Finished extracting species:", and PARSE_JSON (*https://oreil.ly/xXMLO*) can be used to convert the log string to JSON.

Summary

Much like refocusing your diet on eating real food, logging in cloud data pipelines benefits from taking a step back from the constituent components and considering the picture on a larger scale.

In this chapter, you saw how logging practices designed without scalability in mind can negatively impact performance and cost, while in the worst cases can also hinder your ability to use logs for debug and analysis. Be judicious when logging data, and think about how many times a log message may be emitted when running at scale.

When it comes to reducing the costs of logging, setting retention periods and using filters in your cloud logging settings can reduce the amount of data you collect and store. On the code development side, splitting log messages into different levels keeps verbose debug information out of environments where it isn't needed. For especially verbose modules, selectively enabling debug logging can give you more control.

You can minimize logging overhead in Python by leveraging the string interpolation provided by logging methods, rather than interpolating strings ahead of time. Setting up conditional logging will limit logs to circumstances where the additional information is helpful, such as if an exception occurs. This not only lowers log costs and performance impacts but tidies up your logs as well.

Finally, when code can be split across multiple processes, workers, and deployments, including identifying information in log messages is indispensable for identifying the data or processes that produced the message. For further introspection and analysis, logging diagnostic data in JSON format enables you to leverage tools for querying logs.

In this chapter, you saw how to cost-effectively use logging to leave clues for data pipeline debug and observability. The next chapter illustrates how to monitor data pipelines for debug, design, and cost efficiency. Oftentimes, monitoring lets you know a problem occurred, and logs provide more detail to help you root-cause the issue.

CHAPTER 11

Finding Your Way with Monitoring

Operating a distributed system without monitoring data is a bit like trying to get out of a forest without a GPS navigator device or compass.

    —RabbitMQ monitoring documentation[1]

As an avid outdoors person and survivor of cloud data pipelines with scant monitoring, I heartily agree with the opening quotation. The ability to see what's going on in your data pipelines is as essential as a good map in the woods: it helps you keep track of where the system has been and where it's headed, and it can help you get back on track when things career off the beaten path.

In this chapter, you'll see how to create and interpret the maps of good monitoring. Being able to inspect pipeline operation gives you insight on performance improvements, scaling, and cost optimization opportunities. It can also be handy for communicating.

To provide some motivation, the chapter opens with my experience working without a map. I'll share the challenges our team faced and what kind of monitoring could have improved pipeline performance and reliability and reduced costs.

The rest of the chapter follows a similar blueprint, where you'll get specific advice on monitoring, metrics, and alerting across different levels of pipeline observability. Starting with the system level to provide a high-level view, the chapter continues with sections that dig into more granular areas of monitoring: resource utilization, pipeline performance, and query costs.

---

1 The RabbitMQ monitoring documentation (*https://oreil.ly/oUuAp*) is a nice primer on monitoring, even if you don't use RabbitMQ.

A map provides you with information. Acting on that information is where you get real value from the map. Throughout this chapter, you'll see examples of how I and others have acted on monitoring information to cut costs and improve scalability and performance.

Costs of Inadequate Monitoring

Without a map, it's very easy to get lost in the woods. If you've planned for this possibility,[2] you might have some extra granola bars to help you survive a few days before you're found, but it will be a pretty miserable time.

Trying to debug, evolve, and scale data pipelines without good monitoring is similarly miserable. It's also very costly. Much like search-and-rescue crews must be dispatched to find lost hikers, you'll spend a significant amount of engineering time and compute resources making up for insufficient monitoring.

One of the best ways to learn about the importance of monitoring is to work on a system that has very little of it. This was the fate of a data platform team I worked on, where the only debug tools our team had access to were AWS EMR logs and some resource monitoring. There was one alert, which notified the team if a job failed.

Getting Lost in the Woods

If you haven't had the (dis)pleasure of log-centric distributed system debugging, let me tell you—it is a real treat. When a process runs out of resources, you are lucky if you get a descriptive log message clueing you in to what happened. Many times you may get a message that not only doesn't describe the resource shortfall but also makes you think something else is the problem, such as "could not bind to address."

In the EMR-based data platform, large ingestion jobs would periodically fail while trying to retrieve a block of data from one of the cluster nodes. What is a "large" ingestion job? Good question: our team didn't monitor data volume, so it wasn't terribly clear where the cliff was that caused this problem.

Typically when a failure occurred, the on-call engineer had to race against the clock to inspect cluster metrics before they disappeared.[3] For example, our team suspected that autoscaling events were related to these failures, but without monitoring, the only access to autoscaling events was the EMR console, which retained only the most recent events. If the critical time point occurred too far in the past, it would no longer be present in the console.

---

2 Technically, carrying a map is part of good hiking prep (*https://oreil.ly/msJxX*).

3 This setup required a full-time developer to debug job failures.

In addition, these jobs could run for several hours, only to fail after wasting half a day of compute resources. The only recourse was to relaunch the job with more capacity than the failed job. How much more? This also was not clear, since cluster configuration wasn't monitored either, so our team didn't know what had worked in the past. The engineer assigned to on-call that week would double the number of workers in the cluster configuration and hope for the best. Relatedly, because data size and cluster size weren't monitored, a lot of money was wasted due to over-provisioning for smaller jobs.

Our team was deep in the woods with no map, compass, or GPS; just a vague idea that if we bushwhacked downhill, we would eventually find a road leading back to the trailhead.

Monitoring, Metrics, and Alerting

Throughout this chapter, you'll see these three related concepts. Let's take a moment to discuss how they related to one another.

Metrics are discrete values. These can be exported from services, such as the message publish rate for RabbitMQ (*https://oreil.ly/Qkq-t*), or generated from custom metrics, such as emitting a metric for data volume when a batch pipeline job initiates.

Monitoring refers to visualizing metrics in aggregate to observe behavior over time. Using the message publish rate example, monitoring this value would show you how the publish rate changes over time. This can help you identify issues such as a low publish rate when you expect a lot of events.

The trends you observe can be used for scaling or cost savings. For example, perhaps message publish rates are typically highest during a certain time of day. This could indicate an opportunity to scale down your RabbitMQ deployment during these quiescent times.

Alerting uses metrics and monitoring to make you aware of important events and information. Informative alerts, such as a daily summary of data ingestion jobs delivered to a Slack channel, surface important data for consideration but do not require a response.

Most of the time, "alerting" is thought of as a yellow or a red traffic light, indicating a warning of a potential problem or a critical failure, respectively. I've seen warning alerts used when consumer lag is venturing into potentially worrying territory. This gives the team an opportunity to respond before issues occur. Consumer lag is a topic covered later in this chapter.

Critical failures requiring immediate attention generate high-priority alerts. The more critical the alert, the more direct the communication. While messaging systems such as Slack can be good for informational alerts, critical alerts often go to a service like PagerDuty to get an engineer's attention quickly.

It's important to be judicious about high-priority alerting. Returning to the map analogy, some GPS devices provide emergency location services, which can communicate your location if you get into a jam. Much like you wouldn't repeatedly push the emergency button on your GPS, keep alert fatigue in mind. Too many alerts lead to desensitization and distrust that something is actually wrong, which can lead you to miss the signs of real issues.

In addition to engineering and cloud costs, the lack of reliability led to data downtime, eroding trust in the platform. In this case, the customers were a somewhat captive audience, but in other cases, these kinds of issues can negatively impact revenue. Who wants to pay for a data platform that doesn't reliably ingest and surface data?

To summarize, inadequate monitoring resulted in this project incurring unnecessary costs over several areas:

- Engineering hours spent on root cause analysis
- Over-provisioned compute resources
- Extra compute resources for rerunning failed jobs
- Low platform adoption

I presume someone thought this process was less costly than monitoring. Given the system's size and complexity, I doubt the cost of an entire developer was less expensive, particularly when the most senior developers had to stop their work to help debug especially thorny problems.

Navigation to the Rescue

Regrettably, these issues did not prompt changes to put additional monitoring in place. There are a number of metrics that could have been tracked to improve resilience, customer trust, and cost-effectiveness. Many of the specific metrics mentioned here will be described in more detail in the rest of the chapter.

Job metrics

Data volume, cluster configuration, job duration, resource utilization, and job success/failure are essential metrics to track for a pipeline. Tracking these metrics would have helped cut costs by determining right-sized cluster configurations based on data volume and job duration. The metrics could be fed back to a job configuration system that dynamically sized the clusters based on past resource needs of similarly sized jobs, reducing over-resourced small jobs and giving larger jobs a better chance at success.

Additionally, these metrics could have been shared with our users to convey *system throughput* (data volume divided by job duration) and success rate. If the only time stakeholders hear about the system is when something is wrong, they can develop a negative impression, whereas publishing regular metrics gives them a larger picture of mostly successful ingestion jobs.

The cluster configuration also contained customer information. Tracking job details could have illuminated data ingestion costs per customer. This is great data to have when developing pricing plans.

Autoscaling events

Recall from Chapter 2 that while autoscaling can help reduce costs for variable workloads, it also carries overhead and cost. By tracking autoscaling events alongside data volume, you can get a sense of the right-sized cluster configuration. Rather than incurring the processing delays of autoscaling a workload, future jobs of similar size could leverage the autoscaled values from historical metrics.

Job runtime alerting

Rather than waiting for a job failure notification, getting an alert *while* the job was still running would have given the team a head start on dealing with failures. If the runtime exceeded an expected duration, the on-call engineer could investigate to determine whether the job was failing.

Error metrics

Finally, there were specific log messages that could indicate the job was failing. Most CSPs offer the ability to create metrics based on log messages (*https://oreil.ly/tcmNi*), which our team could have used in conjunction with other metrics, such as runtime and data volume, to help identify jobs that might be in trouble.

I mentioned earlier that the EMR console was used for inspecting resource utilization and autoscaling events but that the availability of these metrics in EMR was short-lived. A better option would have been to export the metrics to view them over a longer period. As it turns out, EMR metrics are already exported to the AWS monitoring service, CloudWatch, at no additional cost (*https://oreil.ly/TZY61*). These metrics could have been connected to Grafana (*https://oreil.ly/5ICN3*), a metrics visualization, analysis, and alerting tool, providing the team with a dashboard to look across the metrics to assess system health and performance.

With a dashboard such as this, the correlation of high disk utilization, autoscaling events, and ingestion failures would have been very clear, saving significant engineering time and cloud resources.

Now that you've seen an example of how monitoring can help you get out of the woods, let's take a look at the different types of monitoring that are beneficial for data pipelines.

System Monitoring

System monitoring is your basic map when navigating data pipeline operation. Like the map in Figure 11-1, system monitoring helps you navigate the turns and intersections on a trail, shown with the dotted line. It also makes you aware of major geographical features, such as rivers and roads, that can help you get your bearings.

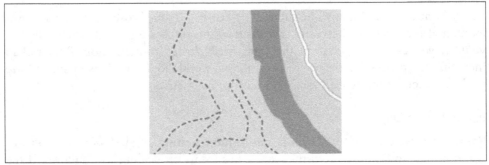

Figure 11-1. System monitoring map; image courtesy of CalTopo (https://oreil.ly/ KYB0a)

With a high-level overview of pipeline performance, system monitoring can help you get to know the baseline conditions, such as typical data volumes and average job runtime. Baseline conditions provide a reference from which you can identify perturbations, such as higher data volumes and longer runtimes. These can be important signals for performance, scaling, and reliability.

Data Volume

In Chapter 1, the HoD team had access to a year's worth of survey data, repeated here in Figure 11-2, to get a sense of ingestion job size. You saw how to use this data to develop an estimate of compute resources. Similar to this initial estimate, monitoring data volume over time will help you refine and redesign pipeline resources as needs change.

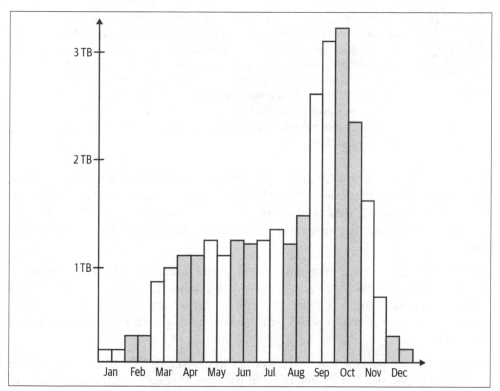

Figure 11-2. Survey data volume per month

For example, in Figure 11-2 there is very little bird survey activity from December through February. Based on migratory patterns, bird surveys peak from September through October, and are otherwise at a fairly consistent level from late March through early August. Assuming this trend is observed over earlier and subsequent years, this can help you budget and choose pricing plans wisely. Trends and seasonality can also help with capacity planning, as you have a sense of when you need more or fewer compute resources.

Monitoring source data volume can also help you track potential system issues; a sudden, unexpected decrease in volume could point to a bug causing data to be lost. I've seen this happen when expired credentials caused input data volumes to plummet. On the other hand, a sudden spike in volume could strain the provisioned compute resources.

If your data storage plan includes creating objects in cloud storage, consider monitoring new object creation. This can help you detect issues such as the recursive AWS Lambda and S3 situation (*https:// oreil.ly/GOBlR*), where an AWS Lambda function is triggered by an S3 PUT event and itself creates an object in S3, which creates another PUT event. This leads to an endless cycle of object creation and Lambda invocation events. Additionally, you can track object size in conjunction with object creation to detect a spike in the creation of small files.

Monitoring data volume as it moves through the pipeline is another place to check for problems. For example, let's say you have a filtering step that you expect will eliminate 20% of the source data. If you observe that the volume of data exiting the filter step is 60% lower than the source data volume, there might be a bug in your filtering logic.

Reading through these last examples, you may be thinking: "But what if there is nothing wrong with the pipeline? Perhaps these data volume changes are due to changes in the source data." You'd be right. Oftentimes metrics are most informative when considered as part of a group and with knowledge of pipeline operation and data characteristics.

For example, one pipeline I worked on primarily reformatted the source data. In this case, it's expected that the volume of input data would roughly match the volume of output data. A significant delta between input and output data would have been cause for concern. Because this was such a cut-and-dried scenario, the pipeline included a size check as part of the data validation.

Another pipeline I worked on had a far less deterministic relationship between input and output data volume. In this case, we combined data volume with other metrics, such as number and type of customers active in the system, to deduce whether a change in data volume warranted closer inspection.

Remember that you have other tools for checking for issues in a data pipeline, such as the validation techniques covered in Chapter 6 and the testing techniques covered in Chapter 7. Consider changes in data volume in light of the other signals you get from the pipeline.

Throughput

With data volume you can also monitor *throughput*, the amount of data processed over a given time period. Monitoring the speed at which a pipeline processes data can give you a heads-up as to performance changes, system stability, and scaling opportunities.

For batch pipelines, throughput can be measured based on job duration. Returning to the scenario I described in "Getting Lost in the Woods" on page 210, if our team had monitored throughput, it would have been apparent that the EMR resourcing strategy was approaching a cliff for larger jobs.

Figure 11-3(A) shows an approximation of this performance issue, plotting data volume versus job duration. Prior to the data points in this graph, the relationship of increased data volume to job duration was roughly linear. While I've omitted this from the graph for brevity, establishing a baseline is essential to know what is within the expected range.

The solid line with the x's shows the increase in data volume for successive ingestion jobs. The dotted line with the square markers shows the corresponding increase in job duration. Notice that while the data volume increases linearly, the job duration increases significantly beyond a certain data volume. Figure 11-3(B) shows the computed throughput based on data volume and job duration.

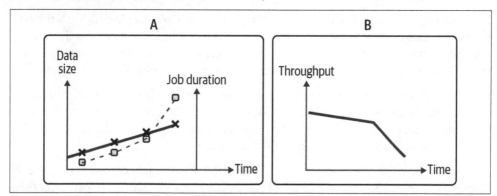

Figure 11-3. Reduced pipeline throughput as data volume increases, viewed as data volume and job duration changes (A) versus the computed throughput (B)

Table 11-1 shows the data for Figure 11-3, annotated with the percentage changes in data volume and throughput. Notice that the changes in data volume from one job to the next are about the same, but the changes in throughput more than double.

Table 11-1. Pipeline throughput example data

Job ID	Source data volume (TB)	Job duration (hours)	Throughput (TB/hr)	Throughput change (%)	Data volume change (%)
1	1.8	4	0.55	—	—
2	2.0	4.2	0.48	−14	11
3	2.2	6	0.37	−30	10
4	2.4	11	0.22	−68	9

Had our team tracked throughput, the correlation between data volume, runtime, and reliability issues would have been visible before jobs began failing en masse. This would have given the team not only time to proactively address the problem, but also the data to go to the product owner and push for engineering time to make the fixes.

In this example, tracking data volume and job runtime would not have been a significant undertaking. At the most basic level, you can record these metrics in a spreadsheet to look at trends over time. One of the teams I worked on looked at throughput metrics on a weekly basis, using a spreadsheet to identify baseline behavior and deviations.

For streaming pipelines, throughput can be measured by looking at the lag between data acquisition at the beginning of the pipeline and data storage at the end of the pipeline,[4] as you will see in the next section.

Consumer Lag

In streaming pipelines, the degree to which consumers are keeping up with the volume of messages from producers is an important metric for system stability. *Lag* is defined as the number of messages published versus the number of messages consumed. To keep things clearer, I'll refer to consumers as "workers" in this section.

Let's take a look at a few examples of lag to get a sense of how this metric can help identify data pipeline issues. Figure 11-4 illustrates a lag profile for a system that is increasingly unable to keep up with the inbound messages. I'll talk through some different data pipeline issues that can cause this to occur.

First, though, a bit about lag profiles. The left side of each case *a* through *d* in Figure 11-4 represents the ramp-up of published messages from the producer. The saturation point, where the curve is flat, indicates that the workers are consuming about the same number of messages as the producer is creating. The ramp-down occurs when the publisher has finished producing and the workers consume the remaining messages.

I'm defining *healthy lag* as lag that gets resolved—that is, the consumer is eventually able to clear all the messages provided by the producer before the next set of messages come in. Cases *a* and *b* illustrate healthy lag, where lag goes to zero before the next group of messages are published.

---

4 Keep in mind startup penalties when using this metric, such as if there is additional latency waiting for resources to scale out when the data load increases.

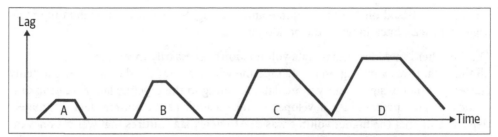

Figure 11-4. Examples of healthy and unhealthy lag

Compared to *a*, the lag in *b* is higher, indicating that more messages are building up from the publisher before the workers process them. You can also see this from the narrower saturation duration. Another thing to note about *b* is the slope and duration of the ramp-down period. These are longer than *a*, another indication that it's taking longer for all the messages to get consumed.

Unhealthy lag occurs when the consumer can't keep up and messages start to pile up. Notice that in the *c* and *d* cases, the lag does not return to zero. If this trend continues, there will be a significant backlog of messages. In *c* and *d*, the trend of higher lag over a longer time period is worsening relative to cases *a* and *b*.

Why does a message backlog matter? For one thing, it means data isn't getting processed as quickly, which can impact performance and SLAs. This can be especially detrimental when sub-second latency is required. From a cost-effectiveness point of view, very low-latency systems are expensive and in many cases are not necessary. To find the right trade-off between cost and latency, work with customers and product owners to determine a reasonable SLA. You can then monitor latency and tune resources to hit the target. If it's going to take a lot of extra resources (read: costs) to hit an SLA, you can bring that information back to stakeholders to reevaluate.

A message backlog consumes resources on the message broker, which is responsible for handling the message exchange between publishers and workers. What starts as sluggish performance due to message backlog can tip over into exhausting broker resources.

You can preempt this failure mechanism by alerting when lag gets into concerning territory. By monitoring over the long term, you'll get to know how much lag the system can clear and what level of lag indicates you might be headed for trouble. Recalling alert fatigue, be sure to consider whether alert thresholds could be tripped by noncritical events, such as heavyweight testing.

Why would the lag changes in Figure 11-4 occur in a data pipeline? It could be that more messages are getting produced as a result of higher data volume. In this case, you would see more messages from the publisher and may need to add more workers to reduce the lag. Thinking back to scaling in Chapter 2, you could address this with scaling rules based on message volume and backlog. Scale out to clear pending messages, and scale back in when the backlog is clear.

On the other hand, changes in data volume don't necessarily mean you want to ingest all the data. I was working on a data pipeline where one of the data sources suddenly started producing significantly more data, resulting in the pipeline lag increasing dramatically. This prompted a developer to take a look at the source data, ultimately determining that the higher volume was due to new data features that weren't relevant to the product. In this case, the extra data was filtered at the source, returning the data volume to its previous size and resolving the unhealthy lag.

Another possibility is that the worker has slowed down. I've seen this happen as a secondary effect of increased data volumes, where data transformation time increases as a result of processing more data. Lag can also build up if the worker is waiting on an external resource. Perhaps another service your pipeline interacts with is under-provisioned or starts throttling back connections. It's essential to root out these bottlenecks in real-time systems, as they limit your operational and scaling capacity.

I've seen this scenario in the field, when working on a pipeline that interacted with several different databases. Our team observed that pipeline jobs started failing suddenly, as if the system was at a tipping point and had just gone over the edge.

Some system monitoring was in place at the time, so our team could see that job-processing times had increased considerably. Unfortunately, there wasn't enough granularity in our monitoring to determine where exactly the slowdown was coming from. Investigating resource utilization on the databases didn't turn up anything. Much like a game of Whac-A-Mole (*https://oreil.ly/c7DSm*), the path forward involved progressively disabling different parts of the pipeline to figure out where the issue was.

The root cause was resource contention at one of the databases. The queries executed by the pipeline were taking a very long time as a result of some recent data changes. The issue wasn't that the databases didn't have enough resources to run the queries; rather, the number of workers and concurrency settings per worker needed to be increased to take advantage of the available database resources. In other words, the current worker settings were insufficient now that database queries were taking longer.

This story is a good example of the multidimensional seesaw (*https://oreil.ly/LHygp*) of managing data pipeline operation. The system was performing well until one of the many data pipeline dependencies changed, throwing the balance off. While I mentioned increasing worker count and concurrency as a solution, our team did more than that. The data changes that precipitated the event were addressed by rethinking our data storage strategy to minimize database contention. The capacity planning for the database was revisited; as with more consumer throughput, the stress point would move from the workers to the database. These changes spanned infrastructure, data modeling, and code.

So far, I've focused on unhealthy lag, what it can mean in data pipelines, and strategies to mitigate it. It's also possible for lag to show where you are over-provisioned, that is, where you've allocated more consumer resources than necessary.

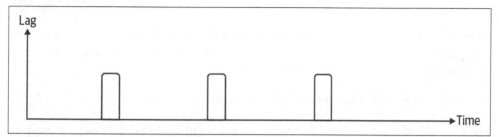

Figure 11-5. Minimal lag example

This can be tricky territory, as you saw in the example of database contention that lag is only part of the story when it comes to data pipeline performance. Notice in Figure 11-5 that the lag is very small compared to the amount of time between message publishing events. If you consistently see very little lag compared to the amount of time available for processing, you may be able to reduce worker resources. To make sure you don't prematurely scale down and create performance issues, keep the following in mind:

Broker resources
Fewer workers means more messages are sitting on the broker.

Consumer variability
Are there scenarios where the consumer could take longer to process a message that could lead to unhealthy lag?

Producer consistency
Are the received messages consistent, such as from a well-characterized, consistent data source, or could messages change without notice?

Alerting
Choose a threshold to alert on unhealthy lag to give you time to reevaluate resourcing.

As an example, I was working on a pipeline where our team observed minimal lag and tried downsizing the Spark deployment to see whether costs could be saved. With the reduced deployment, the lag increased to near unhealthy levels, so the downsizing wasn't possible. While our team couldn't cut costs in this situation, this example illustrates how to look for signals in lag and assess whether changes can be made.

Worker Utilization

While consumer lag gives you information about streaming throughput, worker utilization can illuminate causes of lag and cost-saving opportunities. By comparing the worker settings with the number of tasks executing over a given time period, you can see whether you've saturated your resources or whether you're leaving cycles on the table.

Converting worker settings to the number of tasks that could execute at a given time is dependent on your system architecture. In this section, I'll roughly approximate the total number of slots available by the following:

$$Worker\ slots = Number\ of\ workers \times concurrency\ per\ worker$$

For example, if you're running two workers with a concurrency of four, you can have at most eight tasks running at once. When looking at the total tasks executing, if you see eight tasks running at once, you've saturated your available worker resources. If you see unhealthy lag with all workers utilized, this could be a sign that you need to add more workers or that you need to optimize worker dependencies by providing more resources or changing configurations to allow more tasks to run at once.

If instead fewer than eight total tasks are executing at a given time, you're underutilizing the available resources. This could be due to broker settings that don't correctly share tasks among all available workers or a worker being offline due to resourcing shortfalls. You may also just not have enough messages coming through the system to warrant having eight worker slots, in which case you should consider downsizing to reduce waste.

To illustrate how worker utilization can help you get the best bang for your buck, let's take a look at a case where I was able to halve data ingestion costs with this information.

The product I was working on processed data for customers, similar to the heron identification as a service (HiaaS) example in Chapter 6. Since the processes to be run were common but the customer jobs had to run independently, I used a top-level Airflow DAG for each customer that called a secondary DAG to run the common process. The system started out with eight worker slots for running Airflow tasks.

As is smart when deploying a new process, our team gradually added customers to the Airflow deployment. After we hit about eight customers, performance completely tanked. When I looked at the Airflow web server, I could see that most of the DAGs were failing due to timeouts. My next stop was to look at worker utilization, which looked something like Figure 11-6.

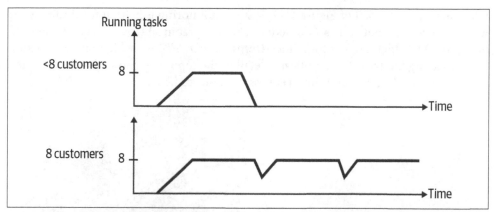

Figure 11-6. Airflow task deadlock

Both before and after the eight-customer threshold, all eight worker slots were utilized. An additional piece of information is that all the DAGs started at the same time. With eight customer DAGs running, all the worker slots were filled by the task that triggered the secondary DAG. For these tasks to complete, worker slots had to be available to run the secondary DAG, which resulted in deadlock. The few DAGs that managed to succeed were just fortunate to be able to get the secondary DAG to run when one of the trigger DAG tasks timed out.

With this information, I refactored the pipelines to eliminate the secondary DAG. Now, instead of consuming two worker slots per task, I could accomplish the same processing with a single slot, effectively halving the cost of running the DAGs.

> Eliminating the secondary DAG wasn't the only solution to this problem. I could have looked at the worker utilization in Figure 11-6 and piled on more workers, which would have solved the issue but at more than twice the cost. This is a key benefit of the cost-effective approaches in this book: having the time to focus on true engineering problems instead of being constantly sidetracked by lack of observability, unreliable systems, and codebases that are hard to change.

As you've seen in this section, system-level metrics (including data volume, throughput, consumer lag, and worker utilization) help you get a high-level sense of how a pipeline is performing. Like a dotted line on a map representing a hiking trail, system monitoring guides you in turning left or right or continuing straight to reach your destination.

Like the map on the left of Figure 11-7, system monitoring is helpful for finding your way in the woods, but you can do better! The topographical (topo) map on the right of Figure 11-7 includes contour lines (*https://oreil.ly/FJ7bg*), which show elevation changes along the trail. The additional detail in the topo map shows you whether the trail ascends or descends and the steepness of these gradients.

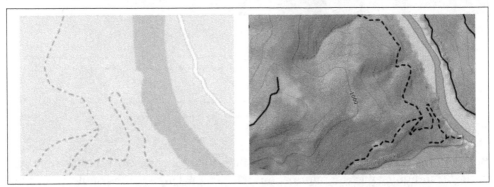

Figure 11-7. Maps representing system-level monitoring (left) versus resource and perfor-mance monitoring (right); image courtesy of CalTopo (https://oreil.ly/KYB0a)

Similar to how a topo map gives you a better idea of what you're in for on a hike, the next section ("Resource Monitoring") and "Pipeline Performance" on page 227 help you delve deeper into the landscape of data pipeline performance.

Resource Monitoring

While system monitoring gives you a lot of information about health and perfor-mance at a high level, resource monitoring drills down to the fundamental elements of memory, CPU, disk usage, and network traffic. Oftentimes these are the root causes of reliability, performance, and cost issues.

This section focuses on how to identify under-resourcing and the issues it can cause. Similar to the system monitoring areas, if you consistently observe low resource uti-lization, this could be a sign that you've over-provisioned and that you could reduce costs by reducing the amount of resources allocated. Consider utilization in conjunc-tion with trends and the amount of overhead needed to accommodate data spikes or high-performance requirements, as discussed in Chapter 1.

Understanding the Bounds

You may have heard processes referred to as being "CPU bound" or "memory bound" to communicate what is limiting performance. For example, the performance of join-ing large datasets in memory is likely to be bound by the memory available in the container or cluster where the process is running.

Knowing which attribute is limiting performance will show you which resource changes will help and which will not. In the large join example, throwing more CPU capacity at the problem is unlikely to help, unless you're trying to help your CSP make more money.

In some cases, you can exacerbate issues by over-provisioning the wrong resource. Let's say you have a data-processing stage that acquires data from another resource. If this process is *I/O bound*, meaning its performance is limited by waiting for the data source, adding more CPU could make the problem worse. Consider that the faster the data processing stage runs, the more requests it can make to the data source. If the data source is responding slowly due to its own resource limitations, the delay between request and response could increase.

Understanding how pipelines process data can help you determine what is bounding your process. In the EMR pipeline example at the beginning of this chapter, the source data was copied to disk and then processed in memory with Spark. Given this, disk and memory were logical assumptions for what bounded that process. You also saw an example in Chapter 1 of how choosing a high-memory machine type performed more quickly and more cheaply for another Spark workload, hinting at the memory-bound nature of that process.[5]

Fortunately, resource monitoring is pretty well established. It's likely you can access this information within your infrastructure. The exception to this is managed pipeline services, where you might be able to get insight into system-level metrics such as lag, but you may not have access to more in-depth metrics such as resource utilization.

Understanding Reliability Impacts

In the most severe cases, processes that overrun resource allocations can keel over. This can impact a pipeline directly if a stage runs out of resources or indirectly if a service the pipeline communicates with is killed due to out-of-resource issues. In one case in which I saw this happen with a database, the pipeline began failing as a result of the database running out of resources and being unable to respond to requests. This is where idempotency and retries come into play, as you learned about in Chapter 4.

If you're working in a containerized environment, monitoring service restarts can help identify inadequate resourcing. A container that consistently restarts unexpectedly may be running into resource issues.

---

5 Spark processes can be bound by other attributes besides memory; this is just one example.

A process getting killed repeatedly is a pretty direct sign that something is wrong. Sometimes resource shortfalls can be more difficult to detect. In one situation, I observed a Spark job get stuck in a cycle of stalling, then making progress when garbage collection ran. The garbage collection freed up just enough memory for the job to move forward a little before running out of resources again. Sometimes the job managed to succeed after several hours, but other times it failed.

It can be tricky to divine whether high-resource utilization is a cause for concern. For example, given a block of memory and no constraints on executors, Spark will consume all available memory in its pursuit of parallelizing data processing. Similarly, Java will also consume available memory, running garbage collection periodically to clean up after itself.

In these cases, simply observing high memory consumption in the container or cluster doesn't necessarily point to an issue. If you see high resource utilization, check your resource settings to help discern next steps. Resource utilization on its own is only part of the picture; consider the *impact* of high utilization to determine whether action is needed.

Memory leaks are another source of instability that isn't readily apparent. Memory utilization that slowly but steadily increases over time can be a sign of a leak. This is a situation where a longer observation window is helpful; if you don't monitor memory long enough to see the leak, you won't be aware that it's happening.

On the other end of the observation spectrum is how frequently metrics are evaluated. This is a trade-off with cost, as frequent evaluation is expensive, and with usability, as temporary resource spikes may go undetected because the evaluation window is too long.

Similar to the Airflow example in "Worker Utilization" on page 222, addressing resource shortfalls by adding more resources isn't necessarily the most cost-effective approach. I worked on a system that used Redis to cache results for common queries. At some point, queries started to fail. Looking into the issue, it turned out that Redis was running out of memory. By inspecting memory use over time, our Ops team noticed that Redis was holding on to a lot of memory outside of the time frame where the queries ran.

This finding prompted the developers to get involved to figure out why this was happening. The developers reevaluated the *time-to-live* (*TTL*), a duration after which a Redis entry is deleted. It turned out that the TTL was too long, so one optimization was reducing this to a more reasonable duration.

The investigation also revealed that a handful of Redis entries were using up most of the memory. After further discussion, it was determined that these entries were no longer needed, having been part of a deprecated feature. With the TTL adjustments and unused entries removed, Redis memory was reduced, which not only fixed the query failures but also reduced compute costs. Had our team simply provisioned more resources to fix the memory issue, we would have been wasting money.

Pipeline Performance

While system-level metrics such as overall pipeline runtime and consumer lag give you a sense of how long it takes for a job to run, inspecting performance within the pipeline can provide details about the processes happening during the job.

Digging into this level of detail is like a higher-resolution topo map, where the contour lines represent smaller gradations. While pipeline throughput gives you the view in Figure 11-8 (left), inspecting performance within the pipeline gives you more detailed information, as in Figure 11-8 (right).

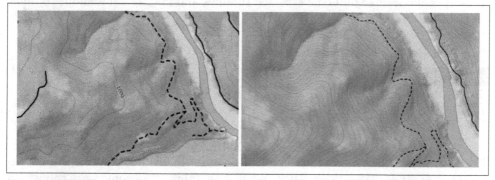

Figure 11-8. System monitoring view with less detail (left) compared to pipeline performance monitoring view with more detail (right); image courtesy of CalTopo (https://oreil.ly/KYB0a)

Pipeline Stage Duration

To dig into pipeline performance at a lower level, let's revisit the HoD batch pipeline from previous chapters, repeated here in Figure 11-9.

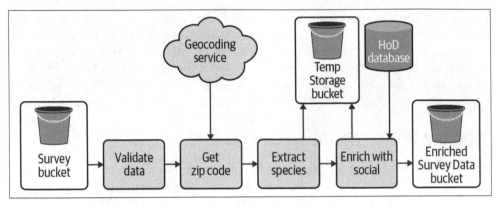

Figure 11-9. HoD batch pipeline

Let's say you've been monitoring the overall runtime of the pipeline for a while and recently noticed some deviations from the expected baseline. Table 11-2 shows the baseline runtime and two cases that have started to appear frequently. In Case 1 the runtime is about three times the expected runtime, and in Case 2 it is about 30 times the expected runtime.

Table 11-2. HoD batch pipeline runtimes

Case	Runtime
Baseline	10
Case 1	35
Case 2	310

The runtime on its own tells you something is amiss, but without more detail it's difficult to know what is going on. Before reading on, think about some ways you would try to get to the bottom of these longer runtimes.

This is the situation I was presented with in the database contention problem I shared in "Consumer Lag" on page 218. Something was taking an unusually long time, but it wasn't clear what it was.

Table 11-3 shows some examples of the more in-depth picture you get when looking at runtimes within the pipeline, with the pipeline stage names abbreviated.

Table 11-3. Runtimes for batch pipeline stages in seconds

Case	Validate	Zip code	Extract	Enrich	Total time
Baseline	2	2	1	5	10
Case 1	2	2	1	30	35
Case 2 (a)	2	300	1	7	310
Case 2 (b)	1	1	2	306	310

Table 11-3 makes it clear where the slowdowns are, but typically you would first observe this information in a dashboard, visually inspecting metrics to look for anomalies. Figure 11-10 shows an idealized trace for the Baseline and Case 1. The top graph shows the overall throughput of the pipeline, and the bottom graph breaks down traces by pipeline stage. For readability, the stage traces are offset on the y>-axis, and I've limited the stage traces to zip code (solid line), validate (dashed line), and enrich (dotted line).

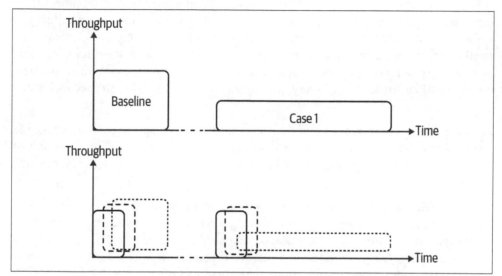

Figure 11-10. Baseline versus Case 1: dashboard view

Getting familiar with the typical characteristics of metrics will help you debug at a glance whether something isn't as expected. In the overall view at the top of Figure 11-10, it's clear that Case 1 has very different throughput than Baseline does, which would prompt you to take a look at the stage traces for further inspection. At the stage level, you can see that the throughput of the Enrich stage is lower than Baseline, and as a result, it takes longer for this stage to complete.

Returning to Table 11-3, let's think through the different cases. Interestingly, Case 2 appears to have two different underlying causes. At this level, you can start drawing on your knowledge of pipeline operation to consider what might cause these deltas. For example, perhaps you recall that there is a five-minute retry when connection issues occur with the zip code API or the database.

A further step you can take here is to consult the logs, as you saw in Chapter 10. If you've left yourself some good breadcrumbs, you might see connectivity errors and retry attempts corresponding to the Case 2 scenarios. From there, you can go back to the API and database to troubleshoot further.

What about Case 1? If there are no connectivity errors, what else could be the problem? If you've logged or created metrics for data volume at each pipeline stage, as suggested in "Data Volume" on page 214, this would be another place to look. Another option for sub-stage level observation is profiling.

Profiling

If you need more fine-grained visibility into where a pipeline is spending time, profiling can help you get to a much lower level of detail. A word of caution: profiling can suffer from the observer effect (*https://oreil.ly/nE3N9*), where the act of measuring runtime can impact the overall duration. Whereas job- and stage-level runtime observability can leverage metadata, such as the task runtime metrics made available by systems like Airflow and Celery, profiling depends on putting probes within the code itself.

Profiling can be expensive from a cost and performance perspective. If you choose to implement profiling, be able to turn it on selectively—for example, on a per-job or per-customer basis, or perhaps only in a test environment where performance isn't critical.

How profiling is implemented and the level of detail required impact cost. If your interests are limited to method runtime, using a wall timer and logging the metric is an inexpensive option. I've seen this approach used to generate JSON logs that were then analyzed in Google BigQuery, similar to this example where the event_id was traceable throughout the pipeline (times here are in seconds):

```
{
    "event_id": "bird-23ba"
    "total_time":10,
    "enrich_with_social": 7,
    "store_result": 0.4,
    ...
}
```

If you want to monitor runtime continuously, setting up a custom time-series metric is another option. Each function you monitor will be a new trace, which can multiply by other factors depending on how the metrics are labeled. More about that shortly.

Many observability services offer application performance monitoring (APM), which includes the ability to profile the full range of resource metrics down to the class and method levels. This can be quite expensive, but it can also be very illuminating to help tune performance.

If you've implemented the code design strategies described in Chapter 6, you'll already have a codebase set up to easily probe the amount of time it takes for discrete processes to run. Continuing Case 1 from Table 11-3, assuming you've separated the concerns of interacting with the database from the join performed in "Enrich with social," you can probe these processes separately, as shown in Table 11-4.

Table 11-4. Profiling "Enrich with social"

Case	Enrich total time	Merge species and social	Store result
Baseline	5	1	5
Case 1	30	20	10

With this level of detail, you can see that, while both the merge and store processes have increased compared to the baseline, the merge has increased by 20 times compared to two times for storing the result.

Errors to Watch Out For

So far, you've seen ways to monitor data pipelines to help you keep ahead of performance and reliability issues, while looking for opportunities to reduce costs. Inevitably, you will also have to deal with failures and errors, the reporting of which is an important aspect of monitoring.

In some sense, you can think about error monitoring as going the last mile when it comes to building data pipelines. A lot of times, so much emphasis is on design and development that it's easy to forget that making a connection from the pipeline to monitoring tools is essential to deal with failures quickly and effectively.

Depending on your infrastructure, you may already have access to some error metrics. For example, Airflow provides various failure metrics (*https://oreil.ly/wWFfI*), as does Spark (*https://oreil.ly/BChvO*). While it's helpful to know that an Airflow DAG failed, being able to convey *why* it failed can expedite prioritization and debug. In addition, frequent failures of a particular type can be signs that the design needs to be updated.

Ingestion success and failure

Knowing whether ingestion failed is certainly important from an alerting perspective. Keeping track of ingestion successes and failures also gives you a longer-term perspective on system reliability. From both a debug and tracking perspective, annotating ingestion failures with a failure reason will help you further isolate underlying issues. The remaining metrics in this section can be rolled up into an overall pipeline failure metric to this end.

Stage failures

The next level of error detail comes from tracking the failure rate of individual pipeline stages. Just like you can get more detail from looking at pipeline stage duration, as you saw in "Pipeline Performance" on page 227, stage failure metrics show you specifically where the pipeline failed.

Tracking stage failures is especially helpful when more detailed failure reasons could be shared by multiple stages. Typically you'll have failures that fall into two groups: those that can be explicitly identified, such as validation and communication failures, which you'll see next; and those that are not identifiable. These unidentified errors could occur at any stage in the pipeline, so annotating pipeline failure with which stage failed can help disambiguate where something went wrong.

Validation failures

As you learned in Chapter 6, an uptick in data validation failures could be indicative of changes in data or bugs in validation code. Monitoring validation failures over time will help you discern which might be the cause. For example, if there is a sudden spike in validation failures following a release, code could be the place to look. If instead you see a steady increase in validation failures across releases, this could be indicative of a change in data characteristics.

Communication failures

When failures occur, it's helpful to be able to isolate the cause. With the number of external dependencies in data pipelines, reporting whether a failure occurred because of a connection issue will show you where to focus debug and improvement efforts. You saw this in Chapter 4 with retries, where it may make sense to retry on a connection failure but not if you executed a bad query.

Authentication failures are a subset of communication failures. It can be tricky to isolate whether a communication failure is due to a failure to authenticate, particularly if you're working through a CSP client library. You saw this with the GCS example in Chapter 8, where failures to upload objects to GCS were due to authentication issues, but because the client library wrapped the exceptions, it wasn't easy to introspect what the root cause was.

Metric Annotation

Oftentimes you have the option to add tags or labels to monitoring data, allowing you to track additional information. For instance, a pipeline metric for job failure could include a label for the failure reason, including values such as TIMEOUT, VALIDATION, or DB_CONNECTION.

The number of unique values for a label, referred to as the label's *cardinality* (*https://oreil.ly/3ZmtD*), has repercussions for cost and overhead. Some monitoring services bill for custom metrics on a per–time-series basis. Each unique combination of metric and labels constitutes a different time-series trace. In addition, more labels mean

---

more time-series traces have to be accessed to visualize the data, which can really bog down monitoring tools.[6]

Thinking back to the zip code example, consider a metric for zip code API call latency. Let's say you add a label for the AWS AZ the pipeline runs in, and you deploy across three AZs. Now let's say you add a label denoting what zip code was returned. There are roughly 41,000 zip codes in the United States. In this case, you would pay for 120,000 traces, and you'd wait for a very long time to see them all rendered in your dashboard.

Instead of adding high-cardinality data to metrics, consider capturing it in logs. This will help you quickly correlate error metrics to specific users or data issues without overwhelming your metrics system or your finance department.

In scenarios where you can isolate authentication issues, identifying failures as being specifically due to authentication problems will really speed up remediation. One pipeline I worked on had a specific error type for authentication problems. As a result, the product was able to surface directly to customers if their credentials weren't working. This completely bypassed the need for debugging by the engineering team, saving engineering costs.

Stage timeouts

As you saw in "System Monitoring" on page 214, changes in how long it takes to run a task can impact system performance, stability, and scaling. Setting timeouts for a stage can help you track performance changes or enforce a certain level of pipeline throughput.

In the error metric setting, timeouts would be a hard failure, where a stage that takes longer than the allotted time fails. You can also set softer timeout limits, such as Airflow SLAs (*https://oreil.ly/E1apj*), that will not fail a stage but will emit a metric when a task takes too long.

Let's consider how the error metrics in this section could be applied to the HoD batch pipeline in Figure 11-9. Table 11-5 shows failure reasons for a few of the individual pipeline stages. All three stages have an UNDEFINED or a TIMEOUT error type, which would be used if an error occurs that isn't related to a specific failure reason or if the stage timed out, respectively.

---

6 Grafana provides a good overview (*https://oreil.ly/A99iT*) of the cardinality problem.

Table 11-5. Failure reasons for HoD batch pipeline stages

Validate data	Get zip code	Enrich with social
VALIDATION	ZIP_SERVICE	DB_CONN
		DB_QUERY
TIMEOUT	TIMEOUT	TIMEOUT
UNDEFINED	UNDEFINED	UNDEFINED

The other failure reasons correspond to specific issues. VALIDATION indicates that data validation failed, ZIP_SERVICE is for failures to communicate with the zip code service, and the DB_CONN and DB_QUERY failures separate the conditions of failing to communicate with the database or a query error, respectively. Note that there are 10 possible failure reasons, which is definitely within cardinality constraints for metrics annotations.

Table 11-6 shows some hypothetical metrics results using the failure reasons in Table 11-5 for a sequential set of ingestion events. Events 1 and 3 show no errors. In Event 2, 1% of jobs failed communicating with the zip code service. This seems like a temporary communication failure.

Table 11-6. Failure reasons for pipeline jobs

Event ID	Errors	Percent errors
1	—	0
2	ZIP_SERVICE	1
3	—	0
4	ENRICH.TIMEOUT	3
5	ENRICH.TIMEOUT	8
6	ENRICH.TIMEOUT	12

Events 4 through 6 show some more interesting behavior, where progressively higher percentages of jobs are failing due to the "Enrich with social" step timing out.

This example is modeled after a pattern I've seen in my work, where a particular stage timing out for a given percentage of jobs meant more resources were needed to complete a process with several database interactions. Typically this could mean that code changes had slowed down the queries or that data volume had increased. You've already seen how to track data volume changes. In the next section, you'll see how to monitor query performance to investigate the other potential root cause in this example.

Query Monitoring

Query performance can give you insight into the efficacy of data modeling and storage layout strategies, and it can surface slow queries that would benefit from refactoring.

Queries can take place as part of data pipeline operation, such as acquiring the relevant data for "Enrich with social" in Figure 11-9, or after the fact, such as queries executed against ingested data by analytics users. In this section, I'll talk about some metrics to help you introspect these processes to improve performance.

At a high level, query monitoring is similar to pipeline performance monitoring in that keeping track of runtime and success/failure rate provides important performance tuning insight. Capturing query plans can give you a sense of how data modeling is holding up to how the data is being used.

Especially if you don't know what queries are executed a priori, such as with a system that generates queries dynamically, query monitoring can be an invaluable tool. Without insight into how data is being accessed, it is difficult to create performant data structures, including data models, views, and partitioning strategies. These decisions trickle back into how a pipeline is designed.

I encountered this chicken-and-egg–type problem when working on a data platform that surfaced insurance data to policy analysts. The analysts ran huge queries that were several pages long, which created a lot of intermediate tables to slice and dice the data. This strategy has its roots in the legacy tools used to query data before the Spark platform was available.

To improve performance, I developed a strategy for surfacing and analyzing user queries, which you can read more about in the article "User Query Monitoring in Spark" (*https://oreil.ly/IAjBu*). I'll walk through the more widely applicable steps here to provide advice on how to generalize this approach:

Get information on queries users are running: the query statement, runtime, and query plan.
> In the article referenced in the preceding paragraph, I had to reverse-engineer part of the Spark ecosystem to get the SQL queries users were executing. Hopefully you have simpler options. For example, the Postgres documentation (*https://oreil.ly/7mPY5*) includes a note on how to log query statements and duration for queries that exceed a certain duration, which are some handy settings for acquiring information on long-running queries.

Identify the highest-impact queries.
> The definition of *highest impact* depends on the use case. These could be the set of queries executed by the most important system users, or they could be a set of queries that are identified as the most critical.

In the Spark platform, there wasn't a cut-and-dried list of queries or personnel to work from. In addition, when I compiled a list of distinct queries, there were far too many to profile independently. If this is your situation, look for query patterns as opposed to specific queries. This is described in the linked article as "query signature analysis." You might find that queries against a particular table are especially slow or that the most common query filters do not coincide with current partitioning strategies.

To identify high-impacting queries, consider looking at metrics that combine the query runtime, the query frequency, and how much the query runtime fluctuates:

Total query time = sum of query times

Average query time = total query time / number of occurrences

Coefficient of variation (CV) = standard deviation of query time / the average query time

Total query time helps you identify how much computation time a given query consumes. The CV shows you which queries are consistent time hogs; the lower this number is, the smaller the deviation is. To get a sense of how to use these values, let's take a look at some example query metrics in Table 11-7.

Table 11-7. Query metrics (time values are in seconds)

Query ID	Average query time	CV	Total query time
1	1	0.1	4,000
2	40	0.2	3,200
3	75	0.8	1,800

Query ID 1 illustrates a case in which the total query time is significant and the variation is low, but the average query time is also low. This could be something like a basic SELECT statement without JOINs or an expensive WHERE clause—the sort of query that may occur frequently but is not necessarily worth trying to optimize. You could filter out query IDs with a low average query time and low CV to further isolate high-impact queries.

Query ID 2 shows a more promising case. The average query time is high and the CV is low, so this query likely takes a consistently long period of time. It also is the second highest consumer of total query time.

Finally, Query ID 3 is an example of a query that, on average, takes a significant amount of time to run, but the high CV indicates the average isn't a reliable indicator. While you might be able to improve execution of this query, the variability in runtime makes it unclear how much performance improvement you will get.

Look for optimization opportunities.

With the high-impacting queries identified, you can now focus on optimization opportunities.

One of the biggest impacts of query monitoring was giving feedback to the analysts. I set up a Databricks notebook that showed the top slowest queries, which the analysts accessed to better understand how they could rework their jobs for better performance.

You might also find that query patterns have changed, necessitating updates to data modeling strategies. For example, in a different project, a job that computed pipeline metrics slowed down significantly over time, starting out running in a few seconds and ballooning to a few minutes. It turned out that a core query in the metrics job was filtering on a value that wasn't an index, and as the data in the system had grown over time, the performance of this filter degraded.

Minimizing Monitoring Costs

Keeping track of metrics over the long term can help you better understand system health, identify trends, and predict future needs. Rather than incurring the expense of storing telemetry data over the long term, you can persist a subset of metrics for future reference. Essentially, you can pull out the important, discrete data points from the continuous monitoring data, greatly reducing the metric data footprint.

When deciding which metrics to persist, keep in mind that you won't have the underlying monitoring data to draw from. For example, perhaps you have a metric for average consumer lag per day. Depending on how you want to use this data in the future, recording the quartile can give you more insight into the distribution of the lag. Another approach is to use percentiles, such as P99, to exclude outliers.

You can incorporate saving discrete metrics into pipeline operation with surfacing telemetry metrics. I worked on a streaming pipeline that published data volume and success metrics to a separate metrics data model. This was cost conscious, as data volume from any time period could be queried from a database instead of saving telemetry data. An added benefit of this approach was that it provided diagnostic information for both the engineering team and our customers. Customers could see their data volumes, and engineers could use this information to plan scaling and architecture changes as well as debug issues.

Similar to my advice in Chapter 10 regarding logging, focus your monitoring on high-impact metrics such as the ones in this chapter, rather than trying to capture everything. If monitoring costs are a concern, remember that having a map is better than having no map. Start with system monitoring and capturing ingestion success and failure metrics, and add detail from here as you are able.

Summary

Monitoring enables you to look across all the decisions about design, implementation, and testing to observe how these decisions hold up to the realities of pipeline operation in the wild. This map can help you improve performance and reliability and save costs across the board, from cloud service costs to engineering costs and the cost of lost revenue due to system downtime.

Throughout this chapter, you saw advice for monitoring data pipelines, from high-level system metrics to more granular insights about resource usage, pipeline operation, and query performance. Like a good map, the ability to introspect system behavior helps you plan for the path ahead, adopting a proactive stance instead of a reactive one.

System monitoring gets you started with a basic trail map. Data volume, throughput, consumer lag, and worker utilization provide a high-level picture of the data pipeline landscape, showing you how data changes impact performance and infrastructure needs.

Having a map is a good start. Being able to both read the map and interpret it alongside other signals is essential for putting it to good use. You saw how data volume fluctuations could be happenstance, as in the case of changes in data sources, or how it could be indicative of bugs in the pipeline. Understanding which of these is the case requires combining the metric of data volume with your knowledge of pipeline operation and data characteristics.

Beyond pipeline performance, tracking metrics such as data volume can help with capacity planning and budgeting. The seasonality in the bird migration data is an example of different data volumes over time, which can be used to determine reservation purchases and adjust cloud spend forecasts.

Changes in data volume and resourcing can impact pipeline throughput, which shows you how much data is processed over a given period. Decreased throughput can indicate under-resourcing, which can escalate to reliability issues, as you saw in the example. Conversely, increased throughput can indicate an opportunity to save costs.

Understanding changes in throughput can require more detailed metrics. For streaming pipelines, consumer lag can show you whether decreased throughput is due to a mismatch between publisher and consumer volumes. Whether due to higher data volumes, producer performance improvements, or consumer performance degradation, a persistent message backlog can limit performance. In extreme cases, reliability can become a concern as well, which is why alerting when consumer lag exceeds a healthy threshold can be helpful.

Monitoring worker utilization shows you how well the pipeline is saturating the resources being provisioned. Consistently using fewer worker slots than are available can indicate wasted resources and an opportunity to reduce workers. Comparing worker utilization and consumer lag can help you determine how to improve performance; unhealthy lag and saturated workers could be a sign that workers or their dependencies need more resources. You also saw, with the Airflow deadlock example, how worker saturation is a careful balance.

Adding more detail to the monitoring map, resource utilization shows you what's going on with memory, CPU, disk, and network resources. Knowing which resources are bounding your processes will help you choose the right vertical scaling solution.

Killed processes, frequent and/or unexpected container restarts, and long job runtimes can be signs that you should check resource utilization. Check these metrics alongside resource limits and configurations to understand where limits are being imposed before upsizing.

While throughput gives you a sense of how the pipeline performs at a high level, digging into pipeline performance at the stage and process levels helps you determine more precisely where improvements can be made. Profiling gives you very finely detailed information about performance, but it can also slow things down. Using profiling in test environments and being able to turn it off selectively will help you benefit from its insights without reducing performance.

Monitoring pipeline failures is good; annotating these error metrics with the failure reason is better. This approach provides a head start on root cause analysis and helps differentiate between intermittent issues and trends that benefit from more immediate attention. Adding low-cardinality information such as pipeline stage and source of error, including validation, communication, and timeouts, gives you this information at a glance. Couple this with logging high-cardinality information to have a solid debug strategy.

Data access is an end goal of data pipelines and can also be part of pipeline operation. Monitoring query performance is another opportunity to optimize cost–performance trade-offs. Analyzing the highest-impact queries, those that consistently take up the lion's share of compute time, can give you insight into optimizing data models or the queries themselves. Improving query performance reduces compute costs and makes for happier analytics customers.

Being able to pull up a dashboard to inspect lag versus data volume versus worker utilization is helpful for point-in-time debugging, but keeping endless amounts of this telemetry data isn't necessary or cost-effective. To track over the long term, capture statistics about continuous monitoring data.

It's always reassuring to know where you've been, where you're going, and what's happening in the present. Without that confidence, things can be pretty uncomfortable, whether you're in the woods or working on a data pipeline. With a map of what to monitor and guidance on different ways this information can be interpreted, you can feel secure in your data pipeline journey and avoid falling off the cliffs of performance, reliability, and cost.

Recommended Readings

- Chapter 18 of *Spark: The Definitive Guide* (*https://oreil.ly/or8gB*), which provides advice on monitoring for Spark and mitigation strategies for common issues
- Chapter 6 of Google's *Site Reliability Engineering* (*https://oreil.ly/mOo_o*) (O'Reilly), which notes the four golden signals for monitoring distributed systems

CHAPTER 12

Essential Takeaways

As you might imagine, my initial research for this book involved reading a lot of material about the cost of cloud services. From shell-shocked graduate students grappling with unexpected bills to large companies feeling trapped with substantial, expensive cloud deployments, it was clear that developing data pipelines in the cloud can be daunting.

It reminds me of learning to ride waves on a bodyboard when I was a kid. Similar to surfing, riding waves on a bodyboard requires that you develop a sense of when to start paddling to catch a wave at the right time. If you don't time it right, you can miss the wave or get dunked when the wave crashes on top of you.

I got dunked a lot in the beginning, ending up with a nose full of saltwater, but gradually I got better. I developed a sense of how the strength of the undertow related to the incoming wave. I figured out how to angle the board to get a better ride. Sometimes I still got dunked.

This was how I felt when I started working in the cloud, a few years after I began working on data pipelines. The steep learning curve was no joke. A big motivation for writing this book was wishing I had something like it at the time. Data pipelines and cloud development are two big topics on their own, let alone together. Add to it the desire to cut costs and you've got quite a lot to digest.

In reflecting on the last 240ish pages, I want to wrap things up by distilling this volume down to what I consider to be the most essential points.

An Ounce of Prevention Is Worth a Pound of Cure

As you've seen in the many tales of woe in this book, and perhaps experienced your-self, debugging and remediating issues in cloud data pipelines can be an enormous expense. Escalating cloud costs with little understanding of driving factors and unde-tected pipeline bugs silently ingesting malformed data are just a few examples of time and money black holes you can easily fall into.

Prevention involves understanding potential risks and how to address them. A key focus in this book has been to illustrate the risks in cloud data pipeline development and provide mitigation strategies.

Reign In Compute Spend

Dynamic pipeline workloads coupled with myriad purchasing options for cloud com-pute creates an environment where it's easy to overspend. While starting out by over-provisioning will help work out the kinks in a new design, you want to work toward a more judicious cost–performance trade-off.

Benchmarking will help you determine the compute configurations needed for relia-bility and performance. This can also give you a sense of resource needs when con-sidering serverless. If benchmarking shows that you need to leave cycles on the table for performance, workload segmentation can help put this excess to use running low-priority maintenance tasks without sacrificing performance for the primary workload.

Autoscaling provides another level of cost optimization, coupling the findings from benchmarking with data workload and pipeline operation variability to right-size compute. Scaling out aggressively and scaling in conservatively keeps performance on track without sacrificing reliability.

Designing performant, scalable data pipelines is another aspect of keeping compute spend in check. Understanding how to get the most out of your data processing engine, be it Spark, Dask, or a relational database, is essential to designing performant data processing code. For large workloads, file structure design and design for hori-zontal scaling have significant performance implications.

Organize Your Resources

It's easy to lose track of things in the cloud. It doesn't take much to create a new stor-age bucket or serverless process or to launch a cluster. The result can be a sort of graveyard, where some of these entities are truly dead and can be removed but are indistinguishable from zombies that may periodically come back to life to perform an important task.

Fortunately, you can prevent this by spending time early in the design process to organize cloud resources. This will help you limit and track costs and avoid zombies.

CSPs provide several tools to help you with this endeavor. You can label and tag compute resources and cloud storage to track what portion of compute costs are due to different projects, organizations, or customers. Lifecycle policies for storage and retention periods and filters for logs enable you to limit the amount of data you collect and retain, tidying things up and reducing costs. Cost monitoring and alerting show you where costs come from and let you know when you're exceeding your budget.[1]

Design for Interruption

Whether due to termination of low-cost interruptible compute instances, hitting API rate limits, or spurious service disruptions, interruptions are a fact of life in the cloud. It is a giant distributed system, after all.

Thinking through where interruption can occur in data pipelines will help you identify where defensive design strategies are needed. Retrying a pipeline stage or low-level service call will help pipelines self-heal from interruptions.

While idempotent design is desirable, it's sometimes not feasible. In these cases, planning a data deduplication strategy will help mitigate undesirable impacts when retrying a job.

Build In Data Quality

In my opinion, the absolute worst thing a data pipeline can do is create bad data, resulting in *data downtime (https://oreil.ly/hFvPA)*—periods where data is incorrect, partial, or missing. Preventing this involves a combined approach of testing, validation, and monitoring.

Use schemas to validate data as it moves through the pipeline, either halting execution on malformed data or dropping the offending row before it causes problems. Rather than attempting to cover all data with a schema, focus on critical fields.

These same schemas can be used to generate data for testing, providing an accurate representation of data sources without connecting to them and incurring costs. With test data generators, you can guarantee that specific data cases will be present for testing, unlike testing against live data, which may only include a subset of cases.

While validation checks data as it moves through the pipeline, unit testing will validate operation in all expected cases, which you can model with test data. At a system

---

1 See the Appendix for budgeting.

level, having a staging environment where the pipeline can run end to end will provide additional coverage. This can be especially helpful for surfacing bugs that show up only at scale.

Even with these preventive measures, you can still end up with bad data. Data quality monitoring can help surface issues. *Data Quality Fundamentals* by Barr Moses, Lior Gavish, and Molly Vorwerck (O'Reilly) has advice on this topic.

Change Is the Only Constant

In the Preface, I mentioned the cost of engineering time as another facet of cost-effectiveness. Part of engineering time can include the topics I referenced in the preceding section of this chapter, but in my experience, the biggest source of wasted engineering time stems from not planning for change.

As you've seen in this book, there are many sources for change in data pipelines. Data sources change, new data sources are added, new analytics users request additional data transformations—the list goes on. Keeping this reality in mind as you design, test, and monitor data pipelines will reduce engineering overhead.

Design for Change

It pains me to recollect the amount of time I've seen being sunk into retrofitting and debugging data pipelines that desperately need to be refactored. Oftentimes there was little support for refactoring because the pipelines worked well enough. Behind the scenes, engineering time was increasingly dedicated to debug and remediation, taking away from a team's capacity to deliver new features. This is a penny-wise, pound-foolish approach.

Don't waste engineering hours with suboptimal codebases. Following software development best practices, aim to create codebases that are easy to change. Modular design will keep pipelines decoupled from specific technologies, making it easier for you to add, remove, or modify dependencies. Isolating code into separate components based on functionality will make refactoring and testing easier.

Configurable design is a powerful tool for accommodating change. Look for opportunities to abstract sources of change into configurations, enabling you to test and deploy updates quickly with a minimum of code changes.

Automated testing is another key element of designing for change. Both unit testing as part of CI and end-to-end testing are essential for verifying pipeline functionality when code or data changes. Relatedly, automating test data creation using schemas will help you keep fake data up to date with changes in data sources.

Monitor for Change

Observation is a must to be aware of changes to performance, cost, and reliability. Has resource utilization dropped? Perhaps you have an opportunity to scale in, or maybe there's a bug preventing data from being ingested.

Monitoring resource-, performance-, and system-level metrics will help answer these questions quickly. Trends in these metrics can illuminate opportunities to cut costs and give you a heads-up that capacity planning or performance needs to be revisited. Once you've made changes, these metrics will help you evaluate the impacts.

Over time, you'll get a sense of what metrics look like when the pipeline is healthy and what changes are signs of distress. Creating alerts based on these conditions will help you stay ahead of issues.

Parting Thoughts

While writing this book, I commented to my partner that I hoped it would be a success. In response, they asked me, "What would success look like?" Perhaps the most common way to measure success would be the number of books sold, which I certainly hope is many. I told them that, to me, this book would be successful if the people who could benefit from the practices that I've described found it useful. I would love to hear that readers sidestepped nasty data bugs with the combined powers of data validation and unit testing, saved themselves from tedious research by using this book and code repository as a reference for design and testing, or saved substantial money with the techniques I've shared.

Writing a technical book is a big undertaking, but so is reading one. If you've found your way to this page, I want to say thanks! I hope that, after reading this book, you find more ease in tackling the multidimensional beast of data pipeline development and have greater confidence developing cost-effectively in the cloud.

Preparing a Cloud Budget

Throughout this book, you've learned how to design and develop data pipelines in a cost-effective way. You've evaluated different options of how to allocate compute and storage, making decisions that are appropriate for your current and near-term data pipeline operational goals. You've put design strategies in place to reduce the chance of data corruption and recomputation expenses, and you've employed development strategies to minimize cloud service costs. On top of this, you have monitoring in place so that you can see how the pipeline performs with the design choices and resource allocations you've made.

Going through this process not only helps you put cost-effective designs in place, it also gives you valuable information about where and why you are spending on cloud resources. Even if your day to day doesn't involve giving budget presentations, communicating how you are saving costs will help propel your career. Engineers who understand cost trade-offs are valuable partners to those who are primarily interested in company financials. You have the ability to act on requests to save costs as well as inform others on what the trade-offs are for doing so.

In this Appendix, you'll learn how to take this information and create a basic budget for cloud spend, using historical billing data, estimated costs, and pipeline workload expectations.

This is just the tip of the iceberg for budgeting and forecasting, but it will help you leverage what you've learned in this book to communicate some basic numbers about cloud spend expectations. If you'd like to learn more about this topic, check out the FinOps Foundation (*https://www.finops.org*) and its official guide, *Cloud FinOps* by J. R. Storment and Mike Fuller (O'Reilly). As stated on the FinOps Foundation website, "FinOps is about making money." By creating visibility of cloud costs and encouraging cross-functional ownership of these expenses, FinOps helps companies invest in systems that contribute to revenue and profit.

This will help your company improve revenue and profit by maximizing the value you get from the cloud.

It's All About the Details

When it comes to looking at the cost of things, everyone likes to know what they're paying for. Say you were in the market for an expensive laptop and came across the two ads shown in Figure A-1.

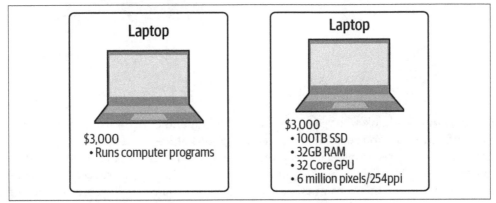

Figure A-1. Laptop ads with varying levels of detail

The cost for each laptop is the same, but there's a dearth of details in the ad on the left. It could be that it performs as well as or better than the laptop on the right, but you can't be sure without more information. You know there are more details about what you are getting for that $3,000. You might even wonder what is being hidden due to the lack of details in the ad on the left.

These are not the sorts of feelings you want the audience for your budget to have. Having the details of your cloud budget available will help build trust with stakeholders and enable you to showcase the cost-effective work you've been doing. You would feel confident about what you were purchasing if you bought the laptop on the right; you want your budget audience to feel that same confidence when reviewing your numbers.

While it's important to convey the details of cloud spend, the business tends to be more interested in the impact of a system. Ultimately, how does this system benefit the company? This relates back to "Requirements Gathering for Compute Design" on page 9: working with stakeholders to determine how to best meet their needs and making the right trade-offs in system design. While this Appendix focuses on the cloud cost numbers, make sure to include the impact of the system in your budget discussions.

At the highest level, your budget conveys the cost of cloud services you expect to incur over a particular time period. Working backward from this point, the next level to consider is the different areas where costs originate. Storage, data egress, and compute tend to be the dominant categories. Other areas include databases, monitoring, networking, and CSP-managed services, such as AWS Lambda or Athena.

Depending on where you are in the pipeline lifecycle, you can get a sense of these costs from your historical billing data or by coming up with an estimate.

Historical Data

If your pipelines have been up and running for a while, historical cloud costs can help you bootstrap your budget. CSPs offer ways to stratify your bill across different services and filter by tags, labels, and projects to help you zero in on the expenses that relate to your pipelines. Figure A-2 shows a very modest cloud bill where you can see different services broken out.

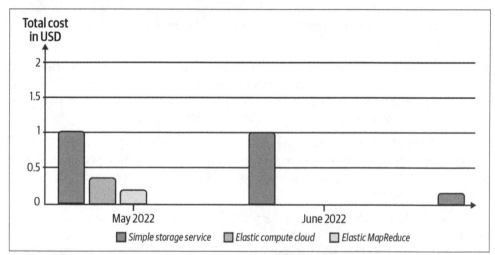

Figure A-2. The world's smallest cloud bill, stratified by service type

If you haven't looked at a cloud bill before, it's definitely an eye-opening experience to see the myriad things you get charged for. Digging into the details can help you get a sense of how costs break down. As you learned in Chapter 3, cloud storage costs include storing the data at rest as well as events to request, create, and delete objects. Figure A-3 shows the breakdown of storage costs for the S3 costs in Figure A-2.

▾ Simple Storage Service		$1.01
▾ US East (N. Virginia)		$1.01
Amazon Simple Storage Service Requests-Tier1		$0.00
$0.005 per 1,000 PUT, COPY, POST, or LIST requests	427.000 Requests	$0.00
Amazon Simple Storage Service Requests-Tier2		$0.00
$0.004 per 10,000 GET and all other requests	127.000 Requests	$0.00
Amazon Simple Storage Service TimedStorage-ByteHrs		$1.01
$0.023 per GB - first 50 TB / month of storage used	43.917 GB-Mo	$1.01

Figure A-3. Simple storage service cost breakdown

In this case, the primary cost driver is data storage, and you can see that there were so few service requests that they didn't add to the overall cost at all.

Combining these billing details with your knowledge of the pipeline will help you create a mental model of how the cloud costs spread out across the system. Even a rough sense of the ratio of compute to storage costs can be helpful when trying to estimate future expenses.

This mental model will also help you evaluate forecasting data. Major CSPs offer forecasting tools as part of their billing services, using historical usage to predict future cloud bills. These forecasts are not always correct. Your knowledge of the system plus the historical usage data can help you determine whether a forecast is reliable.

As an example of how this mental model can help with budgeting, a project I worked on had a one-time event where we were tuning autoscaling settings. Over a few weeks, we ran large test ingestion jobs to assess different autoscaling rules, increasing our cloud compute costs.

When we looked at the billing forecast, this one-time increase was forecast as a month-over-month increase, making it appear as though our future cloud compute spend was going up. This was an important point to clarify to company leadership when reviewing the cloud budget, as the forecast provided by the CSP was not accurate.

Estimating for New Projects

If you are working on a new project or if it's difficult to isolate pipeline costs from other projects in a cloud bill, you can come up with a rough cost estimate. CSPs offer cost estimation tools, such as the AWS pricing calculator (*https://calculator.aws*), the Azure pricing calculator (*https://oreil.ly/TBvRf*), and the Google Cloud pricing calculator (*https://oreil.ly/KPfBn*), that can help with estimating.

Using the benchmarking process from Chapter 1 will help you get a sense of compute needs, which you can scale up for the volume of data and compute complexity you expect over the budget period.

Other costs will vary based on architecture. If you're ingesting primarily to cloud storage, you can estimate storage and data transfer costs based on expected data size. Standing up a small prototype environment can help estimate costs for databases and other services, something IaC practices can help you with. Running this environment for some test ingestion events will populate billing data you can use to seed your estimation.

Whether you use existing cloud bills or come up with an estimate, you've now developed a baseline cost estimate for the pipeline. This might be the limit of what you can provide, which is quite valuable information.

You can think of this as a detailed receipt for the time period you've looked into. A budget goes beyond this to provide an expectation of what costs will look like in the future. In the next section, you'll learn what to look for to determine how your costs might change, enabling you to come up with a budget.

Cloud Cost Reduction Products and Services

As you continue your cost-conscious development journey, you'll come across a mountain of products and companies offering to cut cloud bills by tremendous amounts. With the work you've done learning and applying cost-effective practices and spending time looking at the billing numbers, you'll be in a pretty strong position to evaluate these claims. The expertise you've developed will be invaluable for guiding decisions about investing in further cost reduction services.

When you get a pitch or a product demo that claims to help reduce cloud spend, you'll already have a sense of where you have cut costs or where you need more help. Not only will you be able to assess whether the guidance provided is relevant and actionable, you'll also be able to get the most out of cost-cutting services by having already executed on the highest-value approaches as detailed in this book. Because of this, you can turn to cloud cost tools and services to help with the really thorny issues, instead of investing a lot for some basic advice, thereby maximizing the value you get from these offerings.

Changes That Impact Costs

In the simplest scenario for a budget, your pipeline continues operating exactly as it has in the past; the same data load, the same data processing logic, and the same infrastructure. In this case, the billing history probably gives you a decent estimate of what to expect in the future.

I have yet to work on a pipeline where this is the case, which I suppose is fortunate because otherwise I'd be very bored. Realistically, you'll be experiencing some kinds of changes over the budget time period that can impact cloud costs. In this section, you'll learn some typical changes in data pipelines that can make cost forecasting challenging and ways to address the ambiguity they introduce.

Some of these changes you may be able to estimate, while others are entirely unforeseeable. Remember that a budget is about communicating; if you see changes on the horizon but can't come up with a cost estimate, make note of these changes as possible risks. Even if you can estimate the cost impacts of changes, it is worthwhile to show that you've considered upcoming changes as a part of your budget.

Data landscape

A variety of changes that can happen in the data landscape can impact cloud costs. You might bring on additional data sources or see increased volumes in existing ones. Conversely, you may see reduced volumes or drop data sources from processing. Data source formats can change, which can increase or reduce storage and compute costs depending on whether it makes the data processing more or less complex.

Some of these changes can be anticipated. For example, if you are making a big push to bring new customers on board, you would expect costs to increase. Your sales and marketing team may be able to give you an idea of the number and types of prospective customers they are targeting, which could help you estimate the additional storage, compute, and egress costs.

In another example, perhaps development of an ML product is planned to start in the next quarter, requiring additional data storage to retain a history of raw, unprocessed source data. The costs for developing, training, and running an ML engine would be additional costs to consider if the ML product is expected to be part of the pipeline.

Other changes in the data landscape are difficult or impossible to predict. You don't know whether a third-party API will shut down suddenly, whether the response data will change, or whether changes in API terms will enable you to access more or less data in a single request. In one project I worked on, our cloud compute costs spiked when a third-party API response changed, providing significantly more data than we needed.

Load

Changes in pipeline load can also impact cloud costs. This can be related to changes in the data landscape, such as processing more or less data. Changes in data processing approaches can also impact load. As an example, I worked on a project where our data processing logic increased in complexity to provide new features to our customers, which increased our cloud costs despite the data source characteristics remaining the same. If you know features are planned that can increase or reduce data processing complexity, that will be important to note in your budget.

Other changes in load can come from seasonality. Recall the streaming bird migration pipeline in Chapter 5. Except for seasonal migration events, this pipeline would be quiescent or perhaps entirely off for the rest of the year. When preparing a budget for a given time period, keep in mind how time of year could impact costs.

 You can set up cloud budgets, including alerts if thresholds are exceeded, in Azure (*https://oreil.ly/mAcs_*), AWS (*https://oreil.ly/aKzNf*), and Google (*https://oreil.ly/94BAH*). This can help you avoid nasty surprises at the end of the billing cycle.

Load can also change due to changes in performance requirements for the pipeline. If the pipeline has to increase throughput, you would expect costs to increase as a result of the additional resources needed.

Unplanned changes in load will impact cloud costs but can't be foreseen. Data reingestion due to pipeline bugs is another source of unplanned cost changes. Your CSP may have a major outage in the mainline region where you run your pipeline, incurring the cost of replicating data and running a DR system. While you can't plan for these occurrences, you can make note of them if and when they occur. You'll be able to speak to these impacts on the cloud budget if they come up in the next budgeting period.

Infrastructure

Infrastructure changes can be challenging to budget for. Examples of this are changes in data processing engine or migration from in-house services to managed, such as from an in-house Postgres deployment to RDS, or from managed services to in-house services, such as from an Airflow deployment in Google Cloud Composer to a self-hosted Airflow deployment. Adding a new service, such as the addition of the Lambda function for night heron data in Chapter 7, is another possibility.

When you're swapping between managed and in-house services, you might be able to leverage historical billing data if data landscape and performance requirements remain the same. In the Airflow example, if you provision the same capacity that was provided by Google Cloud Composer and run the same DAGs, you can get an estimate of future costs when moving to an in-house deployment. If you're using these kinds of estimates in your budget, it's good to note this infrastructure change as a risk.

Creating a Budget

Now that you've learned how to come up with some cost numbers and assess budget risks, let's take a look at how to pull these together into a budget spreadsheet. This will help you organize the details of your cost analysis, cost-saving strategies, and risks in a single place. Keep in mind that a budget is dynamic; needs and demand can change, necessitating revisiting prior budgeting decisions.

Throughout this section, I'll refer to the example budget in Table A-1. An empty budget spreadsheet is available at the end of the Appendix for you to apply to your projects (see Table A-2).

Budget Summary

The budget summary is a short synopsis of the budget. This gives the budget audience a succinct description of what the budget covers, the total cost, assumptions, and risks.

Taking a look at rows 1 through 6 in Table A-1, you have the following sections:

Project
> This tells you what the budget covers. In this case, the budget is for the HoD bird identification pipeline introduced in Chapter 6.

Timeline
> The timeline refers to the time period the budget covers. In this example, the budget covers the fourth quarter of 2023. It's important to make sure you present the time period in a way that everyone will understand. For example, Q4 2023 could refer to the fourth quarter of the calendar year, which is October through December. This could be different from the fourth quarter of the fiscal year, so make sure the way you present the timeline is clear to all potential recipients.

Total
> This is the total budget for the time period.

Assumptions
> Anything you are assuming could impact the budget should be spelled out here. In the example, an assumption is that the current data load from existing customers will be the same over the budget period. There are always going to be assumptions when you are forecasting costs. List major ones here to raise awareness of what you are basing your budget on.

Risks
> As you learned in "Changes That Impact Costs" on page 251, there are several things that can impact the budget that you might not be able to plan for. In this section, you can communicate what future changes could impact costs.

Don't try to enumerate every possible scenario, such as detailing that every API you interact with could change. Rather, think about what is on the horizon that you can't estimate costs for. In the example, the uncertainty of what new customer data will look like is cited. In this case, you know there is a push to bring new customers on board, but you don't know how that will impact cloud bills because future customer data is unknown.

Cost-saving measures

This is where you can show off the cost-efficient measures you've taken. If you can put numbers to this section, all the better; for example, "Saved 40% on compute with reservations and improving data processing efficiency."

Table A-1. Example budget

1	Project	HoD bird classification pipeline	
2	Timeline	Q4 2023	
3	Total	$100,000	
4	Assumptions	Load on pipeline for current customers remains stable; expect additional costs to support new customers	
5	Risks	Uncertain impact to compute, database costs for new customers; estimating based on past growth	
6	Cost-saving measures	Spot instances, minimizing data footprint, limited cloud service use in development	
7	Baseline		
8		Number of customers	8
9		Total data processed	160 TB
10		Total data stored	50 TB
11	Expected growth		
12		Number of customers	2–6
13		Data processing	20–50 TB per customer
14		Data stored	1–10 TB per customer
15	**Cost breakdown**		
16	Production		
17		Q3 2023	Estimated Q4 2023
18	Compute	$54,000	$77,000
19	Storage	$4,000	$7,300
20	Egress	$600	$900
21	Databases	$4,000	$7,300
22	Other	$1,000	$1,300
23	Total	$63,600	$93,800
24	Disaster recovery	N/A	
25	Test and development		
26	Compute	$3,000	$3,000

27	Storage	$375	$375
28	Egress	0	0
29	Databases	$780	$780
30	Other	$200	$200
31	Total	$4,355	$4,355

Changes Between Previous and Next Budget Periods

Rows 7 through 14 in Table A-1 communicate important metrics about the system you are budgeting for. This will vary from project to project and can include metrics for system capacity, performance, number of customers supported, or SLAs.

Rows 7 through 10 show the baseline metrics covering the last budget period. Rows 8 through 14 show the expected change over the next budget period. Notice that the expected growth is presented as a range, which helps to further communicate the uncertainty around these impacts.

The metrics in Table A-1 are presented at a system level, but it can also be desirable to break down these metrics in different ways. For example, presenting a per-customer cost distribution can be helpful to inform how to charge for the service.

Cost Breakdown

Rows 15 to the end of Table A-1 are for breaking down the total cost into individual cloud cost categories across different environments. Showing the comparison with the previous budget period gives a sense of how costs are evolving and can also be an opportunity to discuss how costs differed from the prior budget expectations.

The sections you include will depend on where you incur costs. In this example, at a high level are the production, testing, and development environments. Production is, as expected, the largest contributor to the budget and gets its own distinct section. The testing and development environments are combined, as they contribute a fraction of the costs. Make sure to include a budget for all the test and development environments you run, recalling the DEV, TEST, STAGING, and PROD environment example in Chapter 5. In that case, you have PROD and three lower environments to budget for.

There is no DR for this pipeline, so that section is absent. If you have DR, how you represent it in a budget will depend on whether you have a hot, warm, or cold failover system. A hot system, where a production replica is running all the time, will give you a consistent baseline cost to use for a budget. Warm and cold systems are a bit less straightforward, since these only come online at capacity in response to an incident.

In the case of warm and cold DR, you can represent the cost in a budget on a per-incident basis, including an assumption of how long you expect the DR system to be in operation before switching back to the mainline. For example, if it costs $1,000 to bring a cold DR system online and run it for one day, you can represent this as $1,000 per incident in a budget. When estimating DR costs, don't forget the cost of data replication and egress where appropriate.

Within the environments, the breakdown of cost categories, as shown in rows 18 through 22 in Table A-1, depends on your architecture. In the example, the major sections include compute, egress, storage, and databases. An "Other" category rolls up remaining costs that are too small to deserve their own line item. In this case, "Other" would include the Lambda function developed to alert on night heron content.

Communicating the Budget

You've researched the numbers and organized them into a concise spreadsheet. Now it's time for the part of budgeting that technical contributors enjoy more than anything else: talking to other people.

Regardless of whether you relish the idea of presenting this information, the decisions you have made while designing cost-effectively are extremely valuable in budget conversations. A lot of folks can look at billing data and create a forecast, but only those who have designed and developed the underlying system can speak to how these costs translate to a (hopefully) profitable product and can consult on possible trade-offs.

For example, let's say your simulations in Chapter 1 show that you need a 30% memory overhead to meet reliability performance goals for data ingestion. Your monitoring from Chapter 9 shows the amount of data processed over a given time period and the resource utilization of your compute resources, confirming that this overhead is helping you meet performance goals.

When Finance questions your cloud compute costs, noting that you have up to 30% idle compute capacity, you can present this trade-off: "We leave a 30% overhead to meet performance goals. Reducing this will impact performance and stability." It could be that this is acceptable, or it could be that the business is willing to accept a slower data ingestion to cut costs. Because you've evaluated these trade-offs, you can provide this input to budget discussions, enabling the business to make informed decisions.

When it comes to communicating the budget numbers from the example in Table A-1, you'll want to tailor the level of detail you provide based on the audience. The more removed someone is from the day-to-day engineering process, the less detail they tend to need—unless you're talking to a FinOps person, in which case they may be removed from engineering but very interested in the details.

Regardless of who I present a budget to, I like to have all the details available, if not broadcast as part of my presentation. That way, if more detailed questions arise, I can speak to them. You don't want to leave the audience thinking you're just hand waving, so having specifics on hand can bolster your credibility.

Summary

With just a little more investment in understanding cloud bills and cost estimation, you can increase the impact of your cost-effective designs by contributing to a cloud cost budget. Bringing your expertise into budget conversations can increase trust that engineering is using resources wisely, improve the effectiveness of putting FinOps practices in place, and help companies consider cloud costs alongside pipeline performance and scalability.

Combining your design knowledge with historical cloud billing data and estimating tools will help you come up with estimates across different cloud service areas. You can further refine these estimates by looking ahead for changes in the data landscape, load, and infrastructure over the budget period to identify budget risks.

Consolidating your estimates, assumptions, risks, and cost-saving strategies into a budget spreadsheet gives you a single source to refer to in budget conversations. Whether your audience is only interested in the overall cost or wants to know how your compute costs are allocated, this spreadsheet will help you communicate the desired details. This detail and transparency helps create trust and improves visibility into the hard work you've been doing to develop data pipelines cost-effectively.

Table A-2. Budget template

Project		
Timeline		
Total		
Assumptions		
Budget risks		
Cost-saving measures		
Baseline		
	Number of customers	
	Total data storage	
Expected growth		
	Number of customers	
	Data storage	
Cost breakdown		
Production	Previous costs	Budget period costs
Compute		
Storage		
Egress		
Networking		
Databases		
Other		
Total		
Disaster recovery		
Compute		
Storage		
Egress		
Networking		
Databases		
Other		
Total		
Test and development		
Compute		
Storage		
Egress		
Networking		
Databases		
Other		
Total		

Index

integration testing, 136
interfaces
    connectivity testing, 156-159
    mocking generic interfaces, 152-159
    mocking with responses, 153-155
    testing by issuing requests, 155-156
    unit testing, 144
interruptible instances, 6
interruption, designing for, 243

J

job metrics, 212
job runtime alerting, 213
JSON
    as logging format, 205
    as test data format, 177

K

Kubernetes HPA, 46

L

labels
    adding to buckets, 56
    for metric annotation, 232
lag, defined, 218
lifecycle configurations, 57-58
lift and shift migrations, 29
live data, for testing, 174-176
    benefits, 174
    challenges, 174-176
load testing, 137
local development environment, 92-107
    cloud tools, 107
    containers, 93-104
    resource cleanup, 106
    resource dependency reduction, 104-106
    setup scripts and mock options, 106
log levels, 202
log retention, 201
logging, 199-207
    cost reduction, 201-203
    costs, 200-201
    effective, 203-206
    impact of cloud storage elasticity on costs, 201
    impact of scale on costs, 200
low-level processes, 68

M

manual scaling, 39
manual test data generation, 182-184
memory leaks, 226
metric annotation, monitoring, 232
metrics
    defined, 26, 211
    for scaling, 29-30
mocks and mocking, 149-171
    cloud services, 159-164
    complexity versus criticality, 152
    considerations for replacing dependencies, 150-152
    dependency stability, 151
    misspellings in, 155
    mocking generic interfaces, 152-159
    setup scripts and mock options, 106
    test databases as alternative to, 164-169
modular design, 118-128
    DataFrame for, 125-128
    single-responsibility principle, 118-120
monitoring, 17, 209-240
    autoscaling events, 213
    change and, 245
    cluster resource utilization, 17
    communication failure monitoring , 232
    costs of inadequate monitoring, 210-214
    data processing engine introspection, 17
    defined, 211
    error metrics, 213
    job metrics, 212
    job runtime alerting, 213
    metric annotation for, 232
    minimizing costs, 237
    pipeline performance, 227-234
    query monitoring, 235-237
    resource monitoring, 224-227
    system monitoring, 214-224
Moto, mocking AWS with, 162-164, 170
multimodal pipeline (program development example), 112-116
    notebooks for developing code, 113-114
    web UIs, 114-116

N

notebooks, 113-114

About the Author

With over 20 years of experience in the technology industry, **Sev Leonard** brings a breadth of experience spanning circuit design for Intel microprocessors, user-driven application development, and data platform development ranging from small to large scale in healthcare and cybersecurity. Throughout his career, Sev has served as a writer, speaker, and teacher, seeking to pass on what he's learned and make technology education accessible to all.

Colophon

The animal on the cover of *Cost-Effective Data Pipelines* is a red-crested turaco (*Tauraco erythrolophus*). Because their call sounds similar to saying "go away," they are also called go-away birds.

The red-crested turaco is a medium-sized bird with a green body, a yellowish-green beak, red eyes, and a red crest on top of its head. They can grow up to 50 centimeters long (20 inches), and the crest on their head is about 5 centimeters tall (2 inches). Having a long tail and grippy feet helps them keep their balance. In fact, their outer toes are highly mobile and can rotate forward and backward. Additionally, they are the only birds with true green and red pigments in their feathers—other birds that look green and red only appear that way because of light reflecting off of the complex structure of their feathers.

These birds are native to Angola, and are the country's national bird. Their habitats include both subtropical and tropical forests, as well as savannas with trees and bushes. Turacos eat a diet of fruits, flowers, leaves, termites, seeds, acacia, figs, and large snails. They also have the ability to eat berries that are extremely poisonous to humans. In forests, they are essential because they help with seed dispersal. People, however, often think of them as pests because their feeding habits destroy crops and gardens.

While red-crested turacos are locally common, it is suspected that their population is in decline due to habitat destruction. However, they are currently listed as a species of least concern. Many of the animals on O'Reilly covers are endangered; all of them are important to the world.

The cover illustration is by Karen Montgomery, based on an antique line engraving from *Shaw's Zoology*. The cover fonts are Gilroy Semibold and Guardian Sans. The text font is Adobe Minion Pro; the heading font is Adobe Myriad Condensed; and the code font is Dalton Maag's Ubuntu Mono.